D0467832

# POLITICAL WOMAN

# POLITICAL WOMAN

## The Big Little Life of Jeane Kirkpatrick

# PETER COLLIER

ENCOUNTER BOOKS

*NEW YORK · LONDON*

Copyright © 2012 by Peter Collier

All rights reserved. No part of this publication may be reproduced,
stored in a retrieval system, or transmitted, in any form or by
any means, electronic, mechanical, photocopying, recording,
or otherwise, without the prior written permission of
Encounter Books, 900 Broadway, Suite 601,
New York, New York, 10003.

First American edition published in 2012 by Encounter Books,
an activity of Encounter for Culture and Education, Inc.,
a nonprofit, tax exempt corporation.
Encounter Books website address: www.encounterbooks.com

Manufactured in the United States and printed on
acid-free paper. The paper used in this publication meets
the minimum requirements of ANSI/NISO z39.48–1992
(R 1997) (*Permanence of Paper*).

FIRST AMERICAN EDITION

LIBRARY OF CONGRESS CATALOGING-IN-PUBLICATION DATA

Collier, Peter, 1939–
Political woman : the big little life of Jeane Kirkpatrick / by Peter Collier.
     p.    cm.
Includes bibliographical references and index.
ISBN 978-1-59403-604-0 (hardcover : alk. paper) —
ISBN 978-1-59403-605-7 (ebook)
    1. Kirkpatrick, Jeane J.   2. United States—Foreign relations—1981–1989. 3.
Diplomats—United States—Biography.   4. College teachers—
United States—Biography.   I. Title.
E840.8.K55C65 2012
327.730092—dc23
[B]
2012007973


10  9  8  7  6  5  4  3  2  1

# CONTENTS

For my daughter Caitlin
With love always

# INTRODUCTION

"SURE, I'D LIKE TO have an autobiography," Jeane Kirkpatrick once told me. "I just don't want to write it myself."

Someone else might have been trying for a witty paradox. But Jeane, who always held tightly to the idea that she was a Trumanesque plain speaker, was saying here exactly what she meant. She would have welcomed an authentic record of her days, but considered the first-person-singular pronoun such an enemy that she was not willing to attempt it. If pressed, she would claim that in the modern publishing world such books had to be "undignified" to be acceptable, then haughtily suggest that the requirement to present an intimate self was like Coriolanus having to show his wounds. But the fact was that while it was never hard for Jeane to say what she deeply believed, it was often difficult for her to say what she deeply felt.

She had actually tried to write such a book soon after leaving the Reagan administration in 1985. Advanced close to $1 million by Simon & Schuster—a testament to what a hot property she was at that time—she worked fitfully on it for a couple of years before finally giving up. She resisted showing the manuscript to anyone. I kept pestering her about it until she finally sent me a copy, fifteen years after she had put it away. It was fragmentary and stiffly formal, filled with abandonments and new beginnings, resolute only in its avoidance of character and anecdote and, above all, introspection in the discussion of her years as ambassador to the United Nations and paladin of the Reagan Doctrine. No naming names or telling where the bodies were buried; written very much in the manner of someone who had been married for forty years to a former intelligence officer and who seemed to believe that potential readers had no need to know.

Her colleagues and sometime enemies from the Reagan years, Al Haig and George Shultz, were able to erect serviceable personae in their score-settling books, but Jeane couldn't manage this, although she certainly had scores to settle with both of them and a handful of others. One of her core beliefs, fundamental to her anticommunism, was that individuals, not impersonal forces, make history. But she believed with equal ferocity that her own private history was nobody else's business.

Still, in the years that followed her failure with the Simon & Schuster book, people kept urging her to tell her tale. I was one of them. The first time was in 1988 when I happened to be seated next to her at a dinner organized to watch the first Dukakis-Bush debate. I well remembered her from appearances on *Meet the Press* and other Sunday morning news shows a few years earlier—coolly examining her fingernails as a way of gaining time for a response to generally hostile questions, or arching a brow above a hooded eye to express dismay at obvious bias, both signature gestures of someone who had chosen to be a public hard case. Not knowing she had already tried, I asked why she hadn't written the inside story of her role in Reagan's first term. Barely responding (later on I found out that her husband Kirk was quite ill that evening and she had come to the event only out of loyalty to the host), she said that she was not interested in contributing to the "culture of gossip." Her tone indicated that this was not a subject to pursue.

A mutual friend, Jim Denton, reconnected us a decade later, in 1998, when he was executive director of Freedom House, and Jeane and I were on the board. Kirk had died a few years earlier and Jeane seemed more willing than before to escape her own self-imposed confines. I was starting a publishing company called Encounter Books and asked her again about a book, this time with a professional interest. She said that she was already working on one—a "big policy book" on the United States abroad, which she gave me to believe she saw as her legacy project. It was overdue and she needed to finish it before she could even begin to think about anything else. I told her how important I thought the book I was proposing would be, even years later, in telling two major stories at once: the migration she had led of centrist Democrats out of their hijacked party into the Reagan camp, and the major role they had played in fighting the Cold War to victory.

"Present at the destruction?" she asked after thinking for a minute.

"That's it," I replied.

This is when she said in a provisional way that she would like to have such a book but didn't really want to write it herself.

We danced around the subject for a few minutes and then I made her a proposal: I would do the groundwork, interviewing her occasionally, as our schedules permitted; then I would put together something like a syllabus of her own thoughts and memories, which she could work from as an editor as much as a writer.

In what I soon came to understand was a habitual tendency to let people believe they had heard what they wanted to hear from her—thus compartmentalizing that commitment to plain speaking—she gave the impression of being interested in this plan. And so we began to have "conversations."

Most were at her office at the American Enterprise Institute, a place filled with memorabilia that provided context for the project: a "Truman for President" button; the fan letter that Ronald Reagan wrote her after he read her famous 1979 article "Dictatorships and Double Standards"; a battle standard given to her by Enrique Bermúdez, commander of the Nicaraguan Contras; a beautiful piece of quartz that Jordan's King Hussein brought her once when he personally flew his private 747 to the United States; testimonials from Israeli leaders indicating how they had counted on her above anyone else in the Reagan administration to be their champion.

Living on opposite coasts, we had ten or so of these conversations over a period of a few years. Most lasted a couple of hours, but were stop-and-go because of interruptions from the phone calls asking her to testify, participate in panel discussions or be a keynoter at a Republican Party gathering. Constitutionally unable to turn down the invitations, but not particularly anxious to accept them, she would cradle the receiver to her neck and study her nails while speaking in her staccato way to these callers. Then, after hanging up, she would make the transition back to our talk by going through the repertory of tics—rodent-like scrabbling in her purse for buried keys, pens, and prescription pills; noisily adjusting necklaces, rings and bracelets; jerkily searching through a litter of papers on her desk for some conclusive but invisible piece of data—all of which made her seem to be fighting the revolt of the inanimate objects.

She tended to lecture rather than chat, particularly if big ideas were at issue. (She understood that this made her seem a little starchy, and once told me: "It's a problem. I was a teacher long before I got involved in government and I'm a teacher now that I'm not in government. It's who I am.") She didn't like to stray too far from her favorite subjects: how growing up in Middle America at a certain moment in our national life had been a time-lapse civics lesson; how loyalty to the Democratic Party was so deeply embedded in her identity that it required an intellectual bone marrow transplant to get rid of it; how the study of totalitarianism had become her life's work by the time she was twenty years old; how her husband Kirk (full name Evron Kirkpatrick) had been a great man; how her friends Hubert Humphrey and Scoop Jackson were her ideal of public servants; and how she and other centrist Democrats unwilling to regard the decline of America as irreversible had rebelled against Jimmy Carter's presidency, although she herself had done this without any notion that she would eventually embrace and be embraced by Ronald Reagan.

And she spoke of Reagan himself, whom she saw as a quintessential Westerner, drawing strength from his ability to be silent about his feelings just as the men in her own Southwestern birth family had been. "Others saw this as a defect in the president," she said, "but it was part of what made him great—the ability to live within his own boundaries and chart a course without worrying about how he was going to present his drama." Occasionally her words about the president were tinctured with faint disappointment over the fact that he had not saved her when the wolves of his administration closed in. But for the most part there was pure admiration and affection. (And onetime close Reagan aide Richard Allen told me this latter emotion was reciprocal: "Jeane and Margaret Thatcher were the only two women who made Nancy nervous. The president had an intellectual spark with both of them.")

When our talk veered toward more personal subjects, Jeane's quills stood up. If I persisted in heading for areas she had tried subliminally to indicate were off-limits, her manner suddenly defaulted to the hauteur she'd used so adroitly in her public life. Once she interrupted me to say with some asperity, "Talking to you is like filling out government security forms: the questions are endless and intrusive, one after another." Another time, she accused me of being an intellectual stalker. On yet another occasion, after I had asked a relatively innocuous question about her marriage, she showed me her profile: "I'm adopting a position of minimum disclosure."

I came to see that at a certain level the unexamined life was not only worth living for Jeane, but a necessity. She obsessively covered her tracks even though, as I would discover, they didn't lead back to any very dark places. I finally realized that she was just one of those people who hate the idea of being *known*.

Still, for the most part, I think, she took pleasure in the conversations. On some occasions, a tape recorder was present and that encouraged her to treat what she was doing as posterity-talking. But she also just liked to ruminate in an expansive way, in the manner of intellectuals of her generation, about ideas that were important to her. Talking was a form of self-exploration—sending out sonar probes and waiting to see which ones returned a ping.

Surprisingly, one of the subjects to which she kept circling back was feminism, especially the "second wave" that had developed out of the 1960s, which she thought bore that era's birth defects. She regarded these radical feminists as narcissistic and ahistorical, and ultimately antiwoman in their scornful attitude toward marriage and children. She knew what she had accomplished and was defiantly proud to have done it her way—as an individual, without the backing of a movement that would have reduced her existential maneuvers to a dumb show of grievance and reprisal dead-ending in demands for guaranteed outcomes.

Yet she was paradoxically also deeply wounded by the fact that the feminists she scorned had not only ignored her achievements, but disparaged them as inauthentic. She would repeat with a bitter smile some of the things she claimed they said about her: "Gloria Steinem called me a female impersonator. Can you believe that? Naomi Wolf said I was 'a woman without a uterus.' I who have three kids while she, when she made this comment, had none." While she fully understood the source of this animus— her connection with Ronald Reagan and her unique status as the most effective public defender of his policies—there was still a wounded quality to her discussions of it.

She never adopted the grand manner of a former high official and was not inclined to advertise her considerable accomplishments: one of the first female doctoral students in political science at Columba University, one of the few tenured female professors in her early days at Georgetown, and later a "political woman"* who became the United States' first female permanent

---

* *Political Woman* is the title of one of her most successful books and one of the first to examine the surge of women into the electoral arena.

representative to the United Nations. In fact, she always insisted that having children had been far more important to her than having a public life (and she meant this even though motherhood was her least successful role). But being regarded merely as a leading *conservative* feminist never ceased to rankle.

As late as 1994, after being out of government for almost a decade, Jeane raised the issue when she was being profiled by the *New York Times*. The author of the piece, Barbara Crossette, was apparently taken aback by Jeane's stern insistence that she had been traduced by the feminist movement. Crossette evidently did some checking and seemed to confirm the claim when she referred to a Conference on the History of Women at Vassar in 1981, at which the keynoter Joan Scott, professor of history at Brown University, said dismissively of Jeane, at that time the highest ranking and most influential woman in the history of U.S. foreign policy, "She is not someone I want to represent feminine accomplishment."

During the time we were having our talks, at the end of the old millennium and beginning of the new one, Jeane stayed busy but felt that she had been forgotten. She often seemed lonely and reluctant to go home to the large Norman-style house in Bethesda that she and Kirk had bought after she left the Reagan administration and was making an extravagant income on the speaking circuit. Sometimes we'd go to an early dinner to kill time. (On one occasion, we entered a Washington restaurant and people at one large table applauded when they recognized her; she blushed with pleasure and, buoyed by this unexpected token of remembrance, was upbeat for the rest of the evening.) She was a great movie fan, and once I took her to see *Gladiator*, which I'd already seen and thought she would like for the derring-do and vaguely neoconservative political sentiments about courage and country.

When I glanced at her during some of the bloody scenes I was surprised to see that she was flinching and averting her eyes. I commented on it as we were filing out of the theater, and she said, "I've never been as 'tough' as people assumed. I wish I had been."

These evenings ended with her getting into her big sedan, leaning back in the driver's seat with locked arms holding the steering wheel in a death grip, and then suddenly stepping down on the accelerator à la Cruella de Vil and zooming out into traffic without bothering to check the rearview mirror.

She seemed to feel far more at home in her place at Les Baux in the heart of Provence than at her own home during these years. While there she adopted the loose blouses and baggy pants that accented her Hepburnesque ranginess. When I visited her there a couple of times, I was struck, like others who dropped in, by the tasteful elegance of the house that she and Kirk had bought and, in her words, spent "a king's ransom" enlarging and restoring. It sat in the middle of French cultural history. Scenes that Van Gogh had painted were a walk away. Cicadas shrilled in the plane trees outside her kitchen window, giving the scented summer afternoons the feel of a Pagnol novel.

Inside, patchwork quilts from grandmothers on both sides of her family—in lone star, wedding ring, flower garden and Dutch doll patterns—hung over the balustrades of the second floor. There were paintings of Provençale scenes on the walls, including a beautiful Cezannesque landscape by Anna Kirkpatrick, Kirk's daughter from one of his previous marriages, which Jeane always had trouble acknowledging had ever taken place.

Fealty to her husband's memory never moved from the top of her agenda. "I will die in the bed where Kirk died," she would say, more or less out of the blue. "And my funeral will be presided over by the minister who presided over his. And I will be buried next to where he is buried." She took the spiffy little poodle named Jasper with her everywhere, and when people asked about the animal she told them that it had lain faithfully by Kirk's side as he was dying, something she would never forget. Thinking of Kirk led her to try to cinch up the drawstrings of her experiences. At the end of one long rumination about him and them and what she had and hadn't achieved, she said, "It has been a good life . . . a full life . . . I wouldn't call it a big life exactly . . . a big little life, perhaps."

It was a sober and honest judgment.

One of the summers I visited her there, her close friend Margaret Lefever was keeping Jeane company. Another time it was Anne de Lattre, a Frenchwoman who had been Jeane's roommate fifty years earlier at Columbia University and remained devoted to her ever after. They and other visitors accompanied her to the outdoor market at Saint-Rémy, where she would saunter along the stalls, engaging in animated badinage with the merchants. She always came back with bread and cheese, at least, and tomatoes and basil for salad, which she would prepare energetically, cutting and chopping in slightly jerky movements that brought to mind the bloodlettings in *Saturday Night Live*'s parodies of the Julia Child cooking show. In fact, Jeane's kitchen life, like that of so many other women of her generation, had been profoundly affected by *Mastering the Art of French Cooking*. She told me that she had been invited to Child's eightieth birthday party and had gone with some trepidation since the French chef was a well-known liberal. But potential conflicts were resolved through the Gallic refinement they both admired: "Julia volunteered that she didn't approve of my politics but liked the style with which I carried them out. I told her I had always deeply admired her ability to truss a duck. We spent a pleasant evening together."

---

To move our project forward, I finally pulled together some of Jeane's stories about her growing up into a demonstration chapter.* She read it and remarked, "Well, it's accurate and sort of *sounds* like me." She hoped she was in the home stretch of her "big policy book," she said, and finally agreed to take up the "memoir" (subtly downgraded from "autobiography") as soon as she finished. I tried to get her to sign a contract, but she said that "the Simon & Schuster thing"—by which she meant the lacerating experience of having to return a large advance—had made her gun-shy about taking money before there was a manuscript.

As Encounter Books became more time-consuming, our contacts grew more sporadic. I'd call Jeane every so often and ask her how the policy book was going. Not as well as she wished, she usually replied hesitantly. She sent a draft to me and asked for an opinion. It was a hard read, far from the summary statement on U.S. foreign policy she had hoped to produce. (It would be published after her death—heavily edited from the form in which I had seen it—as *Making War to Keep Peace*.)

The last time I saw her was in spring 2005. I knew she'd had bouts of illness, but even so was taken aback by her physical diminishment: bones jutting out of her wrists and shoulders; fingers angled by arthritis; cheeks sunken in a way that enlarged her eyes and gave her a startled look. Perhaps most alarming, strangely, was that her brindle-colored hair, which I'd never realized she'd been dyeing all those years, was suddenly white. She picked at her food and talked glumly of how bad she thought it was for us ever to have gone into Iraq, although she was not about to go public with her doubts, and seemed to feel bad that she was no longer able to live comfortably in the intellectual house remodeled by the new generation of neoconservatives. She talked a little about problems with her eldest son Douglas, an epically self-destructive alcoholic whose decline I'd heard about from others but never before from her.

---

* It appeared in a slightly different form in the *Weekly Standard* shortly after her death under the title "An American Girlhood."

Then she transitioned to the subject of our project. "I'm not making much progress on any of my work these days," she said. "I'm sorry for all your effort, but I don't see myself getting to that book about my life we've been talking about. I'm afraid that this unfinished business of ours will probably remain unfinished."

I could see that the admission had cost her something and told her glibly that if this was the case I might have to go ahead and write it myself. She thought for a long minute and then said, "Well, maybe you should."

At the time I made it, the offer was flippant. But after Jeane died, it gradually took on the feel of a promise to keep. In writing this book, I have drawn on our fragmentary conversations, her draft autobiography and other random, unorganized materials she left behind. I have also used the recollections of friends and family members to fill in some (but by no means all) of the gaps.

It is not the book that I still wish she'd been able to write. But at least it suggests the nature of her improbable odyssey—that of a curious and ambitious young woman who came out of the American heartland with a burning desire to grapple with "big ideas," subjected herself to a grim study of totalitarianism as a way of sharpening her appreciation of freedom, made a significant place for herself in the worlds of scholarship and political activism, and finally, after years as a Democratic Party insider, accepted a cabinet position in a Republican administration where she went on to become, in William Safire's accurate phrase, "the courage of Ronald Reagan's convictions."

And at the foundation of the big little life she built was a truth she always insisted on making self-evident: "I've always been passionately in love with my country."

Not many people could get away with making this statement. Jeane could, because for her it was not just a sentiment but a reflection of her inner light.

# HEARTLAND

Of all the objects in her office at the American Enterprise Institute, Jeane was fondest of a small statue of Will Rogers, which had pride of place on her coffee table. Perhaps five inches high, it portrays her fellow Oklahoman with feet strongly anchored, hips thrust out, hands nonchalantly jammed into pants pockets, head tilted back and wearing a slightly self-effacing smile. It was, Jeane always said, a figuration of the confident Middle America where she was born and to which she liked to think she had always remained tethered, however far she might seem to have strayed. She inferred an order from this place in the way Stephen Daedalus did in his inscription on the flyleaf of his geography book when he said he was from ". . . County Kildare, Ireland, Europe, The World, The Universe." For Jeane, the beginning spot was Duncan, "a small town with a Western feel, ninety miles south of Oklahoma City and forty miles north of the Red River," whose meanings also radiated outward. She always talked about it as a place of hard work, tensile family connections, faith in God and country, unity of belief amidst passionate political debates. This place tugged on her ever more strongly as she grew older because she knew that like all paradises, it was a paradise lost.

It was named after William Duncan, a Scotsman who established his trading post between Fort Arbuckle and Fort Sill on the Chisholm Trail, where the great herds of longhorns were driven up from Texas to Abilene, Kansas. Officially, the town of Duncan was considered to have been born in June 1892, when the Chicago, Rock Island and Pacific Railway first began operation and made the place one of its central stops. Duncan had already come of age by the time Oklahoma was granted statehood in 1907, but was still capable of producing rowdy Wild West moments. Shortly after she was married in 1924, for instance, Jeane's mother was sitting in a matinee in Duncan's only theater one Saturday afternoon, when two men began an argument that escalated into a fistfight and then a shoot-out as the others rushed for the exit.

For the most part, Jeane was too pedagogical to be a good raconteur, always hurrying to italicize the moral of a story before fully *telling* it. But when she talked about the family history, she allowed herself some legroom and rambled a bit in painting the outlines of a saga that seemed to have climbed out of the pages of an Edna Ferber novel.*

Her paternal grandfather, Frank Jordan, had come to Oklahoma on the run in 1896, when he crossed the Red River from Scurry, Texas, after eloping with his young bride Ellen Boles. Ellen's father Levi Boles had already promised her to someone else when Jordan first showed up as a young man with no prospects. Frank was soon a criminal to boot, leaving one of the two horses he owned, a buggy horse, at the Boles' place in exchange for one of Levi's saddle horses for Ellen when he stole her away to get married. It may have seemed like a fair trade to him, but Boles swore out a warrant for horse theft. The newlyweds lit out for the Territory—Oklahoma Territory now, just six years past its prior identity as Indian Territory—roweling their lathered horses toward the border, pursued by the law.

The Boles relented in their hostility to the marriage only after Frank and Ellen's first son James was born. Already expecting again, Ellen was allowed to come and show James in 1898 at her father's Texas ranch. It was there, in fact, that her second son was born, completing the reconciliation. He was named Welcher in honor of

---

* Jeane's brother Jerry—the family's unofficial archivist, with a tenacious memory and a strong grasp of detail—has the more comprehensive view of the Jordans' story and contributed significant facts to its presentation here.

a friend of Frank Jordan's who was the last Indian land agent in Oklahoma, but as a boy he became known as "Fat" because of his imposing bulk and the improbability of his given name.

Frank and Ellen took the baby and his brother back to the small town of Walters, Oklahoma, not far from Duncan. Over the next decade they would have five more children, four of them boys, while Frank made a living by chopping cotton and eventually saved enough to build a mill. His solid citizenship was certified by his appointment as the local justice of the peace. He apparently imposed a strong sense of fair play on his children, because Jeane liked to tell about the time when her father, then twelve, was attending the one-room schoolhouse in Walters and his younger brother Bud ran afoul of the teacher, who caned him with a hickory switch in front of the class.

"Cry!" the teacher ordered. "I'll make you cry!"

Bud refused to give him the satisfaction. When blood began to seep through the backside of his trousers, Fat, who was big for his age, jumped up with clenched fists and said to the teacher, "That's enough!"

When he hit Bud again, Fat repeated, "I said *that's enough!*" and threw a heavy history book at the teacher, hitting him in the head. The school tried to expel Fat, but Frank Jordan, judge and father, appeared in his behalf and he was vindicated.

Fat was a good enough football player to win a scholarship to the University of Oklahoma. But he broke his leg in a sandlot game just before graduating from high school and the offer was withdrawn. He was working in his father's field that summer chopping cotton when a car stopped on the dirt road that ran alongside the property. The driver gave Fat an appraising look and motioned him over, then leaned out of the window and said, "You're a pretty big boy. You want to make a dollar a day?"

Fat asked, "Doing what?"

"Working as a roughneck on an oil rig."

Admitting that he would indeed like to make that kind of

money, Fat said, "Yes, but you'll have to talk to my dad." By this time Frank Jordan had ambled over to the car, and he quickly gave his assent. "This was how," Jeane always ended the story, "my family became involved in a business that would take over Oklahoma as a result of a series of major oil discoveries and make it into an American boom state."

For several years, Jeane said, her father worked in the oil fields as a laborer. One day in 1922, he was visiting a friend in Arlington, Texas, who introduced him to a young woman named Leona Kile. She was living in town with a married sister while taking a business course in shorthand and bookkeeping. Leona was unassumingly pretty, with the long face and agate eyes that Jeane would inherit. Her family stood slightly apart socially from their neighbors, somewhat defiantly displaying a daguerreotype of Leona's grandfather on her mother's side, Captain John Lockhart, who had fought for the Union as an officer in the Indiana Regulars. It had taken two generations of life in Texas to escape the taint of "Yankee."

In 1923, after he had courted her for a few months, Leona allowed Fat to drive her to Oklahoma, where he was then living, and the two of them, each twenty-five years old, "stood up" before a justice of the peace, with no family and just a few friends present. Then they set up housekeeping in Duncan in a rented two-bedroom frame house on Spruce Street. Jeane was born there in 1926.

By then, Duncan had grown to over three thousand residents and was starting to have the feel of a real city, although Don Campbell, whose family lived next door to the Jordans and who became Jeane's close childhood friend, remembered being able to walk three blocks to prairie-like surroundings where he could spend hours shooting rabbits with his .22. Indians occasionally appeared on the streets of the town like extras on a movie set. Blacks were wary. Duncan had been the scene of a near lynching in 1911, which led to an exodus of most black residents. Those who remained had settled into their own rundown neighborhood and lived under a regimen of segregation in schools and other public facilities that would remain ironclad until the early 1960s.

If Duncan felt like a forward-looking place in spite of Jim Crow, one reason was that it happened to be where a young man named Erle P. Halliburton discovered a profitable niche in the oil business in 1919. Starting with a mule-drawn wagon, a portable pump and a few bags of cement, he pioneered a technique for buttressing oil well shafts while they were being drilled so they would be less likely to collapse or explode.

After starting the New Method Oil Well Cementing Company, he soon became a local legend, known for a pragmatic creativity but also for a volcanic temper. (He punched out competitors and occasionally used his growing leverage ruthlessly to put them out of business.) In addition to the techniques for strengthening shafts that would remake the oil business by allowing for deeper wells, Halliburton tinkered with various other inventions and had a modest success when he designed the first aluminum suitcases with aerodynamic lines based on those of the DC3s in whose holds his less sturdy baggage had been battered during the non-stop travels involved in making his company into a major international corporation.

By the time Duncan erected a statue to Erle in its Memorial Park after World War II, his company had already cemented nearly a hundred thousand oil well shafts around the world. It had also developed a sharkish appetite for swallowing rivals, thus gaining the slightly sinister reputation that its future history, particularly in the Middle East, would inflate to epic size.

A casual friend of Erle Halliburton's, Fat Jordan was making his own contribution to the local oil business in the early 1930s. He worked twelve-hour days, always leaving for work early in the morning dressed in the fresh khakis that Leona had laundered the night before and carrying the lunch she had made. A big man with an oblong face, he wore a wide-brimmed hat and a leather jacket when it was cold, looking like the heavy in the noirish films of the era who might be named "Fat Jordan." Exuding a gruff self-madeness, he always seemed to be wreathed in exhaust from the two packs of Camels and the dozen Roi-Tans he smoked every day. At the age of seventy-two, according to Jeane's brother Jerry, Fat saw a doctor for some ailment and was told that he'd feel better if he gave up cigarettes. "The hell I would!" he replied, although he let the doctor badger him into quitting. When he returned a few months later for a follow-up visit, the doctor asked if he felt better now that he had kicked the habit. "Nope, not a bit," Fat replied. The doctor shrugged, "Okay, then, do whatever you want." Fat left the office and bought a pack of Camels and continued smoking heavily until the day he died.

Later on, when Jeane became a newsmaker and journalists writing about her background frequently referred to her father as a "wildcatter," she would indignantly reply that this was false; he had been a *driller*—a contract worker, not a speculator, who had worked hard to raise himself in caste, scrimping to found his own company and buy his own expensive rigs. One of his biggest clients was Carter Oil, a producing company for Standard of Indiana. He got paid by the foot and had no financial interest in the wells he drilled, although Carter sometimes farmed out a low-probability "prospect lease" to him, which occasionally paid off. Leona always referred to these serendipities affectionately by name when telling friends what they had provided for the family: "The Kisner well bought my new winter coat," or "The Phillips paid for one of Jeane's years at Barnard."

---

The Jordans' table talk focused obsessively on "all-n-gaz." Although Leona, his bookkeeper, was as deeply involved in the discussions as Fat himself, she was clearly a limited partner and Jeane grew up thinking that even if she'd had the ability to play a meaningful role in the family business it would have been impossible because she lacked the gender. She knew that her brother Jerry, born when she was seven, "would have more opportunities than I and that my mother and father had more respect for male attributes." Yet it was also true that she grew up as the Jordans' prize possession, the first grandchild on both sides, always destined to be a star.

With her long face and impassive features, she looked like her mother, but had her father's blunt temperament and ambition. Her willingness to butt heads with him at the same time she was trying to accommodate his expectations was, in the opinion of her closest friend Margaret Lefever, responsible for the odd mix of aggressiveness and indecision that defined her personality. Her middle name was Duane—pronounced "Doo-aine"—and from the time she was a baby that was what she was called by everyone except Fat, who called her "Sister," even before Jerry came along.

"I could say the alphabet backwards by the time I was three," she recalled, "thus establishing myself as undeniably promising." At five, she furthered this reputation by reading through a multi-volume set of poems, stories and essays designed for older children, committing many passages to memory, which led to performances at the kitchen table. When she hoarded her allowance for months to buy her first book, what it would be was the subject of suspenseful speculation in the Jordan household. When it turned out to be a thesaurus, her father shot her a dubious look as if to say, "That figures."

Her first memories were "Depression memories"—a bad enough downturn in the oil business that Fat had to stack and store his drilling rigs for several months and go off to East Kilgore, Texas, to work again as a laborer. But while there was little money, there was always enough food: "crusty loaves of bread baked on a big wood stove in the kitchen, fried chicken that had been crowing and clucking in the yard a few hours earlier, and freshly churned butter." Also family-enriched visits by car to both sets of grandparents in Texas—the Jordans now living in Scurry on the

Boles' farm, which Ellen had inherited from her father, and the Kiles in Fort Worth.

Jeane and Jerry liked grandfather Frank Jordan but thought Ellen had a tendency toward obstreperousness, a trait that Jerry always believed had passed from her to Jeane through their father. The Kiles were somehow more "normal." Leona's mother was now a widow raising five grandchildren as a result of the death of one of Leona's sisters. She also took care of Leona herself when she came down with rheumatic fever soon after Jeane was born, nursing her at home and then taking her to the "hot baths" at Mineral Wells, Texas, to soak the illness out of her once and for all.

All four of the grandparents were members of the Texas Christian Church. None smoked, drank or played cards—activities not proscribed by the more latitudinarian First Baptist congregation that Jeane's own family belonged to in Duncan. Both sides of the family were addicted to politics. A bitter opponent of big banks and big railroads as a young man, Frank Jordan was weaned away from committed membership in the Socialist Party of Oklahoma only by the advent of the New Deal. Like the rest of the Kiles and Jordans, he became a yellow-dog Democrat. Inheriting his father's views, Fat blustered to Jeane that she could "bring home a black boy, bring home an Indian boy, but better by God not bring home a Republican."

The safe-conduct pass to a black boy was purely rhetorical. Jeane grew up in a world where the use of "nigger shooter" for marble, "nigger toe" for Brazil nut, and "nigger heaven" for the upper reaches of a theater balcony did not raise eyebrows. Race was everywhere, but nowhere: it was an assumption, not an argument.

And yet, despite this deep but invisible scar, Duncan was what Jeane had in mind later on when, writing about democracy, she said that its building blocks existed in the "small, self-governing towns on the frontier" whose politics and culture revealed "the American genius for that 'art of association' which amazed the French philosopher Alexis de Tocqueville."

She walked the three blocks to and from Emerson School every day and usually came home for lunch as well. Don Campbell, the boy next door whose father worked for Halliburton, remembers her as the top girl in the class, reading the bulletin and speaking at assemblies, but after class a long-legged, coltish tomboy, climbing trees barefooted and demanding to be treated as an equal in the rough-and-tumble neighborhood games played in the twilight summer hours between the end of supper and bedtime.

Virginia Sharpe, who lived in the house on the other side of the Jordans and was Jeane's best friend growing up, recalled the two of them as being in and out of each other's homes constantly. While Virginia was a little awed by Fat's bravado, she loved Leona's cooking and her embracing good nature. When Jeane's parents enrolled her in a private "Expressions" class after school, Virginia tagged along. They did two-person plays, learned the Gettysburg Address together and went to what was called the Schubert Music Class, where they dressed up in taffeta and played recitals for each other, beginning with "The Happy Farmer" as an initiation piece. (Their teacher, Mrs. Thompson, was considered a curiosity in Duncan, first because she had married an Indian and second because he had left her to go back to live on the reservation.) Jeane always felt that it was a testament to the place Duncan occupied inside the American Dream that her childhood neighbors Virginia Sharpe and Don Campbell married right out of high school and spent the rest of their lives there.

---

When she was twelve, her Duncan idyll ended. It was 1938, the middle of the Depression, and many of the Jordans' friends had left for California, following the path made into a national metaphor by Steinbeck's Joad family. Fat himself had weathered the worst of the hard times that followed the bottoming-out of the oil market and was now working for himself again. But the easy deposits in the Oklahoma fields were tapped, and drilling there was becoming less certain and more expensive. He decided to move on to the new tri-state fields opening up at the juncture of southern Illinois, Kentucky and Indiana.

Without knowing much about the town, Fat located his business and family in Vandalia, Illinois. Jeane and Jerry were sick over having to leave their friends in Duncan. It turned out to be as hard a transition for their father as for them. There hadn't been much labor organizing in Oklahoma, but the unions were stronger and more determined in Illinois. Drillers were often attacked by goons who blew up the rigs of those who didn't sign up. When the organizers arrived at his site, Fat's employees, most of whom had followed him from Oklahoma, ran them off in bloody skirmishes fought with ax handles.

Entering junior high in Vandalia, Jeane discovered that Abraham Lincoln had served in the legislature there and that her school had once been a stop on the underground railroad. She had what she later called "an epiphany about epistemology." As she put it, "I had studied the Civil War in Duncan and now I studied it again and found that it was a different war, fought by different people, for different reasons with a different outcome. This was one of the big intellectual experiences for me—a basic lesson in the sociology of knowledge. It did not lead to the idea that truth is relative, but to the notion that personal perception is crucial. People understand the world as it is presented to them."

This was the beginning of what she later called "my own personal civil rights movement," a rethinking of all the assumptions that had been part of the intellectual air she breathed back in Oklahoma. She felt that this was when she started thinking about the idea of America as well as the fact of it.

Still, none of the Jordans were comfortable in Vandalia. The town didn't have the "civic spirit" they had experienced in Duncan and by comparison did not feel "real" to them. And so in

1940, Fat and Leona made another move, this time to Mount Vernon, Illinois, about fifty miles south of Vandalia, where they would live out the rest of their lives.

---

Situated in that part of the state known as "Little Egypt" because its river valleys were said to be similar to the Nile Delta, Mount Vernon had around eleven thousand people then. It was still compact, without the sprawl that accompanied its later build-out. The town had been known for decades as a center of railroad car production, but by the time the Jordans arrived this industry was on the decline and oil production was on the rise.

The family's first home was a two-story bungalow on 12th Street—rented, as were the first homes of most of the other oil people who arrived in the middle of southern Illinois's boom. Fat had to drive thirty-five miles every day to the town of Carmi, where drilling was heaviest, but it was an inconvenience he endured so that Jeane and Jerry could attend the highly regarded Mount Vernon school system, at that time run by Superintendent J. L. Buford, who later became a national figure as president of the National Education Association.

Looking for a new teenage identity to go with the new home, Jeane now demanded to be called by her first name rather than "Duane." Tall and slender, she had a noncommittal resting face and "held herself well," in the words of Phyllis Smith, who became her best friend and competitor over the next four years to see who would be the top female student at Mount Vernon High. According to friends from that time, she exuded a kinetic energy that was often manifested in the erratic body movements—flinging a hand out to grab something rather than reaching; rotating her neck nervously as if to relieve vertebral tension—that would always dominate her self-presentation. She was ambitious and opinionated, but tended to wait for an opening rather than rush to the attack; she made friends easily despite cultivating a formidable privacy.

She and Phyllis Smith took piano lessons together, competing in this realm also to see who could do the better rendition of "Oh Dem Golden Slippers." Phyllis was as fanatically Republican as Jeane was Democrat, with the result that at election times, when both worked at the local headquarters of their respective parties, the friendship was on temporary hold. Both appeared in school plays, Jeane winning the lead in the senior production of a parody of 1930s melodrama called "Pure as the Driven Snow, or The Working Girl's Secret," in which she played the sweet heroine, Charity Deane. But Phyllis won the one thing Jeane desperately wanted when she finished first in their class.

Like their schoolmates, the two girls stopped for Cokes on the way home from school at Livingston's Drug Store fountain and then went to The Sub, the youth center in the basement of the Presbyterian Church in the town square, where they danced and played games. An enthusiastic bobby-soxer who was good at the jitterbug and whose slightly bucked teeth gave her mouth a look of pouty sensuality, Jeane had a serious boyfriend named Silas Allen with whom school gossip claimed she engaged in "heavy petting." But she dropped him because he was not interested in ideas. Another boy once asked her to go to the movies and she replied, in words that soon made the rounds of the school, "No, I'm going to stay home tonight and read *The Federalist Papers*." Still, despite her bookishness, a classmate named John Howard who would remain Jeane's friend for the rest of her life says that she also had an aura about her of one who might someday "be capable of being recklessly in love."

On December 7, 1941, she was at the movies in the Granada Theater with her brother Jerry when the lights suddenly came up. The manager, improbably named Mr. Marvel, walked solemnly out onto the stage and stood against the white screen as he spoke into the hush: "I'm sorry to report that the Japanese have attacked Pearl Harbor and we are at war. Anyone in the audience who is in the armed services should report to his base." Eight-year-old Jerry turned to Jeane and asked, "Does that mean we're going to be bombed too?" She shot him a withering look and said, "Not in Mount Vernon, Illinois!" The movie resumed, but the two of them hurried home.

For the next four years, the family hunkered around the radio every evening and followed the progress of the American forces, listening to commentator Gabriel Heater tell of the wins ("Ah, there is good news tonight!") and the losses ("Ah, there is bad news tonight!"). Fat had seen war coming and scraped together enough money to buy two new cars in the fall of 1941—a Chevrolet coupe for the business and a Dodge four-door for the family. Because he was in the oil business, he had "C" stickers and escaped the worst of gas rationing. One of his brothers went off to war and left his red 1935 Ford roadster with Jeane, who drove it until he returned, using a bottle of gasoline she carried in the rumble seat to hand-prime the carburetor every time she started the engine.

As insulated from the conflict as this landlocked Midwestern community felt, the war still came home. Some of the seniors at Mount Vernon High enlisted and went off to fight without waiting to graduate. The band director's son was the first one killed. A boy from Jeane's class who left school early to enlist died in the Normandy invasion at about the same time that she was handing in her senior paper on the novels of George Eliot.

What came next for her became the family's Big Question. She had expectations for herself, but didn't feel that her father shared them and probably not her mother either. More than a glass ceiling, Jeane felt glass walls pressing in around her. It wasn't a lack of love; that was always in full supply. It was a basic social fact: "We lived in a man's world where traditional gender roles were taken for granted. They wanted me to excel but weren't sure where, outside of home and family, this excellence could and should take place."

Her father made it clear that he wouldn't be unhappy if she married a local boy, settled in Mount Vernon and had kids. Jeane directly challenged him as few in his life dared to do. She wanted to go to the University of Chicago, which the "boy wonder" president Robert Hutchins was just then, through a Great Books program, making into a rough draft of what he later called a "university of utopia." But Fat wanted something a little more "feminine." As a compromise, it was decided that Jeane would make her first and perhaps last stop at Stephens College, a two-year school for women in nearby Columbia, Missouri.

The justification for sending her there was that it was close by and gas was still being rationed. But Jeane and her parents both understood that Stephens was a halfway house—half way between their desire that she have a "normal" life and her own intention that the sky should be her limit.

# BIG IDEAS

At first Jeane somewhat resented being stashed at Stephens, but eventually she came to feel that on the whole it wasn't a bad place to spend a couple of years. Established in 1833, it was the second oldest women's college in the country (after Salem College in North Carolina), a red brick campus of over one thousand students. In the past, it had sold itself to families as a place where their daughters would be "finished" as well as insulated from the temptations of the big city; but now, with the postwar world beginning to take shape, it was looking also to equip them for "independent lives," in the words of one brochure, and to prepare them for "leadership roles."

Because of Amelia Earhart and the other female pilots who had created the cult of the aviatrix, Stephens had recently established a flight school. It had its own airfield and some of the affluent students arrived at school in their own planes. It had its own stables for girls with horses and its own golf course. The school even had its own railway car. When Fat and Leona drove Jeane to school from Mount Vernon they stopped in St. Louis, where she boarded "the Stephens Special," which deposited her at the station a short walk from the center of campus.

There was little intellectual firepower on the Stephens faculty (although the playwright William Inge, on the edge of his later fame, taught there briefly just before Jeane's arrival). But it did have an aura of purposefulness. With her roommate Pat Youngdahl, Jeane went to a nondenominational seminar on Sunday mornings called Burrall Class to discuss issues such as the possibility of nuclear holocaust. (Youngdahl preserved a memory of

Jeane as listening transfixed by these issues, unconsciously depilling the small balls of wool that formed on her sweaters and rolling them dreamily around on her fingertips.) The future journalist Sol Sanders, who was then at the neighboring University of Missouri campus in Columbia, met Jeane during her first year at Stephens and saw her as "gangly and quiet, watching people silently from behind an impassive façade."

Jeane never regarded Stephens as anything more than a way station where she incubated her rebellion against her father by telling classmates that her ambition was "to become a spinster teacher at a women's college." Yet it had value as a place where she could try on various intellectual selves. As she later said, "I read Plato, Aristotle and Hobbes at Stephens. I read Mill and became a utilitarian. I read Veblen and became a member of the Leisure Class. I read Virginia Woolf and, delighted to discover a literature that validated my feelings that the distribution of power between the sexes wasn't what it should be, became a feminist. I read Marx and became a socialist."

This last effort never really took, although when Jeane later became associated with neoconservatives who had migrated rightward from socialism, the myth grew (sometimes with cultivation by her) that she had been a member of the Young People's Socialist League.* In truth, she was intrigued by the rebelliousness of socialism, but too wary to make a commitment, although in the spirit of playing with fire she became briefly interested in a boy who went to "Mizzou" and was actually in the YPSL and trying to build the local membership. Jeane couldn't remember his

---

* The Wikipedia entry on Max Shachtman, a onetime friend and supporter of Trotsky and later a leader in the American socialist movement and godfather of the YPSL, falsely claims that Jeane was once a member of the Socialist Party. The fabulation probably arises in part from the fact that she became close in the mid 1970s to former YPSLs such as Joshua Muravchik and Penn Kemble because of their intellectually muscular anticommunism, and they had been influenced by Shachtman.

name, but talking about him always brought a smile to her face: "He seemed fairly Promethean at first, daring to think what the rest of us regarded as unthinkable." But then, as she described it, after organizing a modestly successful antifascist rally he decided that the next cadre-building event would be a socialist picnic. Along with the others who had agreed to help out, Jeane attended countless hours of meetings, arguing over the politically correct way to organize a picnic. When they failed to read *The Communist Manifesto* as he had commanded, the young socialist decided they were frauds and dilettantes and subjected them to a harsh and long-winded critique, leading Jeane to decide that socialism was not for her.

Perhaps the most significant thing that happened to Jeane at Stephens was meeting Margaret Briggs, the daughter of a Methodist minister from Iowa, who was forced to work tables at the school café to help pay her tuition. Margaret noticed Jeane because of her "stunning good looks" and also because she was always trying to generate serious intellectual discussions with other students at mealtime. Jeane asked for Margaret's help in the volunteer job she had accepted of placing placards advertising school events in the windows of local businesses. It was the beginning of a sixty-year friendship that had a brief hiatus after Stephens but resumed when Margaret showed up in Washington in the early 1950s after having married Ernest Lefever, a future player in the Reagan revolution and a political ally of Jeane's.

When her two years at Stephens ended in the spring of 1946, Jeane again faced her father's ambivalence about her next step. It was partly a question of money, as Margaret Lefever recalls, and partly the fact that "Mr. Jordan felt this continuing thirst for knowledge was a little pointless and was frustrated by Jeane's enthusiasm for it." But Jeane steamrolled his objections. She had visited New York City the previous summer with a roommate just after V-J Day and had been so galvanized by the excitement of the city that she applied to Barnard College, and was accepted.

Fat was somewhat appeased when Jeane was offered a full scholarship by the University of Chicago, still her first choice.

She planned to major in political philosophy and wanted to get a head start by enrolling for a summer session. But things seemed hexed from the beginning. When she arrived on the Chicago campus, the registrar's office couldn't locate her file for three days. When they finally found it, all the classes she wanted were full. Student housing was closed and so she was forced to take a room in a boarding house. The last straw came late one afternoon when she was standing in front of Grant Park waiting for a bus to take her to a function at International House. A gang of young black men surrounded her and tried to force her back into the trees. Jeane "screamed bloody murder" to get the attention of passersby. In the ensuing confusion, she managed to escape and ran back toward her boarding house. She sounded so hysterical when she called home that Leona immediately got in the car and drove up to Chicago to get her.

Back home for the rest of the summer, Jeane pondered her next move. The scholarship to Chicago was still good, but her summer experience had soured her on the city and the university. She was beginning to feel, moreover, that she had perhaps permanently outgrown the Midwest. It turned out that the acceptance she had gotten from Barnard was providential. "New York was where the big ideas were," she later said. "And I was definitely interested in big ideas."

———

She arrived at Penn Station in September 1946 and crammed her voluminous baggage into a taxi, which she commanded to take her to Morningside Heights. In her zesty anticipation of the next chapter of her life, Jeane underestimated how forsaken she would feel in the metropolis after living in small towns all her life. A student from France named Anne de Lattre, who was also beginning her studies at Barnard, happened to be walking down the hallway of the dorms the second day of classes when she heard alarming sounds coming from one of the rooms. She went to investigate and found Jeane stretched out on her bed crying loudly. When Anne introduced herself and asked what was wrong, Jeane looked up at her and sobbed, "I'm so *lonely*." She admitted that despite prohibitive long-distance rates, she was calling home at least once a day.

Straight-backed and patrician, with strong Gallic features, Anne de Lattre was just nineteen years old herself and much farther from home, but she was excited to be in America and anxious to form relationships, so she set about consoling Jeane. It was the beginning of another friendship, like the one with Margaret Briggs that Jeane had forged at Stephens, that would last for the next sixty years.

Anne was in many ways Jeane's opposite. She was from one of the wealthiest families in France, the Sellières, whose fortune came from its role as captain of the country's steel industry. She had a strong intellectual pedigree as well, being the granddaughter of Ernest-Antoine Sellière, a philosopher and member of the Académie Française who was also a friend of Columbia University's president, Nicholas Murray Butler, and had in fact used that relationship to help get Anne admitted to Barnard.

Jeane eagerly embraced de Lattre as her first "intellectual friend" and immediately established a two-person debating society, with Anne's background of wealth and privilege providing one of the arguing points of their relationship. In their late-night dorm-room discussions, Anne asserted that class mattered, even in America where it seemed so permeable. Jeane strenuously denied that class had any relevance in the United States. She insisted that Anne come home with her during their first vacation so she could prove her point.

When I spoke with de Lattre in Paris after Jeane's death, she still remembered the visit to Mount Vernon some sixty years earlier as one of the high points in her *tour d'horizon* of America. She

was indeed struck by the paradox the Jordan household presented—a sense of plenty despite its modesty and the obvious
thrift of Jeane's parents. (She remembered too how excited Jeane's
brother Jerry was to meet her, having never before been introduced, as he said with enthusiasm, to someone from "abroad.")

Without knowing about the running argument that Anne was
having with his daughter, Fat unintentionally supported Jeane's
point when he took Anne on a car trip around the Mount Vernon
area, including the southern Illinois oil fields. As part of the trav-
elogue he assured her, "No one is any better than anyone else in
this country. Everyone has an equal chance." And then a final
chauvinistic dig as she was leaving: "You'll never want to go back
to the Old Country now that you've seen the US of A!"

This dialogue about class between Jeane and Anne de Lattre
would continue for the rest of their parallel lives.* In one of the
last times she saw Jeane after the turn of the century, Anne went
with her to a party thrown by some of her "rich Republican
friends." At one point in the evening, the two women found
themselves standing alone in a corner speaking in alternating
bursts of French and English. Anne criticized the gaudiness of the
hosts' display; and Jeane, without conceding any of the larger
points of their decades-long dialogue, agreed that some Americans who tried to use their wealth to jump up in caste were
indeed "parvenus."

Jeane admired Anne's candor, her talent for friendship and
the orderliness of her mind. But that was partly because in her
first year at Barnard she had also fallen in love with France itself.
This development came about because the Spanish courses she
had taken at Stephens hadn't been rigorous enough to satisfy
Barnard's language requirement, and since she had to start over

---

* Anne also got a PhD and became an economist specializing in development issues in Africa, the subject of a lecture Jeane arranged for her to give
at the American Enterprise Institute in 1979 during one of her many return
visits to the United States.

again, she chose French because it was "more intellectual." Soon she was a Francophile in training. Anne helped her with the language, although she candidly informed Jeane that she spoke as if with a mouth full of mashed potatoes. As soon as the school year was over, Jeane further irritated her father by traveling to Montreal to enroll in an intensive summer course in French at McGill. When she returned to Barnard for her senior year, she was able to hold her own in advanced conversational classes.

De Lattre noticed that Jeane didn't date Columbia boys as other Barnard girls did. She preferred self-identified "bohemians" who hung out in the Village. She spent most weekends there and got to know writers and artists, among them James Baldwin, with whom she became well enough acquainted to be allowed to call him "Jimmy." But she was not in New York for culture. As she later said, "The main reason I went to Barnard was because it was well known in those days as the premier bluestocking institution in the country—a place where women could take themselves seriously." In terms of her intellectual development, the next five years—two at Barnard for her BA and three at Columbia for graduate work—bled into one experience.

One of the things she'd been required to do immediately upon arriving at Barnard, since she came in as a junior, was select a major. She was interested in history and philosophy, but decided on political science because it straddled the others. The "science" part of the discipline vaguely reassured her father that what she was doing might eventually pay off.

As she tried to fathom the political complexities of the postwar scene, one event about which she felt she needed to have an opinion was the Alger Hiss trial. Most of the students she knew hated Whittaker Chambers and felt that Hiss was clearly innocent. But Jeane was going out with a boy whose father had been in the British foreign service and after studying the case felt strongly that Hiss could be guilty. Because of his opinions, she began reading excerpts from each day's proceedings in the next morning's

*New York Times*: "Once I started reading the daily transcripts, I found that I agreed with my friend's father—initially a crushing perception because it meant that I was different from the other right-thinking liberal students. But I couldn't deny it. Hiss had told a witting lie about not having been in Washington that summer. I thought that if he would lie about one thing, he might well lie about another. I found myself feeling irritated not only at Hiss himself but at the fact that the students and faculty around me could have caught me up in a net of expectation of his innocence. I never wanted that to happen again."

An even more significant event for her was the 1948 election. The campus seemed split between country-club Republicans for Thomas Dewey and romantic leftists for Henry Wallace. Jeane admired Truman for his strong international moves against Stalin, which meant, as she later said, "that I was regarded as totally out of it by most of the other students." To double-check her feelings, Jeane went to a Wallace rally. Pete Seeger played the banjo, and then the candidate was introduced by Norman Mailer —whose first novel, *The Naked and the Dead*, had just been published. Wallace came on stage and issued a dire warning about the fascist nature of the FBI, which he said would eventually round up all dissenters if not stopped by his election. Jeane was put off not only by these exaggerations but by the fact that most of his entourage were obviously Communists; and Communists, she had already decided, "were always defending the indefensible."

Jeane regarded voting for Harry Truman as a key moment in her life. In the memoir she tried to write forty years later she said of the episode: "I am retrospectively proud of myself for having resisted, at 21, the temptation of radical politics." She always remembered lying in bed in her Barnard dorm room "too excited to sleep" on the night of the election Truman was supposed to lose.

Awash in that undergraduate euphoria resulting from the sense of being agreeably assaulted by all kinds of new ideas at once, she happened at this time also to become close to the family of Jacob Robinson, born Jokabas Robinzmas, a Lithuanian Jew who had fled his homeland after the Hitler-Stalin Pact and wound up in America, where he was now serving as the first representative of Israel to the United Nations. His daughter had been in the intensive French course at McGill with Jeane and they had become friends. For a couple of months after her return to New York, she made weekly visits to the Robinson apartment to have dinner and listen to the Jewish émigrés and Holocaust survivors who gathered there to talk about the night and fog of the death camps. These harrowing personal accounts came at a time when the magnitude of the Nazi genocide was just beginning to be understood, and for months they affrighted her sleep.

---

After finishing her BA at Barnard in 1948, Jeane thought about going to Columbia Law School, where there were three women. Instead she decided on graduate school in political science, where there were four.

One of the first classes she signed up for was a four-semester course on German politics taught by the historian Franz Neumann. A German Jew who had worked as a lawyer in the Weimar government, Neumann was forced to flee to England when Hitler took power. During the war he had come to America to work for the Office of Strategic Services, precursor of the CIA. Afterwards he had worked at the Nuremberg trials under the chief prosecutor, Justice Robert H. Jackson, and helped write the postwar German constitution. When Jeane chose him to be her mentor, Neumann was a star on the political science staff at Columbia, teaching popular courses on his essential subject: how extremists of the right and the left, Nazis and Communists, had collaborated to cause the violent collapse of Weimar as supporters of the Republic stood by impotently appeasing them. This became one of the foundational lessons of Jeane's life.

Neumann's standing as an intellectual was primarily based on his classic work *Behemoth*, a mammoth study of the rise of National Socialism that portrayed Hitler's Germany less as a coherent state than as a cauldron of struggles among competing power groups. Jeane privately wondered about his worldview, an independent Marxism that did not apologize for Stalin but questioned the American role in the developing Cold War. (His two sons would inherit these views, becoming 60s radicals and doctrinaire leftists later in their lives.) But she found Neumann's mordant descriptions of his experiences in Weimar to be extremely powerful cautionary tales, particularly the stories of how Nazi or Communist groups would take over German towns and the Social Democrats would respond by *filing a suit*. "And by the time the suit was heard," she remembered him bitterly concluding these stories, "the totalitarian party had already consolidated control, killed some people and smashed some things."

Amused but also impressed by Jeane's ambition, Neumann urged her to sit in on lectures given by Herbert Marcuse, a fellow member of the Frankfurt School who had also fled Nazism and also worked for the Office of Strategic Services during the war and who now had a position in the State Department. Marcuse was a close personal friend of Neumann's (he would, in fact, later marry Neumann's widow) who helped him get a teaching position at Columbia in 1952.

Neumann also helped Jeane meet Hannah Arendt and attend some talks she gave on totalitarianism. Most important, because of her seriousness and her hunger to know more about the nightmare of genocide the world had just passed through, he allowed her to study files about the inner workings of Nazi governance he'd been given as part of his work consulting on a postwar German constitution. She found them chilling. As she later reflected, "I had led a pretty sheltered life up until then. I had little idea of the human capacity for evil. It was a deeply disturbing view that I acquired from these documents and from the sense I was getting of the magnitude of the Holocaust. It changed me forever."

Under Neumann's direction, she began a master's thesis in 1950 on Oswald Moseley's British Union of Fascists. She chose this subject because she was interested in quasi-popular antidemocratic movements. Moseley's was small enough to be manageable and not yet heavily studied. Moreover, the New York Public Library had an outstanding collection of materials on this subject.

By the time she received her MA in 1951, she had also done course work for her PhD and had begun to develop a dissertation, reflecting Neumann's own strong interests, about the Communist Party's appeal to members of the French middle class during the time of the Popular Front and afterwards. But her father's willingness to indefinitely support what he now feared was an endless dependency had worn thin. Fat let her know that she could complete her PhD if she must, but it would have to be on her own nickel.

Jeane saw this ultimatum for what it was: one last attempt to get her to come back to Mount Vernon and adopt a conventional life. But by this time, in addition to her academic ambition, she was committed to the idea that you can't go home again (having read the Thomas Wolfe novel and fallen under the sway of its woozy vision of a tragically lost past that barred the return of those who had left it). She saw that her personal freedom depended on taking up her father's challenge. She told her parents that she had decided to get "practical experience" in political science by trying to get a job at the State Department that would also allow her to save enough to complete the PhD.

Carrying letters of recommendation from Neumann, she arrived in Washington D.C. in the late summer of 1951 with two interviews lined up. One was with Neumann's friend Marcuse, who at that point was still working in the department's Central European section. She found him "very heavy-handed, very Germanic, very theoretical, very Marxist, and very pompous." But she might nonetheless have accepted his offer if the other interview had not gone so well. It was with a man named Evron Kirkpatrick, who headed a section of State called the Office of Intelligence Research. "Kirk," as everyone called him, might not have had Marcuse's glittering credentials, but he was an influential political scientist and a canny inside player in the intelligence and policy world, and therefore had standing of his own as an "action intellectual." More to the point, as far as Jeane was concerned, he was genuinely American in his pragmatism and patriotic centrism, and in this regard he was Marcuse's intellectual opposite. When he too offered her a job, she immediately accepted, not knowing that she had found the Pygmalion who would intellectually sculpt her in a way that brought her fully to life.

# KIRK

ONCE CALLED "the most famous unfamous man of his day," Kirk had just turned forty when he hired Jeane and was already a man in full. Chunky in build, with a receding hairline and thick glasses that tended to hide his intentions, he habitually wore a pleasant look that was at once noncommittal and knowing. While he had a large circle of friends, even those closest regarded him as someone who revealed few of his surfaces. ("The only way I can tell what he's thinking," Jeane later told a friend only half in jest, "is to study the books he keeps on his nightstand.")

Although he had few publications, Kirk was nonetheless an important figure in the developing field of political science, a sort of scholarly Johnny Appleseed who would strengthen the discipline by strategically helping graduate students get first jobs. He was also Hubert Humphrey's close friend and mentor and a player in Democratic Party politics. And, a final item in this bulging personal portfolio, he had worked alongside William Donovan, head of the Office of Strategic Services during the war, and retained connections with the CIA, its postwar successor.

Austin Ranney, friend and fellow political scientist, conducted an oral history with Kirk late in his life, which I stumbled across when looking at some of Jeane's papers. The family saga Kirk briefly told Ranney about, like Jeane's own, grew out of Middle America, although it had sharper edges. His mother's family—Kirk was always slightly amused to say their name: Shunkweiler—were fairly large landowners in Indiana at the turn of the century. His paternal grandfather, a Scottish immigrant, was a schoolteacher who lived near them. Kirk's father met his mother in his one-room school, married at the age of sixteen, and moved into a farmhouse on 180 acres given to them by the Shunkweilers as a wedding present. It was near the town of Raub, which had a church, a post office and a general store. The closest big city was Lafayette, about forty miles east.

Kirk was born in 1912, when his parents were nineteen. He was four years old when they divorced, and he lived with his mother until he was a teenager. By then, she had remarried to a man named Lawrence Reed, who was also divorced and had a daughter named Doris. Together the four of them made a new family.

As Kirk told Ranney, his mother was poorly educated herself, but understood the role that books could play in a social ascent and saved her money to buy him leather-bound sets of the works of Dickens, Emerson and other writers. The best student in his high school—he graduated at the age of sixteen—Kirk was drawn to the University of Illinois at Champaign by the $25-a-year tuition. His first year there, he took a class from Charles Hyneman, who would become one of the leading political scientists of his day and was regarded by many of his influential students as the most gifted teacher they ever encountered. Hyneman was only ten years older than Kirk, but already had an impressive intellectual gravity to go along with a quirky sense of humor. (He once innocently asked a Chinese graduate student in his class if Chinese people, who wrote from right to left, would also compile an index before writing the text of a book.) Hyneman would establish himself as an important political theorist and philosopher. "Nobody who ever came in contact with him failed to feel that he'd been touched by a great man," said Kirk, who remained his lifetime friend.

Kirk finished his degree in three years under Hyneman's influence and got his master's degree after one more year. Yale offered him a scholarship to study for his doctorate, and he left Illinois in the fall of 1932 at the age of twenty, having never been farther east than Peoria.

By this time, Kirk was a married man—the result, in Jeane's

possibly embroidered retelling, of something like a shotgun wedding. She claimed that Kirk had come home for summer vacation after finishing his master's degree to find his mother and stepfather waiting for him at the train station along with his stepsister Doris. He was accused of making her pregnant and forced to marry her, although the pregnancy, in this Sinclair Lewisesque episode, would turn out to be a ruse.

New Haven was the sort of environment calculated to make Midwesterners feel intellectually provisional and ill equipped. But Kirk bore down and got honors in all of his courses. He came away with the PhD in two years, writing a dissertation on the Federal Communication Commission's regulation of advertising.

The political science department at the University of Minnesota, one of the few places hiring in the middle of the Depression, came to Yale looking for promising young faculty members and offered him a job. He began in 1935 as an instructor making $1,800 a year, mainly teaching introductory courses in American government. His first child, a son named Thomas, was born not long after he and Doris arrived in Minneapolis. A daughter, Mary, came soon after.

Teaching night classes and correspondence courses to make ends meet, Kirk noted that while most books on American government were descriptive, concerned primarily with laying out the legal, constitutional and structural aspects of government, more cutting-edge work was beginning to be done in analysis and criticism. Working with a colleague, he began putting together a book of readings featuring work by some younger scholars who were starting to remake the political science field, such as V. O. Key and Stuart Chase, along with provocative generalists such as Harold Laski and Charles Beard. When it was published a few years later, *The People, Politics, and the Politician* sold over a hundred thousand copies and made Kirk widely known in the profession.

Minnesota in the early 1930s was a laboratory for radical politics. The U.S. Socialist Party had a strong presence in Minneapolis, and the state as a whole was regarded as an important enough target for the Communists that they sent Clarence Hathaway, later editor of the *Daily Worker*, there to organize.

A visceral New Dealer and Democrat who saw the labor movement as the bone marrow of liberalism, Kirk founded and headed Minnesota's first chapter of the American Federation of Teachers. He was also crucially involved in the struggle that defined the state's politics for a generation: between the Democratic Party and the Farmer-Labor Party, a populist movement that elected three governors, four U.S. senators and several congressmen in the 1930s, and eventually drew a significant Communist presence.

Kirk found a kindred soul with whom to discuss the state's unique political situation when Hubert Humphrey enrolled in one of his classes in the fall of 1937. The future vice president was actually slightly older than Kirk, having first begun as an undergraduate at the University of Minnesota seven years earlier, but then withdrawing after a year to help in the family pharmacy in South Dakota as the Depression hit. After getting the family business back on track, Humphrey returned to Minneapolis with the dream of earning a PhD in political science and becoming a college professor.

Humphrey began lingering after class to talk politics with Kirk, and soon the two of them were going out for beer a couple of times a week. Recently married, Humphrey and his wife Muriel began having dinner with Kirk and Doris. Not knowing about its ambiguous beginning, the Humphreys thought the Kirkpatricks' marriage was a good one. Doris was not as well educated as the other three and was still enough of a farm girl to feel a little daunted by big-city life in Minneapolis, but she was a good hostess and a good mother to Thomas and Mary, both of whom attended the highly regarded University Experimental School of Minneapolis along with other professors' children.

Soon other students with an interest in the state of the state began to enter the Kirkpatrick-Humphrey circle: Orville Freeman, a future governor of Minnesota; Eugenie Anderson, a future U.S. ambassador to Denmark and Bulgaria; Eugene McCarthy, a future U.S. senator then teaching at St. Thomas College in St. Paul; and briefly, Eric Sevareid, soon to become one of "Murrow's boys" reporting on World War II from Europe.

The members of the group shared a political vision that was socially compassionate and supportive of New Deal programs but also hard-line anticommunist. They were all appalled, for instance, by the way the Communists had bitterly opposed Franklin Roosevelt's foreign policy until Hitler invaded the Soviet Union, whereupon they suddenly became slavish supporters of the president.

Of all those in this "Minnesota Mafia," as it would become known, Humphrey was distinguished by an ability to galvanize individuals and groups with a verbal fluency whose only flaw seemed to be the lack of an off switch. (Muriel once famously reproached her husband, "Hubert, a speech does not have to be eternal to be immortal.") After helping him get the William Jennings Bryan award for the best senior essay, Kirk contacted his old mentor Charles Hyneman, who was now chairman of the department at Louisiana State University, and got him to give Humphrey a job as a teaching assistant.

Although it was stuck in the hinterlands of the deep South, LSU was just then becoming an exciting intellectual destination. Because of the large budget Governor Huey Long had given the university, Hyneman had been able to attract future stars of political science like Eric Vogelin, Walter Berns, and the brilliant and eccentric Willmoore Kendall.

Kendall, who would continue to play a bit part for several decades in Kirk's own life, was the son of a blind Oklahoma preacher regarded as a prophet by his flock. An intellectual prodigy who graduated from high school at thirteen and got his bachelor's degree from the University of Illinois at the age of eighteen, Kendall had been an evangelist for Marxism when he went to England as a Rhodes Scholar in the early 1930s. But a trip to Spain during the civil war transformed him because of the insight it offered into the murderous workings of Stalinism inside the Republican cause.

Kendall came back to the United States with the god of leftism having failed him. Unable to hold the line as a Roosevelt liberal, he began a slow transition toward the right that would eventually make him a leading theorist of extreme conservatism by the 1950s and 60s. His path would cross repeatedly with Kirk's in an odd pas de deux that included collaboration at the CIA, competition for academic positions and wary participation in the same social circle in postwar Washington.

Another protégé of Hyneman's at LSU who would play a central role in Kirk's life was Howard Penniman, who left Baton Rouge after getting his BA in 1939 to enroll in graduate school at the University of Minnesota. More animated than Kirk and less likely to automatically support what would become known as "Humphrey liberalism," Penniman, who married the daughter of the chairman of the university's political science department, would become Kirk's student and closest friend, standing shoulder to shoulder with him in the political wars that roiled the discipline over the next four decades.

When Humphrey's teaching assistantship ran out in 1940, he returned to Minneapolis. Kirk used his own connections in the labor movement to get him a temporary job training future WPA teachers, which led to a more permanent position as director of the state workers' education project and the opportunity to travel around Minnesota. Humphrey was supposed to be doing a PhD under Kirk's supervision, but by this time both men recognized that his future was in politics.

He wanted to run for Congress, but knew that if he did, the vote would be divided between Democrats and Farmer-Labor, and the Republicans would win. But mayor of Minneapolis was a nonpartisan job, and Kirk convinced him to run for it in 1943. The two of them hired a campaign manager and a former student of Kirk's who was working in a local newspaper to handle the media. The campaign had no money, but it had Kirk's political sophistication and Humphrey's inexhaustible energy. They lost narrowly, getting 47 percent of the vote, but established the candidate as a comer.

---

By the end of this campaign, Kirk was in Washington D.C. He had tried to enlist in the Army right after Pearl Harbor, but was turned down because of a hearing loss he hadn't noticed. A colleague in the University of Minnesota's geography department who had joined the Office of Strategic Services told Kirk that the OSS was looking for specialists in politics and political systems too. He volunteered and was accepted.

Initially he was assigned to the research and analysis branch, working under a former Harvard historian named William Langer as a control officer charged with making a coherent inventory of all the projects the OSS had in the works. As he made his way around the organization, Kirk was struck by the number of Communists working there, especially in the Latin American division. He relayed his concerns to William "Wild Bill" Donovan, head of the OSS. Donovan agreed that it was a problem and agreed too with Kirk's recommendation that Willmoore Kendall, who had by then left his university post to become an Army officer with the Inter-American Defense Board, be brought in to clean out the division. As a result of this episode, Kirk became Donovan's eyes and ears in the research division.

The OSS chief was, Kirk later said, the most interesting person he ever knew. Donovan had raised and helped fund an Army regiment that served on the Mexican border during Pancho Villa's incursions, and then was called into service in World War I. His actions during heavy fighting in France earned Donovan a Medal of Honor and the nickname "Wild Bill." After the war he was a crusading U.S. attorney in New York, who energetically enforced Prohibition. He ran for governor as a Republican in 1932, losing to FDR's successor, Herbert Lehman. Along the way, he developed a significant capacity for self-dramatization. Kirk always remembered sitting in Donovan's office watching him scream at a subordinate over the phone for nearly half an hour, then recline in his office chair and smile calmly after hanging up the receiver. "You've got to know how to do that," he said with satisfaction. "Anger, or what seems like it, can be an efficient tool."

At the end of the war, Donovan left the OSS to return to his New York law practice. When discussions were beginning about creating the CIA to pick up the work of the OSS, he called Kirk: "I want you to get someone to put together one copy of every report that has ever been done by the research and analysis branch of the OSS. I'll have a truck come pick them up." Flabbergasted, Kirk said, "That's illegal. They're classified." Donovan replied imperiously, "Who's going to do anything about it? Look, we're going to be accused of providing wrong intelligence about this and that over the next year or so, and by God I don't want to have a situation where I can't defend us by looking at the reports."

---

Kirk had kept his hand in Minnesota politics during the war. To save candidates like Humphrey from having to deal with the competitive overlap between the Democrats and the Farmer-Labor Party, he and the other members of the "Mafia" worked to combine the two. In 1944, after a series of fractious meetings, they succeeded in kicking the Communists out of Farmer-Labor and created the Democratic-Farmer-Labor Party. There was an immediate and dramatic payoff when Humphrey was elected mayor of Minneapolis on his second try in 1945. He was now becoming enough of a national figure that Saul Bellow—who had recently published his first novel, *Dangling Man*, and was teaching part-time at the University of Minnesota—briefly considered doing a book about his rise.*

During the war, the Kirkpatrick-Humphrey alliance had gained another key recruit in Max Kampelman, a future diplomat and Democratic Party leader. He had come to the University of Minnesota as a conscientious objector to take part in a "starvation project," studying the effects of the malnutrition that American prisoners of war were known to be suffering in Japanese concentration camps. While losing dozens of pounds, Kampelman decided to pick up a PhD in political science to go with the law degree he already had. He was attending one of the parties that political science graduate students threw on Friday afternoons when Humphrey dropped by. The new mayor was impressed by Kampelman's insights into the political scene—his thesis was on Communist Party involvement in the labor movement—and asked him to join in his administration.

Kampelman's "educated" anticommunism was useful. The Farmer-Labor Party was over, but the Farmer-Labor Association that comprised its rank and file persisted, increasingly under Communist control and always trying to infiltrate the new Democratic-Farmer-Labor Party. (When Orville Freeman, a Marine officer who had been wounded in the Pacific, tried to attend a postwar Farmer-Labor Association meeting, for instance, he was physically thrown out as a "spy" by the Stalinists.) To counter their influence, Kirk, Humphrey and Kampelman attended the founding meeting of the Americans for Democratic Action in Washington in 1947 and then formed a chapter in Minnesota to help ensure that the Democratic-Farmer-Labor Party would remain controlled by democrats. As a result, the DFL supported

---

* Bellow met Humphrey through Herbert McClosky, who joined the university's political science department right after the war and became another close friend of Kirk's.

Harry Truman in 1948, while the Communist bitter-enders in the Farmer-Labor Association supported Henry Wallace.

---

When Kirk returned to the University of Minnesota—for good, he thought—at the war's end in 1946, he spent weekdays teaching and weekends giving speeches to labor groups around the state, continuing the offensive against Communists while also laying the groundwork for Humphrey's planned 1948 Senate run. In the summer of 1947, his friend and onetime student Howard Penniman, then at Yale, invited Kirk to come to New Haven to teach two courses. In effect, it was a tryout for a permanent position that had become open in the political science department. In one of the coincidences that marked their personal and professional relationship, Kirk lost out to Willmoore Kendall for the job.

Upon leaving the OSS, Kirk had written a long memorandum proposing that the government continue the associations the spy agency had established with the leading academics during the war, since many of them were doing work he thought would continue to be useful to the government in the future. He didn't hear anything about his proposal for several months, but then Secretary of State Dean Acheson called to say that the memo had been widely circulated and generated positive opinions, and he asked Kirk to come back to Washington to work for the State Department (which had temporarily taken over many of the functions of the decommissioned OSS). He returned in 1947 as deputy director of the Office of Intelligence Research, ultimately becoming director of the Office of External Research, a unit that coordinated the intelligence uses of scholars and research institutions such as RAND.*

---

* Kirk later said that the scholars were "given funding for study of U.S. foreign policy objectives" and had in some cases been placed in U.S. universities. Howard Penniman, whom Kirk brought on as an assistant, said that his job was to "comb the displaced person camps [in Europe] for émigrés who

The following year, Acheson told Kirk that he wanted State to make better use of Soviet spies who had defected to the United States. He wanted to give them jobs, but wanted these jobs to be supported with private funds. He asked Kirk to get Bill Donovan to a form a group of private citizens to raise the money. Donovan, then re-established in his prestigious law practice, agreed to do it if Kirk would work closely with him. Kirk began traveling to New York three days a week.

At the beginning of the 1950s, Kirk, who had now left academia for good, could feel that he—and his generation—had come of age. Hubert Humphrey was now in town too, having been elected to the Senate from Minnesota, with Max Kampelman in his office as legal counsel. Other members of the Minnesota Mafia cycled frequently through Washington D.C., often meeting for dinners at the Humphreys' modest place in Georgetown.

In the next few years, as the postwar world took shape, Kirk became the inside player par excellence—with fingers in the intelligence world, Democratic Party politics, political science, and in the State Department's efforts to bring scholars and research organizations into its new psychological warfare program. He was at the apex of his influence when Jeane chose to work for him rather than Herbert Marcuse and thus gained entrée to the complex world he had created.

---

The first assignment Kirk gave Jeane was to edit a cache of papers containing accounts of life in the prewar Soviet Union. Some of these had been collected by the Nazis after intercepting Russians who were using the chaos of war as cover to flee the USSR. Others

---

might be able to answer sensitive questions about the USSR and Eastern Europe." These comments were made in 1989 to Christopher Simpson, author of *Blowback*, a book about the postwar recruitment of former Nazis by U.S. intelligence services.

came from debriefings by Allied military personnel of desperate émigrés after they had managed to reach Western Europe.

These documents were different from the materials about Nazism that Neumann had shown her a couple of years earlier: raw and unedited, a dark tunnel leading inexorably toward the bedrock evil of totalitarianism. As Jeane assembled them, the jagged pieces of this testimony formed a mephitic saga of purges and show trials; the use of famine to compel political consent; the beginnings of the industriously evil project that became the Gulag. The papers were supposed to yield a better understanding of the structure of Soviet society, but editing these materials—which, Jeane later said, "revealed a hell purposefully created by government"—left her with two questions about totalitarianism that she would spend the rest of her life wondering about: "How could people do this? How could other people let them?"

After she had been on the job for a few weeks, Kirk began stopping by her office to discuss these and other issues with her. Because of his professorial manner and background, it was easy for her to fall into the role of student with him, particularly since she was supposedly still working on her doctoral thesis. She was flattered when he asked her out to lunch and when, after a few months of deepening association, he began introducing her to impressive friends such as Hubert Humphrey and Max Kampelman.

By the late spring of 1952, Jeane had been drawn into an intimate relationship whose impulsiveness, according to Anne de Lattre and other friends with memories of these days, disturbed and disoriented her. It was not just that Kirk was fifteen years her senior, or that his worldliness made her feel callow and incomplete by comparison. The cause of her disquiet went deeper. As Kirk told her about himself, revelations coming out serially rather than in one conversation, she saw that beneath the surface of this uniquely successful and engaged life was a complex psychological underworld.

He told her about his marriage, and how, over the years, he had outgrown Doris ("a lovely woman," in the verdict of his friend

Max Kampelman, "but certainly no intellectual") as much as he had the childhood milieu that produced them both and caused their marriage. If they had stayed in Minnesota, perhaps it would have worked; but once he came to Washington and discovered the wider world, the relationship couldn't survive. By 1949, Doris had agreed on a divorce and moved back to Sheldon, Illinois, with the children.

Part of the reason for the breakup was Kirk's roving eye, a surprising attribute in someone who otherwise appeared so staid. He'd had a couple of relationships after the war. At a political science function in 1950, he met Evelyn Petersen, a pretty and energetic woman working as a journalist in Washington D.C. As the daughter of Minnesota's governor Hjalmar Petersen, someone Kirk had known and worked with over the years, she had good political genes. As a talented writer who became the first female editor at *National Geographic*, she had ambition and drive.

Evelyn was apparently pregnant when she and Kirk married in 1951. Soon after, in what must have seemed a judgment, his first-born, Thomas, was killed at age sixteen on a lonely rural road in Illinois when he lost control of his car and plowed into a semitrailer that exploded in flames. This event "cast a shadow over Kirk that lasted a long time," Father Jim Evans, husband of Thomas's sister Mary, said later on. When Evelyn gave birth to a daughter, Anna, shortly after Thomas's death, this second marriage was already disintegrating.*

Just twenty-four when she entered this picture and provided

---

* Many years later, when doing his oral history with Austin Ranney, Kirk talked at length about his first marriage, but didn't mention his second. Jeane followed the same strategy except that she didn't even mention the first one unless it was unavoidable. Kirk's son-in-law Jim Evans, who had an affectionate but somewhat wary relationship with Jeane, told me, "She had trouble acknowledging that Kirk had a life before he met her. She wanted badly to be the first and only. But then, she wanted to be the first and only in everything."

another degree of difficulty, Jeane, who had not yet experienced a mature relationship, was agitated by having done something she previously considered herself incapable of: falling in love with a much older man, who had two broken marriages behind him and two children, one an infant. It did not seem coincidental to her that she became seriously ill twice over the next year, suffering through episodes of a mysterious malady that doctors called simply a Fever of Unknown Origin. The first time it struck, she was hospitalized for a few days in Washington; when the second and more serious bout occurred, her parents brought her home and took her to Barnes Jewish Hospital in St. Louis. She was released after a week as a result of what her doctor ominously called a "remission," although he had not yet been able to diagnose the disease.

Back in Washington looking for a way out of her dilemma, Jeane heard that the French government had begun a program for American students modeled on the recently established Fulbright grants. She immediately applied, and was relieved in the summer of 1952 to hear that she had been awarded a fellowship to attend the Institut de Science Politique at the University of Paris. In the beginning of September, she booked a third-class passage aboard the *Ile de France* and sailed away from what she did not yet want to believe was her destiny.

# AMERICAN IN PARIS

ALTHOUGH IN some sense fleeing from herself, Jeane was thrilled to be an American in Paris at a time when leftovers were still on the table from the moveable feast of two decades earlier. The city may have been supplanted by New York as capital of the world, but it was still a place where living well was the best revenge; a place where "the soul and spirit could open up," in the words of Julia Child, who had just begun teaching American women in her Paris kitchen. Jeane sent home a contribution to Adlai Stevenson as the U.S. presidential campaign entered its home stretch, but otherwise intended, as she said later, to "go native."

She rented a room on the Rue de Lübeck, near the Trocadéro metro stop, from a French war widow, and ate breakfast and lunch every day with her and her young children. The routine into which she settled involved informal classes at the University of Paris and research at the Bibliothèque Nationale. Postwar austerity still had a hold on Paris. As winter approached, staying warm called for layering. There were occasional food shortages, and getting enough hot water for a bath at the widow's house required deep strategy. But still it was Paris; and Jeane, having left her troubles behind, had a strong sense that she was in for the time of her life.

She haunted Saint-Germain-des-Prés and saved up for skimpy meals at Les Deux Magots in hopes that she would see a famous writer or painter. She walked the city with methodical rigor, as she had New York when first arriving there. Always on the lookout for cues that would help form her dissertation on the appeal of communism for the prewar French middle class, she sometimes found them in the raucous clashes of competing parties in the streets, the Parti Communiste Français always chief among them.

The French government set up excursions into the country-side and meetings with intellectuals and politicians for the thirty-five fellows in the program. One of her classmates was a young German, the first from his country to receive a fellowship. Jeane remembered him as "blond and rather good-looking according to the Aryan ideal." He asked her out to dinner, and midway through the appetizers made a casual reference to having once been in the SS. As she later recalled, "I felt something like an electric shock go through me. Seeing my reaction, he explained that it was only at the end of the war when the SS couldn't fill its quota by volunteers and had to draft people like him. But stereo-typing took over and the guy changed before my eyes into a Hollywood Nazi and that was the end of that."

Jeane always considered herself fortunate to have arrived in France just in time to get a good seat for the event that everyone was talking about in Paris just then: the fierce battle of ideas between Camus and Sartre, which carried with it echoes of the deepening conflict between the Kremlin and the West, and eventually helped crystallize her own view of the stakes in this clash.

Although Camus had been involved in the underground struggle against the Germans and Sartre had not, the two men had become close friends toward the end of World War II; indeed, after Camus's early death in 1960, Sartre said that although they had not spoken in eight years, he still regarded Camus as his best friend. They'd taken parallel paths after the war—Camus as editor of *Combat*, the leading newspaper to have emerged from the Resist-ance; and Sartre as the head of *Les Temps modernes*, the leading intellectual journal of the day. Both were associated with existen-tialism, the first intellectual rage of the postwar world. In time, Camus would try to walk back from his involvement in this move-ment. Nonetheless, as Simone de Beauvoir said, he and Sartre had "provided the postwar world with its ideology."

Their friendship had always been a balancing act in which the two men, opposites in so many ways, tried to make their differences compatible. Camus, the *pied-noir* from Algeria, Bogart-handsome and filled with personal intensity, had a novelist's eye for human nature and the concreteness of experience, and had developed an austere hope in works such as *The Myth of Sisyphus* and *The Stranger*, where life was "absurd" in its denial of the human need for meaning but offered a grim freedom to those who accepted this condition.

Sartre, a privileged product of the École Normale Supérieure who was "toad-like and wall-eyed" in his own pitiless self-inventory, was the more remote theoretician, concerned with large philosophical projects such as *Being and Nothingness*, and increasingly convinced that the imperatives of History, with a capital "H," drove individual choice and destiny.

In the first postwar years they had shared a general commitment to "third way" socialism, but in the intensifying confrontation between East and West, a decision about communism was unavoidable. Camus, who had befriended Arthur Koestler and been deeply influenced by *Darkness at Noon*, was ambivalent toward the United States, but clear in his feelings about the USSR, as was seen in his simple formulation "Communism = Murder." For Sartre, on the other hand, Stalin's Russia might indeed be a charnel house, but must be supported nonetheless because it stood on the side of History as embodied in the revolution of the working class.

It became impossible to paper over their differences any longer when Camus published *The Rebel* in late 1951. In it he said that communism was a crime of logic and that the emancipatory impulse on which it stood was a one-way street to totalitarianism. Sartre gave the book to one of his underlings to savage in *Les Temps modernes*. When Camus wrote to complain about the brutal piece, Sartre published his notorious "My Dear Camus" response, filled with condescending ad hominem attacks. ("I do not reproach you for its pomposity," Sartre said of Camus's letter, "but rather the ease with which you handle your indignation.") He scorned his former friend's anticommunism as a "refusal to live in the real world." To Camus's criticism that the review of his book had not mentioned Stalin's prison camps, Sartre replied flippantly, "My God, how serious you are."

The *Temps modernes* issue featuring Sartre's attack sold out, was reprinted, and sold out again. Camus fought back, criticizing those whose choice of Communist means and ends made them "gravediggers of freedom." But he found himself isolated by the intellectual bloc that solidified around his former friend.

More a *Kulturkampf* than a mere literary feud, the conflict between the two men was a definition of one of the crossroads at which Western culture now stood: between the "intransigent reformist" and the "engaged revolutionary"; between the view that the "cult of history" is a dead end, offering only oppression, and the assertion that in the extreme circumstances of the Cold War, nothing short of "revolutionary violence" can free the wretched of the earth.

The aftershocks of Sartre's attack and Camus's doomed efforts to defend himself were still battering the intellectual world that Jeane entered when she stepped off the *Ile de France*. She soon found a copy of *The Rebel*, not yet translated, and read it in French. When Sartre gave a lecture on his position at a Paris bookstore, she forced her way through the crowds to get close to him and came away impressed by his gelid intellection but also appalled by what one of Camus's outnumbered defenders called his "intellectual delirium" about the USSR.

Then one of the University of Paris professors working with the French government fellows arranged for an appearance by Camus. Despite her reckless infatuation with Kirk, Jeane still thought of herself as a cautious person. But she felt "galvanized" by Camus. In part it was his good looks and electrifying presence.* Even more,

---

\* She had a soft spot for Mediterranean types. Many years later, a friend was with her at a restaurant when the Peruvian novelist Mario Vargas Llosa,

it was her recognition that he had a moral voice rather than simply a moral presentation. And most of all, she was seized by what she described to me as "his suspicion of abstract theory and its friendship with totalitarianism; his elevation of the human dimension over the political one; his focus on the impact of ideas and the personal consequences of ideologies."

She declared herself an unambiguous partisan of Camus and began to follow the struggle that continued between him and Sartre like the desperate fan of a brave but overmatched fighter, hoping against hope that he can score a knockout in the final rounds. But there was no such comeback. As the politicized Parisian literati increasingly ganged up on Camus, she later said that it felt like watching the intellectual equivalent of mob violence.

She saw Camus several more times during her stay in France and exchanged a few words with him on a couple of occasions, each time finding the experience "mesmerizing." (In describing these changes she would always add, "And despite my youth, I wasn't all that easy to mesmerize in those days.")

In arguments with the other French government fellows, many of whom were aligning themselves with Sartre, she fiercely defended Camus with the feeling that she was defending herself as well. (In our conversations about this time five decades later, she was pleased to note that Camus had been justified by the fall of the Berlin Wall after a long eclipse by Sartre, whose reputation had correspondingly plummeted, and she associated this volteface with a vindication of Reaganism itself.)

---

Her French had been fairly good when she arrived in Paris. Within a few months she was speaking fluently enough to

---

whose dark good looks were similar to those of Camus, came over and introduced himself. The friend noticed that Jeane was pleased by his attention.

impress even her demanding friend Anne de Lattre. She began seeking out and interviewing middle-class Frenchmen whom her advisors, knowing of her doctoral topic, identified as having been sympathetic to communism in the Popular Front. She was beginning to organize her dissertation when the malaise that had incapacitated her before she left the United States returned with even greater fury.

She gamely tried to continue attending the functions and field trips arranged by the French government for the fellows; when these outings became too much for her, she simply tried to get through her days. Increasingly, she stayed in her room on the Rue de Lübeck, not bothering to get out of bed. Her landlady finally insisted on taking her to see her own family doctor. He told Jeane that her symptoms made him fear that she might have leukemia or lymphoma. He made an appointment with a specialist at the Sorbonne who had the poetic name Stéphane Mallarmé and the august title Professor of Blood. So eminent was Mallarmé that the referring physician, excited himself to see this famous man, insisted on accompanying Jeane to the examination.

The Professor of Blood told her that she would have to endure a breastplate bone puncture to get a firm diagnosis. She underwent the painful procedure, without anesthetic, in the hospital. (Telling me about it a half century later, she couldn't keep from flinching.) Fearing the worst, she returned to Mallarmé a week later for his verdict. He gave her the good news—she was not dying—then the bad news: she had rheumatic fever and would suffer from heart irregularities the rest of her life. He prescribed massive doses of penicillin that she would have to take for months.

With what she had feared might be a death sentence having been lifted, she tried to become re-engaged in the large political questions. The one agitating most of the French students she met was the looming execution of the Rosenbergs, whose appeals had finally run out. As the date—June 19, 1953—approached, Paris was convulsed by Communist-directed demonstrations of solidarity with the couple. Jeane reacted in typical fashion by making an appointment with the press officer at the U.S. embassy and requesting a transcript of the trial. Somewhat taken aback, he told her that she was the only person ever to have asked for it. She spent days closely reading the document. Concluding that the Rosenbergs were indisputably guilty, she then spent the last days of their frantic appeals protesting against the French protesters who camped out at the American embassy. "I was a determined opponent of capital punishment then and always have been since, and didn't relish in the least their execution," she later said. "But I was appalled by the ignorance and cynicism of those who used this event to gin up anti-Americanism. The huge mound of flowers at the Place de la Concorde on the day they died seemed to me to be the most vulgar kind of political kitsch."

Being in Paris for ten crucial months was for Jeane what it had once been for Wordsworth: very heaven. She learned from her French contemporaries who had perfected disputation into performance art. In addition to sharpening her intellectual rigor, she had been an engaged witness in the cultural politics of the Camus-Sartre conflict; and she had also learned about good food. (A lasting lesson was that it was actually eating well that was the best revenge.)

She was still sick much of the time, although after filling Professor Mallarmé's prescription she began imperceptibly to improve. But more troubling than her physical problems was her inability to outrun the moral issue Kirk represented. He had continued to send her letters all during her absence. In the summer of 1953, with the French government fellowship nearing completion, she tried to delay crossing the Rubicon that lay ahead, telling her parents that she had decided to stay in France indefinitely. After he hung up from the phone call in which she conveyed this intention, Jeane's father, according to her brother Jerry, said to him, "Get ready to go to France with your mother to bring Sister home." But the emergency preparations were called off when Jeane rang a few days later to say that she had changed her mind and would be returning to the United States after all.

The reversal was caused by Kirk, who had turned up in Paris in full pursuit of her. Anne de Lattre, who had watched with interest what she came to regard as something of a *folie à deux*, was struck by his determination. "He was really chasing her. If he hadn't, she might have resisted. But he was erotically obsessed, and I think she came to feel that way herself."

Years later, Jeane told her lifelong friend Margaret Lefever, in a patent falsehood, that Kirk had used his intelligence connections to find out when she was sailing for home and had surprised her by suddenly appearing at the door of her cabin on the ship. In fact, the two of them, after several brightly lit Paris evenings together, had sailed home as a couple.

---

Back in Washington in the fall of 1953, Jeane now found it necessary to live provisionally. She and Kirk had to observe proprieties because of his career and her qualms. She had to support herself, but didn't feel it would be right to go back to work for Kirk at the State Department.

She got a job working at the Economic Cooperation Administration, assisting its director, Henry Price, in a book he was writing on the successes of the Marshall Plan. When it was published, *The Marshall Plan and Its Meaning* contained no acknowledgement of her contribution, a fact she later bitterly attributed to "prejudice against women."

She was making no progress on her dissertation but could still feel that she was vicariously part of the political science profession because Kirk introduced her to friends of his such as Charles Hyneman, now chairman of the department at Indiana University, Herbert McClosky, an increasingly important scholar who intrigued Jeane with his ideas on the use of survey instruments to research political attitudes and ideologies, and Harold Lasswell, an influential liberal often spoken of in the same breath as Walter Lippmann who had famously defined politics as "who gets what, when, and how."

In mid 1954, her illusions that she would soon pick up her doctoral work were destroyed by news that Franz Neumann had been killed in a car crash during a European holiday. Devastated by the loss, she traveled to Columbia University a few weeks later to talk about her academic future. She was told that there was no one else in the political science department familiar enough with French intellectual and political history to guide her and that she would have to find another topic and another advisor. The prospect seemed so daunting that she decided to give up on the PhD.

She could do this in part because she was still intellectually engaged in issues that interested her, especially those involving varieties of the totalitarian experience. Kirk had helped get her a job at the Human Resources Research Organization at George Washington University as part of a team working on recently transcribed interviews with Chinese Communist soldiers taken prisoner in Korea. The project was run by psychologists and sociologists from the University of Chicago—"a very savvy group," as Jeane described them—who had interviewed Chinese who had surrendered at the unit level and refused repatriation. (Many would eventually be relocated to Taiwan.) The consumers of these interviews were policy people at the Defense Department, which underwrote the project. The effort was informally referred to as Project Tick (as in "we've got to learn what makes the Chinese Communists tick") and was intended to get a focused picture of what was happening behind the Bamboo Curtain as a result of the Communist takeover there.

What she found in these files parlayed what she had learned from the other papers about Nazi and Soviet brutality. These verbatim accounts painted a picture of a society that had been systematically and totally revolutionized as Mao's army consolidated control of China village by village. The subjects were normal people, who described the methodical effort to break down individuals and create politically compliant automata from that human debris. "I felt that I was seeing something much different from what I'd seen in my academic work," Jeane later said of the experience. "It was perversely fascinating to watch through these interviews as a version of the New Man was created by the slow drumbeat of daily psychological violence."

The insight she had would stay with her and become part of her intellectual repertory: "What had gone wrong for most people in China wasn't political per se. It was change in the nature of everyday life that made their existence miserable: the doctor who could no longer practice; the engineers commanded to build bridges they knew would collapse; the family that was forcibly separated and commanded to denounce each other."

As she saw it, she had been given a privileged look into "systematic violations of the human being." The conclusion she drew from these papers was enduring: "I became convinced that a diabolical vision of the public good is the greatest horror and the source of the greatest evil in modern times."

---

During these months, there was increasing diplomatic activity with Mount Vernon. In a series of talks with her mother and father, she had gradually told them about Kirk. Fat Jordan's response surprised her. He said in effect that he'd rather have her be married to a man paying alimony and child support than be a spinster. Her brother Jerry, now twenty years old, had helped things along by coming to Washington for a visit. He met Kirk and came back home to tell their parents that he was "a helluva guy" (creating a memorable moment in which Leona accepted his evaluation but reproached him for his bad language). The next step involved the Jordans coming to Washington for a formal meeting during the holiday season of 1954, when their blessing was asked for and given.

Two months later, on February 22, 1955, Jeane and Kirk exchanged vows in front of her family's Baptist minister in the Jordans' living room in Mount Vernon. The bride was twenty-eight; the groom was forty-three. The wedding cake was double-tiered. Jeane wore an aqua chiffon dress designed by Oleg Cassini that she had saved her money to buy, although there were only six people present at the ceremony. Her father wore a look of relief as much as happiness, what he had wanted to happen at once having finally happened at last.

Jeane's most cherished wedding gift came from her mother: a handwritten book of recipes that recapitulated the Jordan family's history in Texas and Oklahoma. By the time the wedding announcement appeared in the local paper the next day, she and Kirk had already left town for their honeymoon—at the annual convention of the American Political Science Association at Northwestern University.

# "A Lousy Decade"

As the newlyweds moved into their row house on Potomac Avenue in Georgetown and began their life together, Kirk heard that the American Political Science Association was looking for an executive director. With the State Department undergoing a reorganization that would build more bureaucracy and reduce his intelligence functions, he decided to apply for the job and was hired by the retiring president of the APSA, Ralph Bunche. His first months were spent working with the incoming president, Harold Lasswell, who became a close friend of both Kirkpatricks, to increase the organization's membership and make it more significant, a task made difficult by the fact that the APSA was so poor that Kirk had to drastically cut salaries (including his own) and institute a rule that he personally had to authorize any expense of more than five dollars.

Jeane's income became important. Pregnant now, she continued to work through morning sickness at her job at the Human Resources Research Organization. She had reconnected with Margaret Lefever, her old friend from Stephens College who had just moved to Washington D.C. with her husband Ernest, a former international fieldworker for the YMCA who had taken a job in Hubert Humphrey's office that brought them into the Kirkpatricks' orbit. But for the most part, Jeane's social life was dominated by Kirk's friends. Some of them apparently still regarded her as a homewrecker (enough so that in a rare allusion to this issue in one of our conversations she singled out Max Kampelman as having been "very kind and not antagonistic like some of the others"), but her élan and the tenacity with which she chewed on ideas gradually won them over. Soon she was an accepted part of a remarkably tight and durable social circle that would remain intact for decades, until death claimed its members one by one.

Social science was its common denominator, along with the middleness of their Americanism as indicated by the Louisiana-Minnesota axis on which their relationships turned. Hubert Humphrey, who continued his interest in political science even after becoming a U.S. senator, loomed over the group. But at its core were Kirk and Jeane, and Howard and Betty Penniman, their close friends and frequent traveling companions. The two men had acted as each other's patrons over the years, Kirk bringing Penniman to the State Department in 1947, and Penniman bringing Kirk to the political science department at Georgetown to teach the introductory graduate course after he became chairman in 1957. Although they rarely talked about intimate matters, they became so close over the years that they bought adjacent burial plots ("so they could spend eternity discussing political science," a common friend said).

Also included in this close, at times almost incestuous group was Leon Crutcher ("lean and civilized," in Jeane's terse description) and his wife Anne. Like Hubert Humphrey and Howard Penniman, Leon had been a political science student of Charles Hyneman's at LSU and through him had met Kirk, whom he ran into again in Washington after the war when he took a State Department job helping implement the Marshall Plan. Anne Crutcher, who later worked as a food critic and eventually an editorial writer for the *Washington Star*, would become one of Jeane's closest friends, admired, in the words of the elegant obituary Jeane delivered at her death in 1983, for "a habitual, unflinching encounter with whatever life presented her—without denial, euphemism, self-pity or excuses." All through their thirty-year friendship, according to Anne's daughter Claudia Anderson, the two of them would pursue long-running arguments over questions such as whether Lear was senile or a fool, with Jeane arguing the latter position.

The wild card in the group was Willmoore Kendall, traveling to Washington occasionally from New Haven. His second wife, a vivacious Norwegian blonde named Anne Brunsdale, had herself been on the edges of the Minnesota Mafia while studying in Minneapolis during the war. Kendall had provided gossip for the group, having had an affair during the war with Anne Crutcher while her husband Leon was away fighting in the Battle of the Bulge, and later throwing a knife at Brunsdale during a heated quarrel that convinced her to leave him. More problematic than his erratic behavior, however, was the fact that Kendall was moving too far to the right too quickly—so quickly, in fact, that by the early 1950s he was eschewing both rollback and containment as strategies for dealing with the USSR, in favor of preemptive attack.*

Kendall was controversial enough that when Kirk was being interviewed for the job of executive director of the APSA, the relationship was raised as a red flag by those questioning him. As his politics became ever more conservative, Kendall himself felt less comfortable with the solidly liberal D.C. group and didn't wait to be ostracized. When he moved on, however, Anne Brunsdale, who stayed in Washington after their divorce, continued to be a

---

* And too quickly for Yale University as well, where he had beat out Kirk for a job a few years earlier. The liberal faculty there was so embarrassed by Kendall's views that it finally convinced the administration to buy him out of his tenured professorship in 1961. Kendall, who had been a mentor to William F. Buckley at New Haven and would briefly become a force at Buckley's *National Review* (where he was famously said never to have been on speaking terms with more than one staff member at a time), eventually became a Catholic and landed at the University of Dallas. There he continued to attract protégés and write conservative polemics until his early death in 1969, his later years having been enlivened by an unlikely friendship with the political philosopher Leo Strauss, regarded by some as the holy ghost of neoconservatism.

key member. She was an accomplished individual in her own right, eventually co-editing an influential magazine called *Regulation* along with a young Antonin Scalia at the American Enterprise Institute, and joining Jeane in the Reagan administration later on when she served on the International Trade Commission.

The members of this social set were mostly inlanders, not Ivy Leaguers. Claudia Anderson, who saw the group close up as the daughter of Leon and Anne Crutcher, later compared them to the Jews of New York City College in the 1930s: very American, yet slightly alien among the elites that began to form in postwar Washington and create the American Century. Almost all of them were the first of their families to attend a university. They all came from modest circumstances. (Howard Penniman's father was for a time a sharecropper; Claudia's own, Leon Crutcher, had to hitchhike between his family home in Oklahoma and LSU in the years he studied there.) They made their way by sheer intellectual force rather than by networks—except those they built with each other. They were pragmatic "show me" people, and unapologetic in a patriotism that would not be shaken even during the turbulence of the Vietnam era.

Most of these couples also already had young children. In July 1956, Jeane and Kirk joined them in this regard when their son Douglas was born. A month or so later, Kirk was off with Humphrey to the Democratic National Convention, where Humphrey tried vainly for the vice-presidential nomination that Adlai Stevenson had thrown open to the delegates. While he was gone, the baby had what Jeane later described as "nonstop colic," which became so bad that she finally got on a train and went home to her parents. Her father told her confidently that all the baby needed was to be put on a schedule. A week later, Fat had bags under his eyes like everyone else in the house forced to endure the interminable screaming. Jeane always remembered the moment in the visit when her mother suddenly stood up, put on her coat and went to the door. Jeane asked where she was going. With a desperate look in her eyes, Leona replied, "To a prayer meeting at the church to ask the Lord to make Douglas be quiet."

Over the next three years, Jeane had two other boys—John and Stuart—as the family moved to a ranch-style home on Granby Street in Bethesda, Maryland. She was moving fast because of Kirk's age. It was maybe too fast for Douglas, who had an imaginary friend named Louie. When Stuart was born and Douglas was asked how he liked the baby, he replied, "Fine, but Louie wants to feed him to the lions."

Quiet and self-possessed, Kirk connected with the kids naturally, neither expecting nor demanding much from them. "He was helpful," Jeane later said, "but more or less went on with his life. I was deeply involved with my children for many years. He was not an equal partner in this. No man is. It didn't have the impact on his life that it did on mine. Nor would I argue that it should have."

Jeane accepted the role of "800-pound gorilla in all the rooms of the boys' lives" (as one close friend put it) because she deeply romanticized motherhood, insisting that it was absolutely necessary for a woman to experience completion in her life. Eventually this point of view would develop into a provocation, as in a comment in an interview she gave in the mid 1980s when she had become one of feminism's bêtes noires: "Having and raising babies is more interesting than giving speeches at the United Nations. Believe me." Yet mothering sometimes seemed an act of will more than instinct with her—"painting by numbers," in the words of a friend. She and Kirk occupied each other's lives so completely that there didn't seem to be much room left for anyone else. But there was also in Jeane herself a restricted zone of privacy that even those closest to her were barred from entering. She was, in the revealing words of her second and closest son John, a "distant hugger" who once confided in him that for the most part she didn't like to be touched—by her children or anyone else.

The professorial air she adopted with the boys struck some observers as odd, in particular her tendency to refer to them in their presence in the third person—as in, "Douglas Kirkpatrick has the idea that he should stay home from school when his finger hurts"—and the way in which the affectionate irony she used with them sometimes shaded into ridicule. Her mother, who visited frequently, told one family friend that she thought Jeane's constant instruction was intended to affirm her own parenthood as much as to improve the children themselves, and believed it had created an edgy atmosphere in the Kirkpatrick household.

In these early years of marriage and motherhood, Jeane smoked fairly heavily and apparently had sessions with a psychiatrist for a brief time. Although she despised the counterculture of the 60s and its long half-life in the following decade, she became interested in the work of Wilhelm Reich, a figure this movement rehabilitated and made iconic. Jeane started with *The Mass Psychology of Fascism*, where Reich defined communism as "red fascism," a kissing cousin to Nazism, and stayed on for a little bit of Reichian psychology. Even her closest friends did not know of her brief but intense dalliance with Reich's ideas about the primordial potency of orgone energy—an absence of which he believed caused decreased libido and a variety of illnesses. According to one of her sons, Jeane went so far as to have one of the boxes called "orgone accumulators" built for her bedroom closet. (It is not easy to imagine her sitting in it and waiting for the orgone energy to be absorbed and take effect.)

Balked ambition may have had something to do with the tensions she felt during this period of her life; equally if not more responsible was the fact that Kirk, rather than pressuring her to be a traditional wife, "pushed her hard to achieve," in the observation of her friend Anne de Lattre. He also led the way to the areas in which the achievement could take place.

He himself was focused on communism in his first years with Jeane. (And friends couldn't help noticing that with his round-rimmed glasses, white goatee and receding hairline he had a slight resemblance to Trotsky.) He was appalled by Joseph McCarthy primarily because the Wisconsin senator's wild excesses made anti-anticommunism respectable. His own opposition to the Communist Party had hardened since his OSS days, when he had gotten to know James Burnham, onetime Trotskyist leader turned fierce anti-Stalinist. The two became close after the war when Burnham made himself a father figure to William F. Buckley and other young conservatives. Other Humphrey liberals were a little worried by Kirk's association with someone willing to wage "World War III," but Kirk saw Burnham as someone Jeane could learn from and frequently brought him home to dinner.

He also introduced her to another friend, Sidney Hook, a former Communist who had broken with the party over the purge trials and was also become a leading anticommunist—although unlike Burnham he continued to think of himself as a democratic socialist. Hook in turn brought people to the Granby Street house such as Freda Utley, the former British Communist who had lived with her Russian husband in the Soviet Union until he was arrested and sent to the Gulag; and Hede Massing, who had trolled for recruits to communism in the FDR administration during the 1930s and testified against Alger Hiss at his second trial.

In 1956, Kirk edited *Target: The World*, a book whose sensational title was belied by sober contents describing and analyzing Communist propaganda activities around the world during the previous year. (*The New York Times Book Review* said that "it ought to be read by every thinking citizen concerned with world affairs and the survival of our way of life.") He followed this with a companion volume, *Year of Crisis*, in 1957, and in his introduction he described Soviet policies as presenting "special problems and special opportunities" as a result of the Red Army's crushing of the Hungarian uprising and Khrushchev's revelations about Stalin at the 20th Party Congress in Moscow.

Following his lead was easy for Jeane because of the insider's view of the connections between communism and totalitarianism she had already acquired. She got a part-time job doing research for one of the volumes on American communism in a Fund for the Republic series sponsored by the Ford Foundation. While working on it, she heard that the *New Leader* magazine had scheduled a symposium of essays on "The Younger Generation," and she submitted one. To her surprise, it was accepted—the only one in the issue by a woman and the only one to be cautious about the cultural euphoria ignited by the New Frontier. Her essay was published alongside pieces by Norman Podhoretz and other writers beginning to make their mark, although to her dismay it was retitled as "The Distaff View."

But the project had an added dividend: an invitation from Sol Levitas, the *New Leader* publisher, to co-edit with him a book of essays on Communist takeover tactics in countries around the world. Commissioned by Farrar, Strauss, it was to be called *The Strategy of Deception*. Jeane jumped at the chance, noting that the only advantage in having three children under the age of four was that they napped at the same time and allowed her a brief opportunity to do "intellectual work." When Levitas died suddenly midway through the project, Jeane became sole proprietor.

Her introduction to *The Strategy of Deception* showed a scholarly mind and a combative polemical sensibility not at all awed by the fact that this was her intellectual maiden voyage. The ideas may have had something to do with Kirk, but the authoritative voice crackling with irony is hers alone. Writing about the bankruptcy of the Communists' goals, for instance, she says:

> It is now well known to historians and social scientists outside the circle of Communist orthodoxy that the class struggle described by Marx, and thought by him to be the motor of historical change, has failed to develop as predicted. In the most industrially advanced nations, the working classes have not been kept at a subsistence level, the middle classes have not been pauperized, the cycles of prosperity and depression have not become shorter, nor

the depressions more severe. The "inevitably" catastrophic development of capitalism has failed to occur. . . . "Socialism" is imposed on pre-feudal societies; Communist parties serve as a "vanguard" of the proletariat in nations with no proletariat; conquest, subversion and *coups d'état* are substituted for proletarian revolution; the elites of intellectual freebooters are substituted for the working masses.

The book became a Featured Alternate at the Book-of-the-Month Club and put Jeane's name in circulation. With Kirk's help, she got a part-time job teaching two classes of political science at Trinity College, a Catholic women's school founded by the Sisters of Notre Dame at the turn of the century. But she refused to admit that it represented a stirring of dormant ambition, instead (typically) explaining it as simply a way of making enough money to finance some housecleaning and child-care help so that she could be a more effective mother.

By the mid 1960s, as the boys were all enrolled at Sidwell Friends School, the question of her future was an ongoing subject of discussion with Kirk. She always remembered the afternoon he staged a discussion with her about finishing her PhD. She argued the "no" position, using the children as a reason not to take on such a task. He ignored the excuse: "Getting the degree is crucial to doing the things in life you really want to do. You need to do it."

A possible subject for a dissertation arose out of their discussions: Peronism after Peron in Argentina. She wrote a prospectus and sent it to the American Association of University Women, which at that time had a program to help women who had dropped out of professional life and were now looking for re-entry. Her proposal was flatly rejected. Not only that, but an AAUW representative brazenly followed up with a hectoring phone call insisting that at this stage in her children's lives Jeane had a responsibility to stay home.

The irritation caused by this episode, as much as pressure from

Kirk, helped mobilize Jeane in the spring of 1963 to take the train up to New York, where she made arrangements to get back in the doctoral program at Columbia. The political science department was, she felt, not particularly sympathetic to her situation as a mother with three young children, but it readmitted her nonetheless and assigned a scholar named Dankworth Rustow as her advisor. He was not the major figure Franz Neumann had been. But Jeane was no longer a starry-eyed graduate student and probably wouldn't have had much patience any longer with Neumann's "independent Marxism" in any case. Helped out by a grant from the Andreas Foundation, set up by Hubert Humphrey's friend and largest contributor Dwayne Andreas, she began her research.

---

Jeane felt that the 60s was a "lousy time." Kirk agreed, although his disenchantment began even before the apotheosis of the New Left and the appearance of the counterculture. He had worked hard on Hubert Humphrey's 1960 campaign for the presidency and had seen the Kennedys in close enough focus to become a cynic about the New Frontier. (He also got Jeane involved in a minor way, her first experience as a campaign insider, by encouraging her to write a subtly pro-Humphrey article on the Wisconsin primary for the *New Republic*.)* The two of them were at the 1960 convention in Los Angeles where there was early talk about Orville Freeman, governor of Minnesota and part of the

---

* The article, never included in Jeane's bibliography or mentioned by her, was published on April 15, 1960, the only piece in the issue that had no author's bio. After analyzing the vote, it ends by suggesting that Humphrey's appeal to blacks was superior to JFK's: "Since election experts have attached great importance to the urban Negro vote in the swing states of the North, Humphrey's great strength [with] Wisconsin's Negroes deserves special mention. . . . In the two [Milwaukee] wards which are 90 percent colored, Humphrey outpolled Kennedy and Nixon by three and four to one."

Humphrey-Kirkpatrick circle, as a possible vice-presidential nominee. But Kirk told Jeane that the "Kennedy machine" would never choose him. They were in Freeman's suite when word came from Bobby Kennedy's staff that it would be Lyndon Johnson.

Jeane and Kirk felt vindicated in their mistrust of the Kennedys by the Cuban missile crisis, which he particularly believed was the result of their incoherent leadership. Jeane spent the dangerous hours of October 1962 glued to the television set, coming up for air periodically to ask Kirk why they hadn't thought to build a fallout shelter in their back yard.

In the early stages of the Vietnam War she attended teach-ins, one of them at the Pentagon, where she was surprised to see wives of figures in the Johnson administration in attendance. At one point she listened to the political scientist Hans Morgenthau talk about how he opposed the war not because it was immoral but because it was not in the nation's interests. This was half right, she thought to herself: "I didn't have a moral issue about Vietnam. I thought we were morally right. But there was a policy argument. One of the responsibilities governments have to citizens is not to ask them to make impossible sacrifices—in this case, sacrifices ordinary Americans can't understand, identify with or accept. But Kirk and I were never under any illusions that Ho Chi Minh was just some peasant nationalist."*

Her views about the antiwar movement were always much stronger than her views about the war itself. She thought Lionel Trilling was exactly right in his ideas about the "adversary culture," the term he coined in 1965 to describe the perdurability of the romantic revolt against bourgeois society and the legitimization of

---

* If she was disgusted by the intellectual attack on U.S. motives for entering the war, she was even more disgusted years later by the eventual U.S. withdrawal—the manner more than the fact of it. She wrote Hubert Humphrey in 1975 of her "indescribable distress and anguish" over this event and called it "the most shameful display of irresponsibility and inhumanity in our history."

the subversive. But as the antiwar movement intensified and began to flow osmotically in and out of the counterculture to produce a wholesale disaffection from everything America represented, Jeane believed that the divisions it created were deeper and affected more domains of our national life than any pondered in Trilling's theory. Decades later the subject was still raw for her: "I deeply opposed attacks on the integrity of our government and culture. I always believed in the importance of truth, law and authority. Military kids grow up with such values. So do Oklahoma kids."

Outraged because the New Left was so cavalier about an issue—Communist totalitarianism—that was central to her intellectual life, Jeane felt herself pulled for the first time toward the right. It was a tendency she fought against; the example of Kirk's old friend Willmoore Kendall existed as a cautionary tale about how hard it was to stop the slide after the first doubt. But the same thing was happening with many of her friends as well. The earlier social group that she and Kirk were part of had morphed into an informal club called the Winetasters. They held monthly meetings—sometimes in the rumpus room the Kirkpatricks had added to the Granby Street house—where everyone pitched in small sums of money to buy what were then cheap but would later become expensive foreign wines, sometimes put in paper bags for blind tastings. The nucleus of their old group had expanded to include people such as conservative activist Chuck Lichenstein; political scientists Karl Cerny, Roy Godson and Austin Ranney; Seymour Bolton, an American Jew who had been captured by the Nazis in World War II and survived a concentration camp and who was now serving in the CIA as assistant for clandestine service; sometimes Eleanor Dulles, sister of John Foster and Allen; and occasionally a stray academic who had benefited from Kirk's patronage, such as Aaron Wildavsky of the University of California at Berkeley.

The Winetasters' get-togethers had some of the academic tweediness of the faculty lounge, although from the perspective of some of the participants' children, who were often part of the mix, they also had some of the qualities of trial by ordeal. Anne Crutcher's youngest daughter Colette, for instance, was always struck by the loud and dominating presence of the three Kirkpatrick boys, who insisted on playing roughhouse games they invented on the spot, such as one called "TV dodgeball," in which they described a television show to one of the other kids and began to smash him with a soccer ball if he didn't immediately name it.

For the adults, the gatherings were only nominally about wines (French and German only, no Italian or Californian). The politics of the day were the real reason for gathering. Howard Penniman, always the most conservative of Kirk's close friends and now an unapologetic Republican, occasionally put a sharp polemical edge to some of the meetings by getting "very excited," in Karl Cerny's words, about the increasingly turbulent domestic scene. With his slightly world-weary air, Kirk tended to believe that fears of the New Left and what it represented were overwrought. But here Jeane disagreed. The antiwar street actions sweeping the country called to her mind the mobs she had studied in her research on the Chinese revolution. (She later referred to them as "American Red Guards" in her draft autobiography.)

The PhD thesis she was writing reflected some of these concerns elliptically. Juan Peron might have been an admirer of Mussolini, but he was no Hitler and Peronists were not Nazis. The *personalismo* he used to gain power was different from that of Fidel, for instance, in that it was "non-revolutionary." The Argentina he shaped (that "haunted house" whose ghost he was and would be) was governed not so much by an anti- as a non-democratic movement—"a contemporary Caesarist movement," Jeane would call it when she turned the thesis into a book.

Harold Lasswell provided its title, *Leader and Vanguard in Mass Society*, as well as an introduction. The book was written in junior-professor academese, but its concerns reflected issues Jeane had been pursuing since her days at Barnard. In particular, she was

intrigued by the indeterminate nature of the Argentine system—
not totalitarian but not typically authoritarian either because of
the legacy of Peron, a "popular dictator whose mass support was
crucial to his power." She examined in detail the "interactions" of
those leaders who followed him in the first post-Peron decade of
1955–65 and also the "wants, goals and beliefs" of the masses who
had been mobilized by Peronism. To achieve this, she used her
social science skills to design a survey asking them questions
meant to uncover the political motivations of real people living
inside hypertrophied historical circumstances.

In the evanescent manner of such scholarly books, *Leader and
Vanguard in Mass Society* established Jeane more firmly in the academic world and then disappeared. A decade later it was suddenly and unexpectedly (and briefly) exhumed, and examined
more minutely than it had been upon publication, when Jeane
found herself embroiled in the Falklands War at the UN and her
enemies tried to use the book to substantiate their view that she
was friendly to dictators.

---

For Jeane and Kirk, the most distressing feature of 60s radicalism
was its deliberate targeting of the centrist liberalism that had created America's postwar prosperity and committed the country to
the defense of freedom. They were dumbstruck by the fact that it
was not the right-wingers who were the "Nazis" of the New Left's
imagination, but liberals like themselves—liberals who had
helped build the civil rights movement but were now "racists";
liberals who had supported decolonization around the world but
were now "imperialists." An icing of radical chic made this unpleasant intellectual confection infuriating as well as dangerous.
After it published a notorious drawing of a homemade Molotov
cocktail on its cover, Jeane angrily cancelled her subscription to

the *New York Review of Books*, writing the editors: "Please do not ever send me another issue of your revolting rag."

As the grand coalition of the New Deal was systematically dismantled, Jeane felt herself pushed into a we/they polarization. As she later wrote,

> "We" affirmed the validity of the American dream and the morality of American society. "They" adopted the characterization of intellectuals like Charles Reich [author of the New Age tract *The Greening of America*] who described the U.S. as a sick society drunk on technology and materialism. "We" rejected the effort to revise American history, making it a dismal tale of dead Indians and double dealing white settlers, imperialism and war. "They" rejected facts and truths we hold dear. "Their" extravagant attack on American culture and institutions made "us" progressively aware of our attachment to both. "Their" urgent utopian schemes for reform of almost everything made "us" more aware of our fundamental caution concerning radical reform.

The political became as personal for her in the late 60s as it was for any New Leftist when *Ramparts* magazine opened the floodgates of revelation about the CIA's Cold War uses of domestic institutions with its exposé of the agency's clandestine support of the National Students Association. *Encounter* magazine, Radio Free Europe and other Cold War institutions that had received the same secret backing were soon also attacked as "fronts." Kirk was caught up in this net because of a side enterprise he'd begun in the late 1950s called Operations and Policy Research, whose work he later described in the lengthy interview conducted by his friend Austin Ranney as "identifying people who could do jobs on various problems of interest to the government and figuring out how to get money from the foundations to pay them." The emphasis was on sending academics to Latin American countries to do studies there. Dwayne Andreas, Humphrey's wealthy backer, made the first grant to OPR. Others came from the Sidney and Esther Rabb Foundation and from the Pappas Charitable Trust, both eventually accused of serving as "conduits" to funnel CIA money into ostensibly independent institutions.

OPR and Kirk were named by Neil Sheehan of the *New York Times*, in an article that appeared shortly after the *Ramparts* exposé in 1967, as having secretly aided the CIA. Max Kampelman, who was working closely with Kirk at the American Political Science Association when the controversy erupted, says that what Kirk did was relatively modest: helping U.S. Information Agency libraries around the world know what books were worth stocking, and working to foster free elections in Latin America. Jeane always answered the question of the nature of Kirk's intelligence ties with frosty ambiguity: "What did I think about all this? I thought it was his business. Kirk knew a lot of people and was involved in a lot of things when I met him. It was always clear to me that he was going to continue to be.... [P]romoting maximum utilization of information and information gathering techniques, including public opinion surveys, was one of his passions. I became aware that Kirk was advising the CIA on public opinion polling—sampling, interviewing, analyzing data—during the Vietnam War.... Anything he did for the CIA in his later years was peripheral to his involvement in the American Political Science Association. But if in his spare time he wanted to do something for the government that he and the government thought was useful that was fine by me.... I have no doubt that his activities were honorable and his purposes were good and that I would have been proud of them if I'd known more about them than I did."*

---

* The issue of Kirk and the CIA continued to simmer for years and became a convenient way for the left to hit Jeane with a carom shot after she became ambassador to the United Nations. In February 1981, Alan Wolfe wrote

The other battleground where Kirk had to defend himself from the new radicalism was the APSA itself. He had rescued the organization from virtual bankruptcy and doubled its membership, also making it into an institution that encouraged scholars to answer the long-standing question "Where's the 'science' in political science?" But in 1969, a radical group calling itself Caucus for a New Political Science tried to take over the association. The members of this rump disrupted the national meeting, demonstrating what Kirk later described as "the angry behavior already seen on their campuses." Worse from his point of view was the way in which eminent members of the profession who did not agree with their politics were attacked from below by this academic lumpen who made it clear that they regarded these leading scholars as "collaborators."

Aided by Samuel Huntington and other important figures in the discipline who rallied to his side, Kirk managed to quell the rebellion. Because of the fight he waged, the APSA—unlike the American Historical Association, the Modern Language Association and other professional societies—was not taken over by radicals. Jeane always called this "one of my husband's finest hours."

---

She may have hated the 1960s and the 1970s (a decade she saw as "underrated for badness"), but Jeane owed the era a debt for helping

---

an article in the *Nation* in which he called Kirk an agent and said that he had received subventions from the agency at OPR. The eminent political scientist Theodore Lowi, no conservative, responded with a withering letter to the editor (printed as "McCarthyism of the Left") attacking Wolfe for the sloppy mistake in identifying Kirk in the article as the brother of CIA inspector general Lyman Kirkpatrick, for claiming erroneously that the APSA had passed a resolution asking him "to sever his connections with the CIA," and other inaccuracies, and called the piece "a small drop of poison in the American political discourse."

her sharpen her sense of what was at stake in the left's attack on America and sharpen her intellectual skills as well. She was combative but not overly aggressive: a counterpuncher. (One person compared arguing with her to playing tennis against a wall: the ball came back at you just as hard as you hit it.) She could be evasive herself, but was capable of scathing contempt toward anyone else who seemed to duck the big questions. Jim Evans, husband of Kirk's daughter Mary, remembers visiting the Kirkpatricks in 1966. He was having a conversation with Jeane, at her instigation, in which she asked a question he didn't want to answer for fear of becoming embroiled, so he replied with a polite truism. She gave him a shriveling look, said "Everything you say is inconsequential," and walked off.

Those who had watched her evolution as Kirk's protégée saw that she had now become much more than that. In 1967, hearing that her thesis was nearing completion and knowing of her teaching success at Trinity College, Karl Cerny, Howard Penniman's successor as chairman of the political science department at Georgetown, offered her a tenure-track position. Because Cerny was also in her social set as a part of the Winetasters group and might be seen to have a conflict of interest, she asked him to look over a draft of her dissertation so he wouldn't have buyer's remorse. He read it and told her it was excellent. She became the second woman ever on the political science faculty.

In May of 1968, which she would always regard as America's *annus horribilis*, she deposited a copy of her approved dissertation at Columbia's Low Library—a building she could reach only through a tunnel, accompanied by a policeman, because the university was then under assault by student radicals who were engaged, as she put it, in "objectively fascist behavior."

Kirk had also pushed Jeane into a deepening involvement in Humphrey's 1968 campaign for president. After her first tenuous involvement in 1960, she had written speeches for him in 1964, when he ran for vice president, but was still present only at the edges of the campaign. In 1968, as Humphrey battled Eugene McCarthy and Robert Kennedy for the nomination, Jeane was more closely involved than Kirk himself. Partly as a result of her use of surveys and statistical data in her dissertation, she had developed abilities in public opinion sampling that helped her play a role in the campaign's decisions on how such data should be organized to shape the candidate's image.

Kirk thought the divisions in the country and Humphrey's identification with LBJ would make it difficult for him to get elected, and difficult to govern even if he did. As the convention drew near, he had the idea of asking Nelson Rockefeller, just beaten by Richard Nixon for the Republican nomination, to run as Humphrey's vice president on a unity ticket. After Humphrey gave his assent, Kirk and Max Kampelman, working through David Rockefeller, got an invitation for Kampelman to speak to Nelson over dinner at the family estate at Pocantico Hills. Happy Rockefeller urged her husband to accept the offer, but Nelson, after giving it a few hours' consideration, decided against it.

In late August, Jeane and Kirk were at the Palmer House Hotel in Chicago, looking through their window at surreal cloud formations of tear gas below, as police skirmished with demonstrators. When the radicals put uric acid in the hotel air conditioning system, filling the rooms with the smell of vomit, they ran outside gagging with the other guests.

Inside the convention center, Jeane watched with disgust as Humphrey was branded a warmonger because he didn't sign on to the plan of the McCarthy and McGovern delegates to commit the party to unconditional unilateral withdrawal from Vietnam. "It was so unfair to see a decent man such as Hubert so ruthlessly attacked," she later said. "I never forgot that disgraceful display."

In that fall's campaign, some of Humphrey's supporters urged him to dramatically repudiate LBJ. Kirk didn't agree: "Hubert's position on Vietnam was not because of LBJ but because he believed in the war and [repudiating it] would have involved more than breaking with LBJ; it would have involved breaking with himself." Kirk met with a small group of Humphrey brain-trusters under the leadership of Orville Freeman in Washington at seven o'clock every morning from the time of the convention until the election to help Humphrey deal with the crises that arose each day.

In the last week or so, as the race tightened with momentum in Humphrey's direction, Jeane dared to hope that he might win. But Kirk said he wouldn't. As the returns came in on election night, their feeling that Humphrey and they themselves had been betrayed by their own party deepened.

Jeane later said, "The Democratic Party was, for people like me, a primal identification—what some women mean when they refer to something being like 'the father of my children.'" She always remembered a conversation with Kirk after Humphrey's defeat in which he told her that he thought this might be the beginning of the end as Democrats for people like them. She remembered her reaction too: *Unthinkable!*

---

Both to get perspective on what was happening and to get away from it, Jeane took a sabbatical and Kirk took a leave from the APSA in 1969 so the family could spend several months in Aix-en-Provence. One of the many pies in which Kirk had a finger was the Institute of American Universities in Aix, one of the first study-abroad programs for U.S. students. He was on the school's board of directors and arranged to teach there for a term while Jeane wrote.

They rented a place in the shadow of Mont Sainte-Victoire—a subject that Cézanne painted more than fifty times—and put their three sons in a local school. This was a temporary relief for Kirk, who often complained that three tuitions at Sidwell Friends School was "ruinous." The boys were forced to make their way as foreigners in the Darwinian French schoolyard. When they came home bloodied from combat, Jeane was upset enough to talk about packing up and going home. But Kirk said they would accommodate, and they did.

It was on this trip that Jeane decided she would try to turn herself into a serious French cook. She learned about local fresh ingredients and fell in love with such things as *aioli*, *anchoïade* and *haricots blancs*. She became quite accomplished, although, according to the memories of Kirk's daughter Anna (from his second marriage with whom he managed a rapprochement when she was eighteen), Jeane's kitchen was always perilously kinetic: eggs bursting after their water had boiled away; pots of oil smoking ominously; sauces bubbling too furiously while Jeane stood off to the side intensely involved in a book. "But somehow the day would always be saved," said Anna, "and as if by magic, dinner would eventually appear and be quite spectacular."

Being in France in 1969 was a prestige moment for the family, and the first of many trips that would turn into an annual summer sojourn for Kirk and Jeane, and eventually led to a house of their own in Provence. They would all look back on this time with nostalgia. On weekends they piled into the car and traveled throughout the South of France—"Kirkpatrick's Follies," Kirk called these jaunts. The boys would be bickering in the back seat and complaining of car sickness, while Jeane, with a map on her lap to help Kirk navigate, would read aloud from books such as *The Iliad* and *The Odyssey*, and, more mysteriously for her sons, works by Wilhelm Reich and the essays of Bayard Rustin. She would later speak of this as "the best time."

# PUBLIC INTELLECTUAL

THAT JEANE was in an existential sense increasingly on her own now was brought home by the passing of her parents. Fat Jordan died in 1973, feeling in his later years that he was living in a country of rules and regulations very different from the place in which he had grown up and made a life for his family. (His son Jerry remembered that his father, toward the end of his life, underwent an operation to treat a subdural hematoma and when he saw that Medicare had paid the $6,000 bill he expressed the opinion that America should not have to provide such benefits to people like him who could pay their own way.) Leona died of leukemia five years later, having stayed for extended periods with the Kirkpatricks and with Jerry's family in Ohio in the years following her husband's death, but always feeling more comfortable at the family home in Mount Vernon. Jeane's growing sense of political urgency during the 1970s was connected to her fear that the unique American experience that had produced people like her parents was increasingly under assault.

The sense of personal transition was also quickened by Kirk's move to the background of their joint enterprise. He had launched her into the world and given her confidence, by her own acknowledgement, but now, in his sixties, with the American Political Science Association safe from radical takeover and with the Democratic Party he had grown up in leaving him behind, he was ready to stand back and let Jeane be his proxy. (As Tom Mann, his longtime assistant and eventual successor at the APSA, later said, "Kirk just closed the door to his office many afternoons and sat there with his feet up on the desk reading Karl Popper for the seventy-sixth time.")

Entering the middle of her own middle age now, Jeane had acquired her mature self. She had stopped smoking and gnawing at shreds of cuticle on her fingernails. She gave the impression of being without affectation, showing up for classes at Georgetown each day with scant attention paid to her appearance—stingy makeup; hair parted severely in the middle; dressed in the equivalent of academic uniforms. She made so little effort to romance the camera that photos taken of her at this time often have the quality of police mug shots, even though in person she was attractive, her face animated by wit and intelligence.

She still dithered sometimes over decisions on small matters as well as large; but this was not because she didn't know what she thought. Her opinions were case-hardened; her outlook marked by a formidable commitment to empiricism. Anyone who proposed some grand theoretical notion in her presence could expect her to immediately bite down on it with skepticism to test its authenticity. She didn't bother with emollients, and someone who made careless or airy assertions about the goodness or evil of some policy would receive an abrupt response: "Compared to what?" Her pragmatism was a sharp weapon against the "isms" she associated with the European intellectual tradition and considered quintessentially un-American.

She passed on the lessons she had learned in her intellectual and personal life as edicts. "It isn't war that's the greatest danger," she would tell someone bemoaning the perdurable inhumanity of military conflict. "It's tyranny. Tyranny has killed the most millions of people . . . ." And when the issue of large historical forces came up—History with a capital H as science or law—she did not hesitate to make her firm opinion known: "No! That's wrong! *People* make history. *Human purposes* make history . . . ."

She was a loyal friend, but so committed to being the managing partner in the relationships that she sometimes seemed tone-deaf to the needs of those she otherwise cared deeply about, and thus acquired a reputation for making unintentionally wounding comments. When, for instance, Margaret Lefever, at a difficult mid-life turning point, told her that she had decided to return to school for a master's degree in librarianship, Jeane dismissively asked why she would bother with such a second-rate discipline when for a little more effort she could get a PhD in political science.

But if she sometimes stomped clumsily through friends' inner lives, Jeane also often surprised them with her keen appreciation of what they needed at some critical psychological juncture. In 1971, soon after her friend Anne Crutcher's daughter Claudia married a man who was obviously unsuited to her, Jeane visited the couple with a wedding gift and during a private conversation said that she liked the new husband, which Claudia took to be "an intentionally generous and supportive statement, since no one else, no family member, no other friend bothered to say such a thing."

She had built a reputation as a diligent and insightful teacher at Georgetown, someone who insisted on grading her own papers and who was always accessible to students—but was not in the least inclined to trim her ideas to fit the modish fashions of post-60s academe. (During the vogue of the "free university," she volunteered to teach a mini course on the origins of radical political theory, but she made it clear that she meant the dangerous political radicalism of the left.) She worked hard to advance the careers of her graduate students, and brought some of them home for dinners of Provençale cuisine—including, most memorably for her sons because of his service in the battle zones of Korea as a chaplain, Cardinal John O'Connor, whose PhD thesis she supervised.

The emergence of radical feminism in the early 1970s was a problem for her. She believed that she herself was a successful feminist, but also thought her accomplishments had value precisely because they had been achieved without the institutional brace of a movement, the ululations of victimhood, or maudlin sympathy from the media. Obtusely, she also couldn't see why her path—that of rugged female individualist plowing through what the new feminism saw as insuperable structural obstacles—shouldn't be regarded as a default option for women.

She was impatient with what she regarded as the psychological extortions of "second wave" feminism, even before its leaders had made her a hate fetish. She was offended by the vulgar Marxism of the movement, especially the notion that well-adjusted traditional women were guilty of false consciousness; and she thought its cadres were guilty of bad thinking in their conviction, as she read it, that "culture is ideology, social structure is conspiracy, the enemies are men, and feminists are the most oppressed political caste in history. From this perspective, the women's movement is analogous to other movements of oppressed people. The goal is overthrow of an oppressive system; its method is struggle."

She took particular aim at Betty Friedan, godmother of the new movement, saying, "Anyone who tries to define reality for a huge category such as women is engaging in a kind of tyranny. I finished *The Feminine Mystique* thinking that all the 'comfortable concentration camp' stuff was quite ridiculous. All she had to do to escape the oppression she felt was not to look for an underground railroad or stage a slave rebellion but simply *feel differently*."

But Jeane too was concerned with core questions about women in the new age, especially whether a woman like herself who believed she was well integrated into marriage and family life could also make it to the top in her public life. Could such a woman "have it all"?

She addressed this issue elliptically by embarking on a study that would be published as *Political Woman* and billed by its publisher, Basic Books, as "the first major study of women in American public life." It was an outgrowth of a 1972 conference convened by Rutgers' Center for American Women and Politics involving fifty women, including senators and representatives from twenty-six state legislatures, who participated in this three-day event. Jeane and her associates talked to as many of them as she could, in discussion groups and personal confidential interviews, about "the private price they paid for being a public person."

Stipulating that "the proportion of women playing any real part in political leadership is ridiculously small," the book asks ground-zero questions: "whether women have the capacity to participate fully in the power processes of society, why they have so rarely sought to do so, and if or how they differ from men when they do . . . ." Looking for answers in the character and experience of those who successfully participated in politics, Jeane employed tables and statistics, as well as interviews, Lasswellian typologies and other devices from her social science toolkit. But someone acquainted with her own efflorescing life at this time might also have seen qualities of the interior monologue in this doggedly empirical book. The "average" member of the fifty political women she interviewed was (more or less like her) a "fairly attractive, forty-eight-year-old mother of two nearly grown children. Although she has a college education, she has rarely worked outside the home. She lives in the small town where she was born and is financially supported by her reasonably successful husband, who has encouraged her to run for office. Running for office was an extension of many years of community service."

Although their political achievements have involved "crashing the gates" (glass ceilings had not yet been discovered), these successful women not surprisingly resembled Jeane herself more than someone like Gloria Steinem: "Few of these legislators believe that women are 'an exploited group,' that women are 'most unfairly treated'. . . . Few of these legislators believe that they are deprived, denied freedom and self-fulfillment, exploited by men and society." For that matter, "Nor do they ever use male resistance to excuse themselves for failures to achieve a desired goal. Instead they react with the same determination, persistence and hard work with which they have confronted challenges in other areas."

These were, moreover, "normal" women "who marry, have

children, nurture their families, love their husbands . . . [and also] develop skills needed for political success . . . without shrinking or collapsing." While they may appear to be "conventional women whose lives conform to traditional values . . . they are profoundly non-conformist." And then the kill shot: "These women find much that is offensive to 'common decency' in the public behavior [of] . . . the 'stars' of the women's liberation movement."

---

If *Political Woman* was a shot across the bow of the new feminism, it was also a memo to self about the possibility of making a serious bid for power at the dawning of this new era when fundamental beliefs about the nature of women's aspirations were changing. But for the handful of people who knew of the Kirkpatricks' intimate drama, the book had a melancholy subtext. Jeane might insist that women's political ambition was normalized by marriage and particularly motherhood, but just as she was ready to take wing, her own family was, in Tolstoy's formulation, becoming unhappy in its own distinctive way.

Jeane always portrayed it to friends as a tight-knit unit brought even closer by travels in France and elsewhere, with three promising and active boys being educated at Sidwell Friends to play a role someday in the life of the country. She repeated and probably embroidered upon her sons' clever sayings. Once asked by a family friend about how a small fire at Sidwell had gotten started, for instance, Stuart, her youngest, was alleged to have replied sententiously, "The authorities suspect arson." At times it appeared that she edited the comments into little homilies. One of them concerned the time when the first-grade teacher was quizzing the class about their backgrounds; the other children answered "Italian," "Irish," "German," etc., and when it came his turn, Douglas said "Democrat." Another involved Stuart's statement that he and his brothers were never really punished, but sent to their rooms to write an essay on what they had done wrong and why they wouldn't do it again. Then came his punch line: "At times I wished we could get a spanking like other kids."

Kirk had a comfortable relationship with his sons that was, because of his age, somewhat avuncular as well as paternal. Jeane was always intensely engaged, although she was occasionally the odd woman out in this redoubt of maleness. When Stuart wrestled at Sidwell, Jeane sat through one match, but never watched again because she feared he would break his neck. When John, largest of the boys, was on the football team, Jeane happened to attend one big game in which the players shaved their heads as a sign of commitment to victory. She took one look at her bald son as he ran onto the field, said 'He's an idiot," burst into tears, and stalked out of the stadium.

As it was perceived by outsiders, the family had a sort of sitcom normalcy. There appeared even to be an emotional surplus: when their housekeeper Eluisa Barrantes became pregnant and had a son, Ricardo, Jeane and Kirk refitted the basement of their house so that mother and child could live there for several years as almost-Kirkpatricks, participating in holidays and birthdays and the normal rhythms of family life. When Ricardo went through an obstreperous period, Kirk, whom he called "Daddy," paid for him to go to military school for a couple of years and then welcomed him back in the house. Jeane included Ricardo's name with those of her sons in the dedication of one of her books.

She wanted the boys to be intellectuals—primarily, it sometimes seemed to family friends, because it would validate their parentage. As a result, she helped them too much on their papers at Sidwell, just as she allowed them to take her courses (where they received high grades) when they went to Georgetown later on. She tended to blame some of their doings and undoings as teenagers on the permissive culture. After receiving news of yet another mishap involving cars, girls and substances, she said half jokingly to a friend, "God, I wish we had some sort of ritual like the Indians did where you could send your sons out to kill a bear or something and they'd come back men."

But there was a real tragedy in the family that went beyond teenage mischance or the fact that none of the boys gave evidence of the serious intellectual ambition that Kirk and Jeane valued. This was the alcoholism of the first son Douglas. It began while he was in high school and had escalated into a drama of bottles under his bed and in other hiding places by the time he graduated—the onset of a forty-year lost weekend that would have profound consequences for them all. It seemed to have no cause and no conclusion; it was just a plague that had been visited on them.

By the time Douglas was in college, his "problem" had become the dirty little secret of their lives. Margaret Lefever remembers calling Jeane after the publication of *Political Woman* to congratulate her on a favorable review she'd read. They talked for a while, with Jeane agreeing that most of the notices had been good and that the book was actually making money. Then, for the only time in the more than sixty years that they were friends, she suddenly broke into tears: "I'd trade it all, this and everything else, if only Douglas could be normal."

As the Kirkpatricks integrated their first son's increasing personal disorganization into the architecture of their lives, those close to them looked for an explanation. Were Jeane and Kirk so involved with each other and in the public life they had created that some crucial nutrient was missing in the family? Did Kirk's remoteness and Jeane's over-involvement create bad chemistry? Did the idyll of marriage and motherhood she wrote about function as one of those "theories" she otherwise condemned for obscuring the complex truths of individual experience?

The public life that Jeane increasingly embraced in the late 1970s was at least in part a screen behind which she could hide from these questions.

She played an important role as speechwriter and pollster in Humphrey's doomed 1972 presidential campaign—prepared for the worst because Humphrey, trying to patch together a temporary unity among warring factions at the end of the 1968 convention, had been forced to put his onetime close friend George McGovern in charge of revising the rules for delegate selection in 1972. She had watched with dismay over the following four years as these rule changes, combined with the cultural revolution in the party, made it a vehicle for what was now being called the "new politics," a term Jeane always wrapped in contempt.*

The mandate of the Commission on Party Structure and Delegate Selection was to open the party to wider participation and presumably create a more democratic framework for the selection of delegates. But the new rules rammed through by the McGovernites encouraged quotas for blacks, women, young voters. (This was officially denied, of course, but McGovern himself let the cat out of the bag when he told a reporter for the *National Journal* in 1972, "The way we got the quota thing through was by not using the word 'quotas.'")

If party bosses had wielded too much power in the past, now they had virtually no power at all. The result was a convention in 1972 that featured, rather than a new grass roots, what Jeane would later call a "new elite" tilted in favor of affluent "limousine liberals" at the expense of the party's lower-middle- and working-class constituents. (While 42 percent of rank-and-file Democrats had not completed high school, nearly 40 percent of the delegates to the convention in 1972 reported that they had done postgraduate work, she pointed out, and one half of all McGovern delegates were lawyers, teachers and other professionals.) These new elite delegates overwhelmingly chose a candidate, McGovern, who had won

---

* In her draft autobiography she wrote and underlined, "The new politics treats danger as a psychological category rather than an objective condition. It recommends therapy, not self-defense."

no more than a quarter of all the votes cast in the primaries—fewer than Humphrey and only slightly more than George Wallace before he was wounded in a mid-May assassination attempt.

As Jeane said later on, "George McGovern was the only candidate who understood the rules. Nobody else understood that the people who were outside in the streets in Chicago in 1968 would now be inside in Miami in 1972. It was a revolution by rule changes." In her view, those who had killed the party four years earlier were now adding insult to that injury by busily inhabiting its corpse. The Democrats had turned themselves inside out so quickly that Tom Hayden, architect of the 1968 riots at Chicago, was now a party regular. Chicago Seven defendant Jerry Rubin flashed his multiple credentials on the convention floor at Miami in 1972 and bragged, "I've got three and Daley isn't here." (Indeed, Mayor Richard Daley's slate of delegates had won the Illinois primary but been disqualified by the national party on a technicality.)

The 1972 election was the first time in her life that Jeane voted for a Republican. Later on she said, "When I voted for Richard Nixon I didn't do it easily and I wasn't proud of it. But I knew McGovern was going to lose and thought he should."

Other centrist Democrats had also seen the handwriting on the wall of the McGovern campaign in the summer of 1972. Ben Wattenberg, then an aide to Senator Henry "Scoop" Jackson, came up with the idea for a new organization to reassert a center of political gravity inside the party. Picking up the former outlook of the old-line liberal Americans for Democratic Action, which had also now been "turned" by leftists, it would be called the Coalition for a Democratic Majority (CDM). It was formed in Norman Podhoretz's living room by a small group that included, along with Wattenberg, Podhoretz and his wife Midge Decter, and the ubiquitous activist Penn Kemble as executive director. They decided not to go public until after the election, to avoid blame for the certain outcome.

The CDM's birth announcement was an ad placed in the *New York Times* and the *Washington Post* on November 8, 1972, a few days after McGovern's apocalyptic defeat. Headlined "Come Home, Democrats," it was intended as a riposte to the signature line in McGovern's convention acceptance speech, "Come home, America," which members of the new group believed summarized his campaign's isolationist narcissism. It called on "common-sense liberals" to reject the "new politics" and return to the road of success taken by the New Deal Democratic coalition since FDR.

In addition to Scoop Jackson, the big names in the CDM included, among others, Bayard Rustin, Daniel Patrick Moynihan, AFT chief Al Shanker, political scientist Samuel Huntington, Scoop Jackson's assistant Richard Perle, George Ball, and Jeane and Kirk (who had to keep his involvement quiet because of his job at the APSA). It was the nucleus of what some later commentators would call a "counter-establishment."

Much of the organization's heavy lifting would be done by young activists such as Kemble and Joshua Muravchik, who didn't know Jeane very well at this point and assumed that she was there more or less as Kirk's wife. But Jeane noticed them immediately. They were all tough-minded anticommunists who had come up through the Young People's Socialist League in the 60s under the mentorship of onetime Trotsky protégé Max Shachtman and had become, along with Carl Gershman, Social Democrats close to Moynihan and Scoop Jackson in the 70s, strongly advocating democracy promotion and human rights as well as anticommunism.

Jeane was more cautious on these issues than they were (believing, for instance, that America's goal should not be "the moral elevation of other countries but the pursuit of a civilized conception of our own national interest"), but she was attracted to their ideological sophistication, their record in combating the anti-American elements of the New Left while being part of that

milieu in the 60s, and most of all to the fact that they took totalitarianism as seriously as she did.*

The CDM, which Jeane insisted (echoing Irving Kristol) was
not an organization at all but rather a "state of mind" and a "clear-
inghouse of ideas," met every month or so at the Federal City
Club over the next couple of years. She later said of it, "Beyond
agreeing on specific issues, we agreed on broad approaches and
convictions. We saw ourselves as an embodiment of the mainstream Democratic Party traditions from Truman to Kennedy.
We felt we could re-influence the party, if not entirely recapture it.
As political scientists, we shouldn't have been so optimistic."

This was a period of maximum frustration for Jeane. In addition
to participating in the CDM, she had agreed after the 1972 debacle
to serve as a Humphrey representative on a national Democratic
commission on rules reform. She saw the job at hand as "reforming
the reforms of the McGovernites," but was aware that the Democratic Party, as now constituted, would never let this happen.

---

If Irving Kristol's response to a crisis, as he once famously said,
was to start a new magazine, Jeane's was to write a monograph.
Over the next year she wrote two: *Dismantling the Parties: Reflec-
tions on Party Reform and Decomposition*; and *The Presidential Nom-
inating Process: Can It Be Improved?* The thinking she put into
them led to her next book, *The New Presidential Elite*, the result of

---

* In "The Origins of Neo-Conservative Support for Democracy Promotion,"
an MA thesis submitted to the University of Calgary history department in
2007, Bill King traces the migration of these key figures from the YPSL, to
the Social Democrats, to the remnants of liberal centrism that coalesced
around Moynihan and Jackson, to a central role in defining the "second
generation" of neoconservatism, which moved that "tendency" from the
domestic concerns emphasized by Irving Kristol and others in the "first generation" to a focus on foreign affairs.

a systematic, detailed survey of 2,449 delegates who had attended the 1972 Democratic and Republican conventions. (The Republicans seemed to have been included to give a sense of objectivity to a work concerned primarily with the reconstituted Democratic Party.) Based on nearly 2,500 completed questionnaires and over 1,300 interviews, and filled with tables, graphs and figures, it was perhaps her major effort as a political scientist per se, and was fittingly dedicated to Kirk.

What she found in her study of the Democrats was a de-emphasis of delegates from state parties and an increase in ad hoc delegates associated with a certain candidate or cause, which she believed was the most radical electoral change since the Progressive movement created the referendum and initiative and the presidential primary over fifty years earlier. "Skill-based professionals" such as teachers were rising in importance as people from business and blue-collar trades faded. The result was the advent of what she called "rectitude specialists" more interested in ideology and moral causes than in winning elections.

In an allusion to Daniel Bell's ideas about a "new class" dominating the media with profoundly antibourgeois values centered on "personal freedom," she saw this new elite as "symbol manipulators" who understood how to use their media sophistication and connections to destroy the legitimacy of established institutions while creating the rationales for new ones overnight. The new breed might see themselves as "people of principle replacing the opportunistic bosses and machine politicians of yesterday," but they were really "the people who arrived early and stayed late"—a veiled allusion to the old Communist technique for infiltrating organizations.

*The New Presidential Elite* was generally well reviewed. Still, it was an 800-page work of political science, not meant for a general readership. More important for Jeane's future was her first piece written for *Commentary*, which appeared at about the same time as the book—a broadside about what had happened in 1972, titled

"The Revolt of the Masses." (The allusion to Ortega y Gasset's classic work about the evolution of "mass man" was intentional.) In it, she compared the old New Deal coalition, concerned with "issues of economic status, security and opportunity," to the "strange new coalition of the disconnected, the disadvantaged and the alienated" that had formed around the McGovern campaign. She noted that most Americans, including "traditional" Democrats, viewed the counterculture which had backed McGovern as "the enemy" and, unlike it, did not see America as "a sick or repressive society, or crime as a quasi-legitimate form of political protest." She also condemned McGovern himself—whose "Come Home, America," she charged, was about a retreat not just from Vietnam but from "materialism" and other aspects of middle-class life. She accused him of having "challenged the central beliefs of the traditional political culture." Among them:

> ... the belief that freedom is rooted in law; that equality of opportunity and individual achievement constitute a just basis of reward; ... that those who cannot work should be supported by public funds and those who will not should be treated less generously; that work has intrinsic value for persons and societies; that citizenship requires obedience to law with which one disagrees; ... that order is a prerequisite to both liberty and justice; that patriotism is a social virtue; that the U.S. is a basically decent and successful—though imperfect—society.

Where this essay appeared was as significant as what it said. *Commentary*'s editor Norman Podhoretz had himself evolved from aggressive liberalism in the early 60s, to a position—strongly supportive of Israel and tough on the Soviet Union, and strongly critical of the cultural left—that would soon be called neoconservative. His magazine mirrored his journey, becoming a literary and political homeland for intellectuals who felt they had been mugged by the 60s and were now forced to watch from the side-lines as the New Left began its long march through the institutions of American life, chief among them the Democratic Party. Podhoretz brought these nomads into *Commentary*'s fold and also encouraged contributions from Social Democrats, who had been the only element of the New Left to maintain an anticommunist stance and who were now trying to bring issues such as the plight of Soviet dissidents into the public consciousness. (Bayard Rustin compared what they faced to what blacks had faced under segregation, with the proviso that Soviet totalitarianism was "much worse.")

In becoming a contributor to *Commentary*, Jeane was joining figures who would be friends and allies in the future, such as James Q. Wilson, Michael Novak, Irving Kristol and his wife Gertrude Himmelfarb, in addition to Podhoretz and Decter. The magazine offered her access to a brainy political environment where issues rather than elections were at the center of things. More than a scholar or political operative, she was now becoming established as a public intellectual.

---

With the 1976 election approaching, foreign policy issues became more pressing as the Soviets, sensing U.S. vulnerability after Vietnam, began to escape the confines of containment and acquire new clients in the Third World. The Committee on the Present Danger was formed at the beginning of the year as a blue-ribbon lobbying group of civic and former military leaders concerned about America's loss of nuclear superiority and the "windows of vulnerability" the United States faced as a result of the USSR's expansion. Jeane joined the committee and there met individuals such as Admiral Thomas Moorer, future CIA director William Casey, future secretary of state George Shultz and others she would later serve with in the Reagan administration.

An issue for the CPD, in addition to what Jeane and others like her regarded as the appeasement of McGovernism, was the policy of détente designed by Henry Kissinger during the Nixon and Ford administrations. The strategy itself they found questionable—using arms control and other incentives to rein in Soviet ambitions. Even more contentious was the declinist vision of the future that accompanied it, epitomized by an indiscreet comment that Admiral Elmo "Bud" Zumwalt claimed Kissinger had made to him: "The U.S. has passed its historic high point . . . [and] we must persuade the Russians to give us the best deal we can get." This version of realism they found as bad as the self-hating appeasement of the McGovernites.*

With Soviet expansion raising the electoral stakes, the Coalition for a Democratic Majority looked for a candidate who would stand against these trends. While still admiring Humphrey for his good fight, Jeane was aware that the gabbiness that made him the "Happy Warrior" also made him seem a bit antique in the new age. ("I loved Hubert," she once remarked to me. "But he was a 'politician'—the sort of guy who, if you asked him how he was, was likely to say, 'Well, I'm so glad you asked that question . . .' or something like that and off he'd go.") Scoop Jackson was more serious and less oblivious to context—someone who had a strong record on civil rights, conservation and especially military preparedness. He had dealt the Soviets a blow in 1974 by authoring a major piece of legislation, the so-called Jackson-Vanik amendment, that in effect used trade restrictions to pressure the USSR to allow emigration of dissidents, refuseniks and Jews. Jeane's fellow CDMer Ben Wattenberg was on Jackson's staff, as were Richard Perle and Elliott Abrams, two other centrist Democratic intellectuals now in her orbit.

Becoming (with Wattenberg) an "issues person" for Jackson during the primaries of 1976, she traveled with the candidate as

---

* Kissinger denied having made the statement.

he campaigned across the country, working on his polling as she had for Humphrey four years earlier. Possessing the thoughtful gravitas required by the office, as well as a keen awareness of the implications of Cold War issues, he was, she believed, supremely qualified to be president. She was disappointed when he was out-positioned by Georgia's governor Jimmy Carter, who had adroitly run as an outsider to capitalize on the revulsion for career politi-cians and "Washington" resulting from Watergate, and as a mod-erate on the simmering issue of Soviet aggression that would finally come to a boil in the 1980s.

Serving also with Wattenberg as the Jackson representative on the platform committee for the Democratic convention, Jeane was disturbed by the reluctance of the Carterites to include the USSR in condemnation of human rights abuses, and by how they insisted that any mention of it be put into moral balance with U.S. aid for "right-wing dictators." It still rankled twenty-five years later, when she told me that "Carter and his *people* just couldn't get with the idea that it might be good and necessary to be morally censorious of the Soviet Union."

Despite their doubts, almost all CDM members (although not Jeane herself) grudgingly supported Carter over Gerald Ford dur-ing the general election. Afterwards they presented the president-elect's transition team with a list of their members to be considered for positions in the new administration. Of the more than fifty names handed to the new chief of staff, Hamilton Jordan, only two CDMers were chosen, according to Joshua Muravchik, who was part of the negotiation. One was Sandra Bregman, wife of a party donor who received a low-level appointment to the Department of Energy only after a deputy to Jordan lectured her on how she would have to abjure her relationship to the CDM itself. The other went to Peter Rosenblatt, briefly president of the CDM, whose selection as ambassador to Micronesia gave birth to Elliott Abrams' mordant quip that passed through the group's membership: "They couldn't even give us Polynesia or Macronesia, only *Micro*nesia."

Among the names on the CDM list that were passed over was Jeane's—for assistant secretary of state for educational and cultural affairs, the least prestigious of the assistant secretary positions. It was providential. If she had been selected, she would have labored for a year or two in obscurity and been so tainted that Ronald Reagan probably would never have chosen her for his administration.

---

Jeane experienced a metaphysical lurch when Kirk almost died in the spring of 1977. He had been in Bloomington to receive an honorary degree from Indiana University when he contracted what he thought was a bad flu. By the time he got home, he was desperately ill and had to be hospitalized at George Washington University hospital. He was diagnosed with Legionnaire's disease, which had burst into public view the previous year when over two hundred people attending a convention of the American Legion became seriously ill, more than thirty of them dying.

The doctors thought Kirk too might be a terminal case, but Jeane, according to her friend Margaret Lefever, "simply refused to let him go." She approached the crisis as a social scientist, systematically contacting other guests who had been at the Bloomington hotel at the same time to determine the extent of the outbreak, and intensively researching what little was known about the disease. She learned enough to decide that the treatment Kirk was being given was inadequate and demanded that he be transferred to Georgetown and put on a different regimen of drugs. He gradually improved, although people close to the family always believed that he never fully recovered.

As Kirk got better, Jeane could take stock. She would note later on, "I'm not much of an activist by nature; I'd rather sit around and read books. What drove me to get involved in politics was the anti-Americanism of the 60s as it came to take over the mainstream. If not for this, I would have been an academic who dabbled in politics because of her husband's associations."

As the CDM got active again at the end of Carter's first year in office, Jeane, like the others in the organization, used it as a sounding board for their growing fears that the USSR was taking advantage of what it perceived as U.S. weakness. This position seemed validated by the findings of "Team B," a group of sixteen "outside experts" including the Sovietologist Richard Pipes, Paul Nitze, Paul Wolfowitz and others commissioned late in the Ford administration by George H. W. Bush, the CIA director, to evaluate the Soviets' capacities and intentions in a "competitive analysis" against the agency's own investigators. Team B's report, leaked to the press shortly after Carter took office, found that the U.S. was at a disadvantage as a result of a Soviet arms buildup that was aggressive and expansionist in nature, rather than merely the defensive paranoia of a nation that had been invaded three decades earlier, which was official CIA dogma. Team B sounded the alarm about mobile missiles, MIRV technology, increased antiballistic missile capacity and other issues in terms that reaffirmed what groups such as the CDM and the Committee on the Present Danger (CPD) had already been saying.

But Jeane was bothered less by disparities in missile throw weight and deployment than by the mood of defeatism that seemed to be settling like an airborne toxic event over American foreign policy. When the CDM raised an alarm about the ten thousand Cuban internationalist mercenaries sent to fight in Ethiopia to pay back Soviet financial support, the secretary of state, Cyrus Vance, replied: "To oppose Soviet or Cuban involvement in Africa would be futile." The CDM's worst fears were confirmed when the president himself congratulated America for having gotten over its "inordinate fear of communism."

Jeane later said, "Although we had supported Scoop in 1976, almost no one expected that Carter would turn out as bad as he did. . . . I didn't like that the Carter administration had decreased

U.S. military strength and cut budgeted plans for weapons development, insisting on non-verifiable arms control agreements. During the Carter years, the Soviets achieved military parity because the administration thought the effort to maintain supremacy was unbecoming. In the years between the fall of Saigon and the election of Ronald Reagan, twelve countries fell under Soviet influence. Terrible things happened to a lot of people."

In her draft autobiography, Jeane wrote a little political haiku to summarize her sense of the new worldview of "liberalism from McGovern to Carter":

Weak is strong

Vulnerable is safe

Rich is guilty

Hostile is neutral

Friendly is suspect

There's nothing to worry about anyway.

In 1977, the only blank spot on Jeane's résumé was filled when William Baroody, president of the American Enterprise Institute, invited her to spend a sabbatical year there. The invitation had been finessed by the Kirkpatricks' omnipresent friend Howard Penniman, who had come to AEI in the mid 1970s after retiring from Georgetown. He had talked up Jeane to Baroody and to Austin Ranney, the head of the political science "department," who already believed that she was a "brilliant, very much underrated intellectual."

AEI was just then coming into its own. It had begun in 1938 as the American Enterprise Association, a corporation-supported research institute studying and promoting capitalism. Baroody, son of Lebanese immigrants, had reconfigured it as a sort of think tank university with "departments" and chairs, a conservative mirror image of the more liberal Brookings Institution, focusing on government policy and issues ranging from health care to foreign policy.

Former president Gerald Ford increased AEI's profile when he agreed to become a "distinguished fellow" in 1977, and Antonin Scalia, Robert Bork, Laurence Silberman, and others from his administration became AEI "distinguished scholars." But now, Baroody was also recruiting former liberal Democrats who, like Jeane, were in transition—figures such as Irving Kristol (an AEI adjunct scholar in the mid 70s), Michael Novak and Ben Wattenberg (who would later compare the group to *shabbos goys*, gentiles who lit the stoves of observant Jews on the Sabbath). Soon these intellectuals were associating AEI with ideas—in addition to supply-side economics and welfare reform—revolving around the rejection of détente policy toward the Soviets, which would eventually put the organization in the storm center of the Reagan revolution.

Generously endowed by corporate and individual gifts, AEI was beginning to acquire the amenities—plush meeting rooms, a subsidized lunchroom, ample secretarial and research help—that would distinguish it as a great place to work. Most of all for Jeane, it provided colleagues who were very different from the scholars and Democratic activists she had associated with until then. She once told Kirk that the casual hallway conversations with figures such as Novak and Scalia were like seminars. She found Kristol in particular to be a kindred spirit, among other reasons because he too hated the 60s—the relativism, nihilism, self-indulgence and, most of all, the flatulent utopianism.

One of the subjects she learned more about was Latin America. AEI staged conferences on land reform, extending democratic activism by U.S. labor unions south of the border, and other issues. It hosted leaders from throughout the region, one of whom, José Napoleón Duarte, later the embattled president of El Salvador, Jeane first met at this time.

At the suggestion of her new conservative colleagues at AEI, she read *The Road to Serfdom* and other works by Friedrich Hayek. But she still found conservative thought in general "one-dimensional." In a 1977 essay on the "new right" for *Commentary*, she criticized Ronald Reagan for arguing after the 1976 election that there was a major political realignment on the American horizon and "that the Republican Party can only be revitalized if its leaders commit it to a clear-cut conservative position." She dismissively compared the view that there was a "hidden conservative majority" ready to be mobilized to McGovernism's belief that a coalition of the alienated poor, young, idealistic and ethnic was waiting to take power.

The neoconservatism associated with Irving Kristol, on the other hand, was more to her measure. A "tendency," in Kristol's term, rather than a movement, it had first begun to make an impression in the 1960s in articles in its flagship publication, *The Public Interest*, that initially focused exclusively on social problems, especially those involving the "unintended consequences" of Great Society government programs such as welfare (although Kristol insisted that a welfare state per se was not incompatible with conservative philosophy). By the following decade, the neoconservative worldview expanded into foreign affairs too, in reaction to the leftward and anti-American drift of the reconfigured Democratic Party. Organizations like the CDM became neoconservative *après la lettre*.

Jeane had already been breathing the political air of neoconservatism at AEI and moving on her own toward some of its ideas: that the "adversary culture" and its assertion of radical individualism had caused a crisis in America; that the "new class" of intellectuals, academics and bureaucrats that had come into prominence as a result of the 60s was now propagating hostile ideas about identity, morality, what would soon become known as "multiculturalism," and bourgeois life in general. Now that it had broadened its view—partly in response to people like herself—to focus on Cold War issues, this neoconservative "persuasion" (the other term its partisans used to insist that it was in no sense a movement) offered her a rest stop while she recovered from having to sever her umbilical identification with the Democratic Party.

Since it had picked up so many of the concerns of the defeated liberal centrism, neoconservatism also offered her a coherent connection with her own past convictions. ("The differences between neo-conservatism and traditional liberalism," she wrote, "are, I believe, more a matter of mood and degree than of values.") When her French friend Anne de Lattre came to the United States for a visit in the late 70s, Jeane gave her an enthusiastic neoconservative tutorial and arranged a meeting with Irving Kristol that she invested with some of the hushed importance of a visit to the Vatican.

If distancing herself from the Democrats caused her to experience something like a political phantom limb syndrome, she also experienced a new liberation. When Carl Gershman, then head of the Social Democrats, invited her to speak at the organization's national conference in 1977, she surprised him by accepting, joining Penn Kemble and Seymour Martin Lipset on a panel called "The Future of Liberalism." In her presentation she discussed the relationship between liberty and equality, concluding, unsurprisingly for those who knew her, that it was necessary to split the difference because liberty alone would lead to an anarchy inviting totalitarian intervention, and equality alone would require an all-powerful state bureaucracy smothering the individual.

After the presentation, Gershman asked her to join the organization, pointing out that Lipset, one of Kirk's close friends, already had, and that even the former LBJ aide Eugene Rostow was considering it. (He would join in 1978.) Jeane politely declined: "I'm not a Social Democrat. I'm a liberal."

But she was a liberal who knew she would never be acknowledged as such by those who now controlled the revised definition

of the term. And however buoyed she was by the élan of neoconservatism, it couldn't satisfy her yearnings for a presidential candidate who saw the world as she did. A former student later
recalled running into Jeane in the spring of 1979 and asking her
who she was backing for president. Jeane shrugged and said list-
lessly, "Oh, I don't know. Teddy Kennedy, I suppose."

# REAGANAUT

In HER UNPUBLISHED autobiography, Jeane wrote of the despair she felt as the Carter worldview took hold with what she saw as its dominant idea that "it is vulgar and mistaken to take seriously the rise of communist influence or the decline of American power" and the subtext that "maybe we deserve to lose anyway."

Two disparate events in 1979, taken together, came to symbolize for her the way in which American foreign policy had begun to exhibit features of an autoimmune disorder. The first was the fall of the shah of Iran in January and the replacement of his government by an Islamic Republic headed by the Ayatollah Khomeini. Jeane had watched with incomprehension the Carter administration's indecision about whether or not to support this pivotal U.S. ally, and the growing sympathy of some of its members for the revolution (as embodied in UN ambassador Andrew Young's statement that Khomeini was "some sort of saint").

The second event, more lacerating because the Soviet Union was so central a part of the equation (as it had not been in Iran, although Jeane seemed to see its hand there too), was the Nicaraguan revolution that culminated in July when strongman Anastasio Somoza was forced to flee Managua. The Carter administration had hastened the tipping point first by indicating that it favored regime change, then by appearing to validate claims of the Sandinista National Liberation Front that its movement was committed to pluralism and moderation. (The deputy secretary of state, Warren Christopher, went so far as to say that this movement represented the promise of a "new Nicaragua through popular participation that is capable of meeting basic human needs.")

As the Sandinistas methodically marginalized the remaining democratic elements of the junta that had given legitimacy to the revolution and consolidated its own control, the Carter administration was giving it $65 million in aid.

These events were still developing in early August when Jeane and Kirk flew to France, returning to vacation at the place they'd rented in Saint-Rémy for years. She had been planning to work on a chapter for a book of essays on democratization movements, but just before she left, she told her AEI assistant Jackie Tillman, "I've decided to work on something else. Please send me everything you can find on the Sandinistas, Carter policies in Central America, the Somoza regime, etc. Send it to me as soon as possible!"

Mornings were spent at the outdoor market; afternoons in walks with Kirk or perhaps a drive to Arles or Nîmes. After dinner, Kirk read while Jeane worked, poring through what Tillman had sent her—especially Senate Foreign Relations Committee hearings of the past two years and literature put out by left-wing American support groups for revolution in Latin America. Her objective, as she later described it, was "to understand what the Carter administration was doing in Nicaragua and El Salvador, and to understand what it thought it was doing."

She titled the long essay she drafted over the next few weeks "Dictatorships and Double Standards." Here, ideas about the differences between authoritarianism and totalitarianism that had been circulating in a disorderly way since the late 1950s were crystallized into an attack on Carter's foreign policy, with the urgent feel of a manifesto. Using Iran and Nicaragua as case histories, Jeane showed how what she regarded as historical illiteracy, moral incoherence and doubt about American values had combined to produce policies with "catastrophic" consequences for U.S. security, and she argued that the administration's reaction to events in both places recalled American behavior in China before the triumph of Mao and in Cuba before the triumph of Castro:

The pattern is familiar enough: an established autocracy with a record of friendship with the U.S. is attacked by insurgents, some of whose leaders have long ties to the Communist movement.... The "Marxist" presence is ignored and/or minimized ... on the ground that U.S. support for the dictator gives the rebels little choice but to seek aid "elsewhere." Violence spreads, and American officials wonder aloud about the viability of a regime that "lacks the support of its own people." ... Requests for help from the beleaguered autocrat go unheeded and the argument is increasingly voiced that ties should be established with rebel leaders "before it is too late" ... [and before the U.S. ends up] once more on the side of history's "losers." ... Should the incumbent autocrat prove resistant to American demands that he step aside, he will be readily overwhelmed by the military strength of his opponents, whose patrons will have continued to provide sophisticated arms and advisers at the same time the U.S. cuts off military sales.... Only after the insurgents have refused the proffered political solution and anarchy has spread throughout the nation will it be noticed that the new head of government has no significant following.... [T]he U.S. will have been led by its own misunderstanding of the situation to assist actively in deposing an erstwhile friend and ally and installing a government hostile to American interests and policies in the world.

After showing how this pattern had played out in the events of 1979, Jeane transitioned to what she saw as the general truth. Democracy is not created by fiat; it takes "decades, if not centuries" for people to "acquire the necessary disciplines and habits" to support it. Then she came to her central points: "Although there is no instance of a revolutionary 'socialist' or Communist society being democratized, right-wing autocracies do sometimes evolve into democracies—given time, propitious economic, social, and political circumstances, talented leaders, and a strong indigenous demand for representative government." And: "Traditional autocrats ... do not disturb the habitual rhythms of work and leisure, habitual places of residence, habitual patterns of family and personal relations," while "precisely the opposite is true of revolutionary Communist regimes."

Just such transitions from autocracy to democracy had been occurring in Spain and Greece and Portugal in the 1970s. But Jeane noted that these realities were not for the Carter administration. With cutting irony, she said that its chief desire was obviously not to defend America but "to understand the processes of change and then, like Marxists, to align ourselves with history ...."

Her fury about Carterism was especially clear in her critique of its double standards, which in future discussions of the essay would tend to be overshadowed by the "dictators" part of the argument. In its haste to produce change, the administration had targeted for condemnation only those authoritarian pro-American regimes it saw as not having answered History's call. The USSR, greatest human rights abuser in the world, was largely immune to such criticism.* (When the Soviet foreign minister Andrei Gromyko came to the United States in 1977 to discuss the SALT II agreement, Carter broached the topic of human rights hesitantly, reassuring Gromyko that the U.S. did not want to

---

* In another essay written a year or so later, she stipulated more specifically the two aspects of the Carterites' interpretation of human rights that she found disturbing. "First, the concern was limited to violations of human rights by governments. By definition, activities of terrorists and guerrillas could not qualify [for condemnation].... Secondly, human rights were defined not in terms of personal and legal rights—freedom from torture, arbitrary imprisonment, and arrest ... but in accordance with a much broader [and Soviet-friendly] conception which included ... economic 'rights' provided by socialism (shelter, food, health, education)."

appear to "interfere in the domestic affairs" of the USSR "or put you in an awkward position.") Nor did the administration acknowledge, Jeane wrote, that "the present governments of Vietnam, Cambodia, Laos are much more repressive than those of the despised previous rulers; that the government of the People's Republic of China is more repressive than that of Taiwan, that North Korea is more repressive than South Korea, and so forth." She concluded by scornfully pointing out that liberal idealism should not be synonymous with masochism and that "a posture of continuous self-abasement and apology vis-à-vis the Third World is neither morally necessary nor politically appropriate."

"Dictatorships and Double Standards" was Jeane's signature piece of writing and she would have to defend it the rest of her life. Later, her critics would make much of the mortal blow the death of the USSR appeared to have struck to her thesis. But during her government service, the essay was also brought up regularly to justify attacks on her as an apologist for dictatorship. She still bristled twenty-five years after the fact when someone said that she had defended figures such as Somoza: "I simply took the position that it was a mistake to imagine that we were making things better for anyone if we participated in destabilizing those governments when the only alternative to them was a Soviet-backed regime. The Carter administration was catastrophic be-cause it produced such effects. I'll go to my grave believing that."

The argument of the essay also revealed how much of a "realist" Jeane was in foreign policy, a fact sometimes obscured by her growing affinity for the personalities and ideas associated with neoconservatism and the rhetorical brio of the ideological fight against the Soviets. It was not the realpolitik of Henry Kissinger, which she opposed as much as what she considered his Spenglerian sense of doom over the prospects of the West in the Cold War. For her, realism was rather a belief that policy should reflect the realities of "culture, character, geography," instead of the "vague, abstract universalism" associated with a utopian thinking that she believed led inevitably to appeasement of totalitarianism.* Hers was an inconsistent realism that owed more to Burke than to Machiavelli (although a Burke on a war footing, as he was during the French Revolution). It developed over time but did not change much from her early days as a college student backing the worldview of Harry Truman to her last days doubting the worldview of George W. Bush.

---

Jeane finished "Dictatorships and Double Standards" feeling, as she said later, that if she published it "the sky would fall down on my head." Preparing to return home from the summer in France, she told Kirk that she was going to put it in a desk drawer and let it marinate. But he insisted that she submit it to *Commentary*. Seeing its potential, Norman Podhoretz cut several thousand words, excised some of the political science jargon, and buttressed the main points. (Jeane ran into the journalist Sol Sanders, an old friend from her Stephens College days, soon after the piece appeared, and when he expressed some reservations about it, she said defensively, "Well, it *was* heavily edited.") It appeared in the November 1979 issue and quickly became one of the most widely read pieces that *Commentary* had ever published, its relevance

---

* Jeane spent a lot of time trying to understand the intellectual "perversion" of utopianism, as she saw it. In her thinking, it began with "theories ungrounded in experience [that can therefore] never be tested." This led, on a spectrum of debased thinking, to "rationalism," whose political effect she saw in "the determined effort to understand and shape people and societies on the basis of inadequate, oversimplified theories of human behavior." And this rationalism "encourages utopianism.... Both are concerned more with the abstract than the concrete, with the possible than the probable.... Both are less concerned with people as they are than as they might be (at least as rationalists think they might be)."

seemingly certified when the Soviets invaded Afghanistan while it was still on the newsstands.

The Center for Ethics and Public Policy—run by Ernest Lefever, husband of Jeane's old friend Margaret Briggs—reprinted ten thousand copies and sent them all over the country. The Heritage Foundation and the American Enterprise Institute did the same thing. Soon the piece was being talked about in some circles as offering a decoder ring for the failings of Carter's foreign policy.

One of those who read it was Ronald Reagan, then gearing up his 1980 campaign for the presidency. He had been sent the article by Richard Allen, a former staff member of the National Security Council in the Nixon administration who had been active in the Committee on the Present Danger and was now a foreign policy advisor to the former California governor. As Jeane told it, "Reagan had been in Washington and Dick was driving him to the airport to go home. When he got out of the car, Dick gave him the essay and said, 'I think you're going to like this.' Reagan called him from a stopover in Chicago and said, 'It's a terrific article.'"

A few days later, on December 12, 1979, Reagan sent Jeane a letter saying that the essay had had a "great impact" on him. "I found myself reexamining a number of the premises and views which have governed my own thinking in recent years," he wrote. "There is so much food for thought in the article that one hardly knows where to begin to compliment you on your keen insight."* He proposed a meeting.

Jeane was wary. "I didn't know Ronald Reagan read *Commentary*," she said later on. "I didn't know much about him at all,

---

* Because of her well-known absent-mindedness, Jeane kept misplacing this letter over the next few years, although she realized its importance. For a time it appeared to have definitively disappeared. But in 1985, her AEI assistant Jackie Tillman finally recovered it from a mass of otherwise trivial papers and had it framed so it would be more difficult to lose.

in fact, and what I did know was not encouraging from my point of view."

The Carter administration also took notice of the piece and what it represented. The president, worried about a primary challenge from Ted Kennedy, was now anxious to consolidate his standing with those he regarded as Democratic Party malcontents. When he signaled an interest in a fence-mending meeting with the CDM, despite his loathing of the group, Max Kampelman, working through Vice President Mondale, an old Minnesota political ally, set one up.

Kampelman, Jeane, Norman Podhoretz, Midge Decter, Penn Kemble, Elliott Abrams, Ben Wattenberg, Max Kampelman and others got together at the Hay-Adams hotel across Lafayette Square from the White House for breakfast early on the frigid morning of January 31, 1980—a strategy session before the meeting. They discussed whether the president's recent denunciations of the Soviets for the invasion of Afghanistan—Carter had been quoted as saying he had learned more about the USSR from this event than he ever knew before—might be a bridge to reconciliation. They decided to test this possibility by beginning the meeting with praise for this new toughness, and they chose Kirk's friend Austin Ranney as their spokesman because of his mild and diplomatic demeanor. Then they walked to the White House.

When Carter appeared, Jeane thought he seemed "constricted": eyes boiled-looking, jaws working, lips set in a frozen smile that parodied geniality. He had Vice President Mondale with him. Ben Wattenberg later remembered that the president had been erroneously briefed to believe that the CDM was there about human rights, so he launched into what the group, not knowing this, regarded as a bizarrely off-point statement about how its members could help him with a problematic situation that had come up in Ecuador. After a moment of bafflement and earnest throat clearing, Ranney began their presentation by saying that while there had perhaps been disagreements between the administration and the CDM regarding Soviet intentions and how American policy could be more effective, these frictions might now be reduced because the president had altered some of his views of the USSR as a result of Afghanistan. Carter interrupted him with a clenched denial: "Your analysis is not true. There has been no change in my policy. I have always held a consistent view of the Soviet Union. For the record, I did not say that I have learned more about the Soviets since the invasion of Afghanistan, as is alleged in the press. My policy is my policy, and has been my policy. It has not changed, and will not change."

The meeting proceeded in this fashion for another thirty minutes or so, with CDMers asking increasingly probing questions and the president giving increasingly terse answers. Then Carter stood and, claiming that he had another meeting, strode out of the room. Vice President Mondale, closer to the CDM orbit, asked the shell-shocked members of the group to stay and for the next hour tried to pour emollients on the drama with a discussion whose theme Jeane recalled as "the president really isn't as bad as you think he is." She left the meeting feeling that Carter was simply "a disaster." On the way out of the White House she said to Midge Decter, "I am not going to support *that man*."

A few weeks later, she went on a speaking tour of India for the U.S. Information Agency. One of the side benefits of the trip was that her friend Bayard Rustin was part of the group. They stayed up late at night speaking about Rustin's views on Gandhi, civil disobedience, apartheid.

She caught a virus at the end of the tour and came home with a high fever. She was still in bed a few days later when she got a call from Richard Allen. "Governor Reagan is in town for a few days and would like you to be part of a group meeting at the Madison Hotel," he said. Jeane asked, "No commitments implied by attending?" Allen replied, "Of course not."

Another call came about an hour later. The voice on the other end said, "The White House calling for Mrs. Kirkpatrick." Then a Carter aide named Bernie Aronson came on the line: "Jeane, President Carter and the rest of us are concerned about the CDM point of view being adequately represented in platform hearings we're holding across the country, and we'd like you to speak ...." Amused by this disdain for the laws of probability—the hearings just happened to have been scheduled at roughly the same time as the Reagan meeting—Jeane told Aronson that she already had an appointment at that time but didn't bother mentioning what it was.

When Richard Allen met her in the lobby of the Madison on April 6, Jeane was still nervous about possibly being used by the Reaganites. "Listen," she cautioned him, "remember that I'm an AFL-CIO Democrat." He soothed her, "All I want you to do is talk to him. Nobody ever needs to know about this meeting if that's what you want."

Entering the suite, she saw that William Casey, head of the SEC during the Nixon years, was there. So was Ed Meese, Reagan's longtime ally in California politics, and, more comforting, the arms control hawk Paul Nitze and Admiral Thomas Moorer.

For almost an hour there was general talk about the deterioration of America's commitment to stand up against the Soviets. Finally, Reagan looked at Jeane and told her how taken he had been with her *Commentary* essay, which had reinforced his concerns about Central America. As Allen recalled the conversation, Reagan said further that it helped him see that leftist regimes were more deeply rooted than rightist regimes. In a comment that might have surprised those who later came to see her merely as the president's hatchet lady, Jeane replied by cautioning Reagan that it was also true that "unspeakable atrocities occurred under rightist regimes in Spain and Germany and so he shouldn't read too much into that belief."

Richard Allen later said it was "love at first sight" between Reagan and Jeane. But in fact, when she got home that afternoon and Kirk asked her what she had thought, she was still uncertain. "He's not at all like any political leader we've known—more personal, more remote, less sure of himself, less aggressive, less articulate than most major political leaders are, probably less well informed, but that's not certain because he doesn't talk like a college professor or a senator or a journalist." After a pause she continued: "But I like him. At least he wouldn't start by destabilizing the government of Guatemala, say, at a time when Communist guerrillas would be the likely beneficiaries."

The next night, she and Kirk attended the first of columnist George Will's intimate dinner parties for Reagan, and were seated at a table with him and, among others, the AFL-CIO president Lane Kirkland and Meg Greenfield, editorial page editor of the *Washington Post*. Reagan told stories of trying to purge the Screen Actors Guild of Communists, and Kirk, who was sitting next to him, replied in kind about working with Hubert Humphrey to do the same thing in Minnesota politics. It was certainly love at first sight between the two of them.

Jeane spent some time after the dinner researching Reagan's years as governor and was surprised and reassured to find that he had forged a more civil give and take with the Democrat-controlled California legislature than Jimmy Carter had with the Democrat-controlled legislature of Georgia. (One of the calls she made was to her friend Jesse Unruh, the Big Daddy of the California Democratic Party, who gave a surprisingly positive evaluation of the man he had opposed while Speaker of the legislature there.)

After another meeting with Reagan, she contacted Richard Allen and told him, "Dick, I am ready to endorse this man for president." Allen always felt that this was a significant historical moment because Jeane, with her impeccable pedigree in the

Humphrey-Jackson wing of the party, would in effect give permission for others to follow, thus "clearing the way for Democrats to cross the bridge to Reagan."

How momentous a step she was taking became clear to her in a November dinner at Michael Novak's house. One of the other guests was Daniel Patrick Moynihan, now a U.S. senator. Speaking for most CDMers at this point, he reproached her gently for signing on with Reagan. But Jeane didn't back down. She was feeling the euphoria of apostasy, the sense that what had seemed like walking in circles over the last few years might actually have been a purposeful journey leading to this moment. She had also seen an appealing strength and directness in Reagan that offered a potential antidote to all the facile discussion about America's decline. (By now she had no doubt heard Allen's story about asking Reagan, when he first became an advisor, about his vision of the ultimate outcome of the Cold War, and getting the direct reply: "We win, they lose. What do you think about that?") Moreover, as she later said, Reagan was the sort of man she had grown up admiring—comfortable with who he was, not inclined to easy intimacy, and not at all compelled to explain himself: "He does not seek to dominate situations with talk or with an overwhelming presence, but manages effectively, communicates authority, and maintains boundaries between himself and others that are respected even by men who have known him well for many years." A man, in short, a good deal like her own father and like the archetypal Westerner of the American imagination.

At her first meeting of his advisors, Jeane was introduced to the others in Reagan's inner circle. Reagan himself tried to disarm Jeane by saying that he knew how she must feel being among Republicans because he, as a former New Dealer, remembered having the same experience. Leaving the meeting, she mentioned the comment to Kirk's friend, the political scientist Aaron Wildavsky, who had also been present. "It's true," she said. "I've never had much association with Republicans." Wildavsky laughed, "Hell, I never even saw a Republican till I was sixteen."

Despite her enthusiasm for Reagan, Jeane was far from ready to jump ship. About the same time as "Dictatorships and Double Standards" appeared, she had written another piece in *Common Sense* that was less widely read but it just as clearly defined her state of mind. It was called "Why We Don't Become Republicans." In effect, the argument she gave was that even though people like her had been estranged from the Democratic Party for a decade and found many Republican policies preferable, Republicans were still the "country club" party, not sympathetic to the "whole community" and its need for a commitment to the "public good."

Republican Congressman Mickey Edwards and some other young Turks of the party—David Stockman, Guy Vander Jagt and Newt Gingrich among them—invited Jeane to discuss the *Common Sense* piece as a way of learning more about what kept the CDMers from coming over. Or, as Jeane phrased it, "Since we often find Republican policies preferable to Democratic programs, why don't we simply break with the Democratic Party and become Republicans?"

Stockman, a future controversial head of the Office of Management and Budget, immediately launched into a lecture on how Republicans should not be expected to embrace Democratic entitlements and how welfare had created a hereditary underclass. Jeane replied, "Yes, but you can't ignore urgent human needs because of long-term public consequences."

"It doesn't help a person to undermine his character," Stockman pressed.

Jeane shrugged: "That's exactly the kind of reasoning that makes me feel like a Democrat . . . ."

---

After the Republican convention, she became a leading figure among Democrats for Reagan and gave speeches for him around the country, trying to move Democrats disgusted with Carter over the threshold of suspicion. She participated in the mock debates where Reagan prepared for his only face-off with Carter, which advisors knew would play a large role in defining him for skeptical voters. David Stockman portrayed Carter in these sessions and Jeane was struck by the unnerving accuracy with which he captured the president's mirthlessly unctuous smile, the crooning self-righteousness, the computer-like use of facts and figures. Along with George Will and Pat Buchanan, she peppered Reagan with hard questions about foreign policy.

The debate took place in Cleveland on October 28, one week before the election. As expected, the president attacked Reagan as a dangerous right-winger. In a folksy way ("There you go again!") Reagan rebutted the charge and went on the offensive against Carter's weaknesses. Many on Reagan's own team had been prepared for the worst, but his unflappable good humor and respectable grasp of the issues stood in stark contrast to Carter's smugness. By the time Reagan started his closing statement with the devastating question "Are you better off now than you were four years ago?" it was clear that he had more than held his own.

Jeane and Kirk were at the Reagan headquarters at the Hilton on election night and at the Republican National Committee victory breakfast the next morning. Not long after, the president-elect announced the formation of a senior foreign policy group chaired by Gerald Ford to help in the transition. Jeane, Scoop Jackson and Eugene Rostow were the only Democrats on the panel.

The fact that she had established herself as a player was seen in one of these early discussions, when the term "Reaganaut" was used to describe the people around the president-elect, and Henry Kissinger said dismissively that he had no idea what it could possibly mean. When no one else responded, Jeane spoke up to define it pointedly as describing someone who, as distinguished from foreign policy establishment figures of both parties, "shared a view of the Soviet Union and the Cold War and its seriousness and intractable character that Ronald Reagan had been espousing for years, not someone who saw the Cold War as a conventional major policy disagreement. Someone who had a clear conviction that Soviet communism was repressive and aggressive and bent on exploiting its empire through violence—coups, guerrilla war, outright invasion." Her implication was clear: such a person was in no way like Kissinger himself, whom she believed had not acknowledged the uniquely dangerous nature of the USSR when cutting deals under the banner of détente; had ignored moral questions (especially those represented by the Soviet dissidents) in favor of strategic ones; and had put changing the internal nature of the USSR at the bottom of his priorities.*

It was a bravura moment. Jeane walked out of the meeting with Cap Weinberger, who had just been named secretary of defense. Struck by what she'd said, he asked her to join him.

"I know nothing about the Department of Defense," Jeane demurred. Weinberger replied, "That makes two of us. We can learn together."

The offer was still on the table just before Christmas when Jeane was at the Fontainebleau Hotel in Miami giving a speech for the local chapter of American Friends of Hebrew University,

---

* Kissinger did not appreciate these comments. But eventually, as Jeane became a star in the Reagan administration, he and she established a wary friendship. Uncomfortable at being an outsider in the great debates of the era, Kissinger occasionally wrote her petulant letters whose tone was filled with passive aggression, as in one, undated, where he complains, "Apparently you have been warned that I am least to be trusted when I sound most plausible—and by members of an administration that I have been defending with more conviction than it defends itself." Jeane was always interested in his views and respectful of his person, but also always aware that their differences often placed them on the shores of two different intellectual continents, staring at each other with a certain incomprehension. She once told me, "I always felt that there was a big difference between him and [Lawrence] Eagleburger and [Brent] Scowcroft and us [the Reaganauts]. They thought of us as ideologues, and they were right if by that you mean people who perceived and were willing to act on a policy of ideas and principles."

on how Israel stood alone as an oasis of freedom in a desert of despotism in the Middle East. Mixing pleasure with business, she and Kirk went out to dinner later on and then took a long walk. They returned to their room and saw that the message light on their phone was blinking. When she called the front desk, the operator said "Please call Ronald Reagan" and gave a California number.

"How are you, Jeane?" Reagan said when she finally got through to him.

"Great, Governor. How are you?"

"I'll be better if you'll agree to be our next ambassador to the United Nations," he said.

"Are you sure you think I can do the job?" Jeane tried to hide the tremulousness in her voice.

"I am sure and I hope you'll do it."

"Well, I'm very honored that you ask me. I'll do my best."

Reagan gave one of his characteristic pauses and then said, "Jeane, you've made my day."

Shortly after her appointment was announced, Jeane received an invitation to address the Bilderberger Club, the elite group seen by some conspiracy theorists as a sort of executive committee of the ruling class; it was a preview of the higher circles in which she would now be moving. She was asked to speak on "North/South issues," the idea then taking hold in international affairs that the crucial problem facing the world was not the Cold War, but the disparity in wealth and energy and protein between the prosperous Northern Hemisphere and the impoverished Southern one. In her talk, Jeane argued that the very subject was encrusted with ideology and Western self-hatred, and that the future of the impoverished countries of the world lay not in redistributionism but in growth and development. And these, she insisted, could only come from capitalist economics and democratic governance. She closed by saying that it was still the basic East/West issue that mattered: freedom versus tyranny.

She regarded it as a modest talk, but, as she later wrote, a Bilderberger from Switzerland jumped up when she finished and declared that what he'd just heard "sent shivers down his spine and struck horror into his heart." The meeting ended on this note of conflict. The next day, Jeane got a call from David Rockefeller, who had been present, and who apologized profusely for the way she had been treated. When she recounted this story in one of the early meetings of the new administration, George Bush, the vice-president-elect, complained that it "wasn't fair" that she should get to go to meetings of the Bilderbergers when he could not, for fear that he'd be criticized as "too liberal."

Thinking about the whole thing in the days to come, Jeane concluded that the new world she was about to enter would be "strange and interesting."

# Diplomacy without Apology

The three weeks before the inauguration were filled with briefings by the transition team and early meetings of the president-elect's inner circle. Jeane knew that part of her appeal was that she was a fresh face with no political baggage, but she also recognized that not having a constituency, as most of the other appointees did, made her vulnerable. She had the beginnings of a strong relationship with Reagan himself, but knew that this was an asset that would be degraded by overuse. With Kirk advising her, she tried to bolster her position by insisting that the United Nations job be elevated to cabinet rank, and that she also have a seat on the National Security Council. She maneuvered her way onto the powerful National Security Planning Group, where one of her first actions would be to try to commit the new administration to backing the Contras in Nicaragua.

She felt an affinity with Bill Casey, the new CIA chief, in part because he had a background in the Office of Strategic Services similar to Kirk's; she also liked the Californians Ed Meese and William Clark, respectively counselor to the president and national security advisor. But she wasn't so sure about Alexander Haig, the sleek, aggressive secretary of state designate, under whom she would be working even though she was his equal in cabinet rank. While she liked what she'd heard of his military career, she was put off by his self-presentation as the take-charge "vicar" who intended to run foreign policy with papal infallibility and carried a little black book filled with talking points he consulted like scripture. His overbearing verbal style also gave her pause. When Kirk asked how things had gone after one early session with Haig, she said, "It reminded me of why I gave up ping pong." Kirk got the reference immediately: their middle son John, as a teenager, had lured Jeane into games of ping pong that he would then dominate by smashing the ball at her so hard that she finally had to drop the paddle and flee the room.

Haig was annoyed that she had a seat on the NSC and that Bill Clark designated her as an independent counselor to the president, which meant she could telephone Reagan anytime she wanted without going through channels. Initially he condescended to her, describing, for instance, one of those early meetings as being largely taken up "by an interesting if somewhat discursive lecture on the nature of assertiveness by Mrs. Kirkpatrick." Privately he was less circumspect, according to a rumor Jeane heard about a meeting in which he had fumed: "I don't know how anybody expects that I will work with that bitch."

At her confirmation hearings, she gave a preview of things to come when she said frankly that those agencies of the UN which were committed to human betterment could count on her support, but those committed to an "ideological struggle against the fundamental principles and intents of the U.S." would get her opposition. Only a few Democratic senators questioned her closely—all of them on the basis of what she testified was a "distorted reading" of "Dictatorships and Double Standards." She won unanimous approval by the Senate Foreign Relations Committee and then by the whole Senate, and was sworn in by Vice President Bush on February 4, 1981.

The CDM threw a going-away party in her honor. In a brief talk, she promised that her first principle in the UN would be "to agree to nothing before we understood what it meant and to try very hard to make certain that nothing we agree to diminishes freedom in the world."

When she made her first trip to the UN, Donald McHenry, Carter's second ambassador to the organization, showed her around the U.S. mission occupying eleven floors in a building on

First Avenue. Her own office was on the tenth floor and had a spectacular view overlooking Turtle Bay. Jeane asked McHenry why the windows were covered with thick two-ply drapes. He told her they were composed of a special fabric to block the laser-activated listening devices beamed from a nearby building occupied by a front for Soviet intelligence. Later on, he showed her the permanent representative's personal suite on the forty-second floor of the Waldorf Astoria, with four bedrooms and a grand piano in the living area. She sat down and played a few notes of the *Goldberg Variations*.

Still feeling the effects of his bout with Legionnaire's disease, Kirk had finally retired from the American Political Science Association and was able to be with her in her first weeks in New York. He loved the sumptuousness of the scene at the Waldorf—a private chef, a huge selection of the best California wines, an unctuous butler, Dufys on loan from the Metropolitan Museum of Art splashing the bedroom walls with blue. He took an almost paternal pride in Jeane, but was sometimes a little confounded to find himself merely a prop in her drama. (In one well-remembered episode early in her tenure, the roast pigeon at a state dinner with the French UN ambassador arrived not only undercooked but underthawed; when one guest hacked too vigorously at the bird on his plate, it flew across the table onto Kirk's lap. The French ambassador's wife picked it up and put it on her own plate, continuing the conversation without missing a beat as Kirk watched with a look of incomprehension on his face.)

Jeane wanted his daily counsel, and he would have moved into the suite at the Waldorf permanently if he had not still been involved with their three sons, all of whom were having enough trouble finding their way that he felt he should be a presence in their Washington home. He and Jeane were particularly worried about Douglas, whose problems were now entering the public arena, as was indicated by a visit to New York in which he demanded to see her at the UN, had a drunken scuffle with security officers, and later claimed that he had been attacked by "foreign agents."

---

Shuttling back and forth between New York and Washington in the first days of the new administration, Jeane was sometimes struck by how peculiar it was that she should have this job. She was a career academic; more to the point, she was a woman in two very male environments not yet tamed by politically correct pieties about gender equality. At the UN she was the only female ambassador heading a major delegation and she was aware of the institutional perturbation this caused. The feeling was even more pronounced in Washington. At one point she was sitting silently in a meeting in the White House situation room along with President Reagan, the vice president and a handful of others, when she saw a mouse scurry across the floor and thought to herself that it was no more surprising that such a creature should be there than that she, a woman, should be.

"A woman in high office is intrinsically controversial," she commented in an early interview. "Many people think a woman shouldn't be in high office. Kissinger is described as a 'professor.' I am described as 'schoolmarmish.' Brzezinski is called 'Doctor.' I am called 'Mrs.' I am depicted as a witch or scold in editorial cartoons and the speed with which these stereotypes are used shows how close those feelings are to the surface. It's much worse than I ever dreamed it would be. My feelings are hurt."

During her first days at the UN, she felt subtly assaulted by a process of "dequalification." She was sometimes called "tough," but usually for attitudes she believed would be considered normally assertive in a male. On one occasion, someone pointedly referred to her as "temperamental," leading one of Jeane's friends to reply, "What does that mean? Temperamental once a month?"

The bureaucrats on the staffs of State, Defense and the CIA

feared her because while they talked to each other in advance of White House meetings and could prepare for each other's positions, Jeane never advertised what she was thinking on a given issue and thus became a wild card. The press wasn't sure what to make of her either. (The *New York Times* referred to her as "a professor turned diplomat.") But she immediately made one thing clear to the media and other countries at the UN: there had been regime change at the U.S. mission. "Until now," she said, "the Soviets have been playing chess and we've been playing checkers, but no more." She criticized a human rights document turned out by some committee of Third World nations for having "the character of a letter to Santa Claus." To congressmen who told her to lower her expectations and treat the UN as a place where the Third World could "blow off steam," she replied that it was "not a Turkish bath." When another diplomat noted vacuously that the great thing about the UN was that it was a microcosm of the world, she was heard to mutter, "In my worst moments, I fear that this is true." Asked by a reporter from *Life* what she had learned after a few weeks on the job, she said, "That my sentences are too short and my meanings too clear. I must learn to obfuscate."

Around this time, she had a private meeting with Ronald Reagan that she later recounted in her draft autobiography:

> "Mr. President," I said, "I thought the UN was a problem when you sent me there. I didn't have a very high opinion of it. But now I've had an opportunity to learn about it."
> "Yes, Jeane," he leaned forward.
> "Now, Mr. President, I have a much worse opinion of it."
> "I was afraid for a minute that you were going to tell me all my impressions of the last twenty years were wrong."

She inherited a group of more than a hundred career employees who seemed to think that their job was to promote and defend the UN, and who reacted sullenly when she told them that the job of the U.S. mission was representing the interests of the United States. ("Mankind—that abstraction—does not appoint us, employ us, or pay our salaries.") Knowing that they saw her arrival as a "hostile takeover," as one career foreign service officer acknowledged, she made the most of the small number of political appointments she was allowed. In forming her team, she called on Chuck Lichenstein, a longtime friend and former vice president at PBS whose appointment reassured members of the president's "kitchen cabinet" because he was a lifetime Republican. Another friend who joined her was Richard Schifter, a Maryland attorney and Holocaust survivor.

Jose Sorzano, a beloved former PhD student and colleague of hers at Georgetown, was a key hire; he was a Cuban refugee and a canny political infighter whose loyalty she knew she could count on.* She brought on Ken Adelman, who would later head the U.S. Arms Control and Disarmament Agency. When he equivocated about whether to take the position of deputy ambassador, she signaled her impatience by saying, "Well, as Mahalia Jackson says, 'Is you is or is you ain't my baby?'" (It was actually Louis Jordan's signature song.)

Allan Gerson became her legal advisor, loyal friend, and occasional co-author on speeches and essays; he would later write *The Kirkpatrick Mission: Diplomacy Without Apology*, the authoritative account of the Kirkpatrick years at the UN. But perhaps her key hire was Carl Gershman, who had been in the trenches for years with the Young People's Socialist League, doing hand-to-hand combat with Communists. Knowing Marxism-Leninism in theory and practice, Gershman could, as Jeane later commented, "drive the Soviets crazy with his detailed familiarity of their texts and intentions." In October 1981, she asked him to give a speech to the

---

* When Sorzano reported that members of the Soviet bloc were making snide references to the fact that there were so many Jews and Cuban exiles on her staff, Jeane smiled and said, "That's right. I like smart people."

UN Third Committee, the organization's stage for human rights discussions. When he scorched the Soviets for their brutality and referred to the USSR as "the last remaining empire on earth," the demands for replies from Eastern bloc countries was so great that a special session of the committee had to be convened. Despite the institutional criticism directed at her, Jeane was pleased by the result and instructed Gershman to continue "to raise the banner of freedom all the time and everywhere."

Adelman later commented about their early days, "We were like Davy Crockett at the Alamo." Unexpectedly, some of Jeane's bitterest battles were with the bureaucracy of her own State Department. A crucial moment came when she talked to Elliott Abrams, assistant secretary of state for international organizations—and ironically the son-in-law of her good friends and comrades-in-arms Norman Podhoretz and Midge Decter—and he told her that she would be dealing with Secretary Haig through him. He received a frosty response: "The secretary and I will decide that." Despite their political closeness, she and Abrams butted heads until Jeane solved the conundrum by helping get him moved to the more influential State Department job of assistant secretary for human rights, which had been vacant for a year or so after the Senate failed to confirm her friend Margaret Lefever's husband Ernie for the job.

The struggle with State often took the form of petty obstruction rather than open conflict. Jeane's assistant at AEI, Jackie Tillman, who was now heading the office that the UN ambassador maintained at Foggy Bottom, once called "upstairs" at Jeane's request to ask an innocuous question about how many U.S. troops were stationed in South Korea. The anonymous voice on the other end of the line asked, "Why do you want to know?" Tillman replied, "My boss needs the information." The bureaucrat asked, "Why does she need to know?"

Tillman ended this conversation by saying, "None of your business." But State was in Jeane's business during her entire tenure at the UN, and usually in a negative way. When she went on a tour of Latin American countries in 1981, for instance, she discovered that a memo had gone out from State to all the U.S. ambassadors saying, in effect, "Be nice but ignore her."

Jeane forbade her staff from clearing speeches with State. For the next four years they would all scathingly refer to the department as "the Building," as if it were some malign Kafkaesque institution populated by automata.

If Jeane was not wholly surprised by the hostile environment and kabuki politics of the UN, it was because she inherited the experience of fellow Democrat Daniel Patrick Moynihan, who served as U.S. ambassador to the organization from 1975 to 1976 under President Gerald Ford. She had talked with him and read *A Dangerous Place*, his book about his deeply disillusioning time there. In Moynihan's view, the UN's growth in the post–World War II era—from 52 states in 1960 to 157 in 1975, largely as a result of decolonization—paralleled the organization's embrace of a "totalitarian theory and practice wholly at variance with its original purpose." America was on the defensive in the world body because of the Vietnam War and the subsequent policy of détente (which Moynihan regarded as "a form of disguised retreat," although its architect, Henry Kissinger, was his theoretical boss while he was at the UN). But Moynihan decided that he would "make no apologies to our moral inferiors," and would use his time in the organization to defend American interests as well as he could and "to challenge totalitarian ideals and governments around the world." His defiant attitude was summarized by the French epigram posted on his office door: *Cet animal est très méchant: quand on l'attaque, il se defend.*

Moynihan had held the UN political culture accountable for the organization's malignity. Jeane agreed, caustically referring to the United Nations as "the glass house where everyone throws stones." But she was more interested in the political *structure*, and she spent her first months employing her political scientist's understanding of institutions in an effort to understand how the United States could be on the losing end of 145-to-1 votes.

She concluded that there had been "a degree of falsification" present in the organization since the beginning, owing to the bulky presence of the USSR and its satellites, which gave the lie to its ideals. But the situation became worse when the UN was taken over by blocs dominated by its postcolonial members: the Organization of the Islamic Conference, the African bloc, the Latin American bloc and, most powerful of all, the Non-Aligned Movement, encompassing roughly 93 of the 157 member states and cutting across geographic lines and membership in other blocs. This situation made the UN a place where "unlarge, unpowerful, unaffluent" groups banded together to dominate the agenda and activities of the organization. "The UN," Jeane said emphatically, "is their place."

Alliances between the blocs were built on mutual back scratching: "The African bloc supports the Arabs on all matters attacking Israel and the Arabs agree to support the African bloc on all matters attacking South Africa. Soviet clients like Cuba bring along the Non-Aligned bloc." The members always protected and never criticized each other: "Uganda was never targeted for human rights violations. Neither is Ethiopia, nor Vietnam, nor any other member of the Non-Aligned bloc or African bloc or Islamic Conference."

Only the United States and Israel were not parts of a bloc. Even the Europeans had their own tepid bloc, which was utterly "without zest for explaining and defending Western values." In fact, the Europeans, Jeane charged, "have long since accepted their prescribed role, grown accustomed to being 'it' in a global game of dunk-the-clown, and have opted to 'understand' the point of view of their Third World accusers."

Because of this political structure, the UN had become an organization where an endless "political struggle is waged to control the definition of key terms and descriptions of reality. What are human rights? What are human rights abuses? What is aggression? Who is the aggressor and who is the victim? What is a national liberation movement? Who is liberated? All of this is 'decided' by a plebiscite rigged by blocs . . . ."

In any debate, the blocs provide a long procession of speakers "to echo and elaborate on accusations," leading to "the isolation and humiliation of the victim" and an effort to "create the impression that 'world opinion' is united in condemnation of the targeted nation. States that have no economic, strategic or political stake in the issue except for their common bloc 'membership' become involved. The charges become progressively outrageous, the denunciations progressively hyperbolic. . . . The attackers, encountering no obstacles, grow bolder, while other nations become progressively more reluctant to associate themselves with the accused . . . out of a fear that they themselves will become a target of bloc hostility." Such a process seemed to Jeane to "more closely resemble a mugging than a political debate."

After creating this conceptual ideological map—the most rigorous effort yet to chart the topography of the organization—Jeane said that part of the reason for America's isolation in the UN, in addition to pernicious structural developments in the organization, was "a longstanding lack of skill in practicing politics there." In fact, she saw "no difference between our relations with supporters and opponents"; there was "no punishment for opposing our views and values, and no reward for cooperating."

She told her staff that she intended to treat the U.S. mission like a political operation in Chicago, where tough deals cut on the basis of enlightened self-interest trumped the theater of idealistic rhetoric. Success would come not from blandishing enemies or begging nations to like America, but from "good precinct work, canvassing, persuading, getting out the vote." She had posters made bearing the image of Richard Daley, the former mayor of Chicago, and posted them throughout the U.S. mission because "he knew the difference between winning and losing and that winning was better."

No longer would countries that valued placid relations with the United States outside the organization be allowed to attack it without response inside UN chambers. In courtesy calls on ambassadors from Third World countries that continued to count on foreign aid even though they lined up against the U.S. on every issue inside the organization, she made it clear that notice was now being taken of their behavior, reinforcing this idea with the slogan: "We take the UN very seriously. We notice, we care, *we remember.*"

She sent the voting record of every member nation to legislators in Congress. After a meeting of ninety-three foreign ministers and delegates produced a report on the state of the world for the UN filled with what even the *New York Times* admitted was "one-sided anti-Americanism," she sent a letter to forty of these nations that said: "I think you no more believe these vicious lies than I do, and I do not believe they are an accurate reflection of your government's outlook. And yet what are we to think when [you] join in such charges?" She concluded bluntly, "I would very much appreciate hearing from you about it."

In one early address to the General Assembly, she admonished her fellow delegates, "It is not fair to judge one nation or group by the Sermon on the Mount and all other nations on the curve." Then she went on to score the UN as a place where "moral outrage has been distributed like violence in a protection racket"; a place where Israel and South Africa were daily punching bags, but UN agencies "are silent while 3 million Cambodians died in Pol Pot's murderous utopia . . . while a quarter million Ugandans died at the hands of Idi Amin . . . and while thousands of Soviet citizens are denied equal rights, equal protection of the law; denied the right to think, write, publish, work freely or emigrate."

When the Ethiopian foreign minister suddenly interrupted some mundane debate to accuse the United States of racism and genocide, Jeane replied by reading from an Amnesty International report on appalling human rights abuses in Ethiopia. After a Syrian delegate gave a rant about how Vietnam and Cuba deserved the appreciation of the world community for breaking the back of U.S. imperialism, she rose to thank him dryly for his "very useful clarification of the issues." When he angrily asked her if her words represented a "constructive ambiguity or an example of imperialist obfuscation," she paused for a moment and gave a contemptuous shrug, "Oh, probably imperialist obfuscation, but I'm not sure."

Her risky decision to wage "diplomacy without apology" (in the phrase of her legal advisor Allan Gerson) paid off. The *New York Post* wrote, "At last a challenge to the lies of the nonaligned." The *Chicago Tribune* praised Jeane: "Now she should put on a pair of brass knuckles under the velvet gloves and really get to work!" There was some pushback from the career foreign officers in the U.S. mission, one of whom reproached her for overkill by saying, "A dog does not fight with a chicken." Jeane answered, "What if the dog is being attacked by 96 chickens?" When she later told Ronald Reagan about the exchange, the president chuckled and said, "We need to have a little fried chicken."

An early test was Cuba's resolution to condemn the United States for controlling the destiny of Puerto Rico—an event which Jeane later characterized as Castro's annual effort "to lambaste American imperialism and colonialism ... [and] lecture the Assembly on the glories of self-government everywhere but on his island." Old State Department hands counseled her against fighting because losing "would only make our defeat more visible." Jeane rejected such negativism out of hand and set out to block the Cubans with a highly political campaign that featured intense "factual lobbying"; enlisting U.S. ambassadors to make appeals in the capitals of countries whose vote was critical; and making it clear to these countries that their vote would be taken into consideration in bilateral relations with the United States. In last-minute discussions with the UN representatives of Zambia, Uganda and other countries that had routinely voted with America's opponents, Jeane recalled, "I told them that I would never forget their vote on this issue . . . and neither would the Reagan administration. . . . I would see to that."

She unexpectedly won the Security Council vote in an outcome that helped develop what she called "a taste for victory" in the career officers at the mission, who now began to abandon the defensive crouch that had been their habitual posture at the world body. One of them later recalled being locked in a public debate with a Third World representative who "commented to me admiringly that while he didn't necessarily agree with my country, at least the U.S. was standing up for its convictions when they came under attack, something he accurately said other Western countries were not doing."

Some Third World nations were not so complimentary, but diplomacy without apology ignored them. When he heard murmurings that some of these nations were talking about trying to move the UN out of the U.S., Jeane's aide Chuck Lichenstein famously replied that if they did, he and others in the American delegation would be at the dock as their ships sailed, happily waving goodbye.

---

From her first days at the UN, Jeane believed that the treatment of Israel was the presenting symptom of the institutional disease afflicting the organization. In this, she agreed with her predecessor Daniel Patrick Moynihan, who had seen the isolation of Israel as the USSR's "great project," an endeavor undertaken with diabolical ingenuity by accusing the Israelis of racism—the chief sin at the postcolonial UN—and thus making Israel morally equivalent to apartheid South Africa. How far this project had advanced became clear to Moynihan the day he saw the egregious Idi Amin address the General Assembly and receive a standing ovation when he said, "I call for the expulsion of Israel from the United Nations and the extinction of Israel as a state." The offensive against Israel reached its nadir in the General Assembly's passage of the notorious resolution formally condemning Zionism as "a form of racism" in November 1975.

Leaving the organization to run for the Senate, Moynihan felt that things could not get worse for Israel. But then Jimmy Carter's ambassador Andrew Young criticized the Jewish state as "stubborn and intransigent," and secretly met with the PLO observer to the UN. This act cost Young his job, but his replacement, Donald McHenry, went a step further by voting for Resolution 465 condemning Israel's occupation of "Arab territories including Jerusalem."

Jeane was shocked by the level of hatred for Israel she saw at the UN. Soon after arriving, she commented to her colleague Richard Schifter, "I just want you to know that I think the Holocaust is possible again. I didn't think so before I came to the UN. But I think so now." She discussed her fears with the president, who agreed that the United States had to stand against the "obsessive" vilification of Israel. As Jeane pointed out, there was "a systematic totalitarian assault on language and meaning," in which the Israelis were caricatured as "Nazis" and accused of committing "a new genocide" against the Palestinians.

She began by reprimanding the career foreign service officers on her own staff who, still reflecting attitudes of the Carter administration, dismissively referred to Israel's UN ambassador Yehuda Blum by his first name and rudely interrupted him when he came to Jeane's office for discussions. She told them that such behavior would no longer be tolerated toward a man who spoke nine languages and was a Holocaust survivor.

She lectured the Security Council too, pointing out that in

1981 alone it had met sixty times and failed to deal with the Soviet invasion of Afghanistan, Vietnam's invasion of Cambodia, Iraq's invasion of Iran, or Libya's invasion of Chad, while forty-five of these meetings "dealt with complaints by the Arab states against Israel." The sickness was so deep, she asserted, that it had infected the mundane operations of all UN agencies: "A women's conference is suddenly transformed into a forum for the denunciation of Zionism and it will be solemnly asserted by the assembled delegates of what is called the 'international community' that having studied the problem the conclusion has been drawn that the biggest, most important obstacle to the realization of women's full enjoyment of equal rights in the world is Zionism.... A meeting of the International Atomic Energy Agency becomes so absorbed in negotiations and debate over a resolution to expel Israel that it almost forgets to worry about nuclear non-proliferation."*

She got a personal taste of this "mob rule," as she called it, when she headed a delegation to an International Conference on African Refugees in March 1981. The day before it opened, Arab states, led by Libya, moved to expel the Israeli representative. Jeane told the delegates that if this happened, the United States would walk out and withdraw the $285 million it had committed to the refugee problem. They must choose between money that would help people and their "vile rhetoric," she said, causing an Arab diplomatic retreat.

---

* With bitter humor, she told one audience she addressed in 1981 on the subject of UN obsessions: "I sometimes find myself thinking about an old joke about national character, according to which a group of international scholars were each asked to write a book on the elephant and report back in six months with their manuscripts. The German came in with six volumes entitled *The Prolegomenon to the Elephant*, and the French specialist came in with a slim, elegantly bound volume entitled *The Love Life of the Elephant*, and the American came in with a thicker book called *Communism and the Elephant*. Well, if we were to project that today to the United Nations, we can be sure that the Non-Aligned Movement's contribution would be *How Israel Destroyed the Palestinian Elephants*."

A move to expel "the Zionist entity" came before the General Assembly the following year, proposed by Syria and Libya. When the State Department dithered in its response, Jeane went to contacts in Congress, notably Moynihan in the Senate and Jack Kemp in the House. They proposed a resolution that if Israel were to be expelled, the United States would withhold its contribution to the UN, which amounted to a quarter of its budget, and withdraw from the organization itself. Again, the Arabs backed down.

Jeane was in a no-win position on June 7, 1981, when Israeli jet fighters destroyed the Osirak nuclear reactor that Saddam Hussein was building at a secret location outside Baghdad. Although the State Department had immediately denounced the Israeli action as "aggressive," she made her own feelings known when she commented, "If it takes one nuclear missile to wipe Israel off the face of the map and Iraq is deploying the capacity to deliver such missiles, then context is not irrelevant." But she had to walk a diplomatic fine line when Iraq brought a resolution for sanctions against Israel to the Security Council. In a half-hour meeting with the president on May 31, she argued that the United States should abstain. She was ordered to try to reduce the resolution to a simple condemnation. After three days of negotiation with the notoriously rigid Iraqi foreign minister Sa'dun Hammadi, she got this concession, which somewhat mitigated the vote she had to cast to censure Israel. But when the question was called, she raised her hand slowly to half-mast and allowed her face to register the look of one who has just caught a faint whiff of fecal odor.

Reagan praised her as a "heroine" for making the best of a bad situation. Even the press concurred. "The acerbic professor has grown to be a respected diplomat," wrote *Newsweek*. But Jeane still had an unpleasant taste in her mouth a few days later when she and Kirk flew to France for a brief vacation. They had barely settled in at their rented house in Saint-Rémy when the presidential advisor Richard Allen called and read excerpts from stories in the *New York Times* and the *Wall Street Journal,* based on leaks from Alexander Haig's aides, claiming that she had not only been willing to accept a resolution condemning Israel but proposed one herself and it was derailed only by the secretary of state's timely intervention.

It was the latest salvo in a campaign of innuendo that Haig had been waging since Jeane's appointment in an effort to neutralize her as a competitor to his vicarship of foreign policy. Although Allen assured her that the president didn't believe the stories, Jeane told Kirk that she thought Haig was trying to "disappear" her. Half an hour later came a call from Haig himself, earnestly disavowing the stories and promising that "heads would roll" when he found out who was responsible for the leaks.

But the two of them were clearly on a collision course. The secretary of state had always believed that Jeane's appointment represented a coup by "right-wing activists," and he resented her unwillingness to play second lieutenant to his brigade commander. For her part, Jeane stubbornly refused to submit. The conflict became serious enough that Reagan wrote in one of his diary entries, "Back to office to meet with Jeanne Kirkpatrick. She and Al H. have been at each other's throats. Later in the day met with Al. Bill Clark at both meetings—thank heavens. . . . I think we can get a lid on it with no further damage."*

This last sentence was another example of the famous Reagan optimism. Jeane and Haig continued to clash over issues such as Solidarity's challenge to Poland's Communist regime. He was sympathetic to the dissident organization but didn't want to provoke the USSR or unnerve Western European nations worried that Soviet troops would be deployed in response to the democracy

---

* The president always had trouble with Jeane's name, spelling it "Jeanne" or "Jean" as well as occasionally the correct way.

movement. Jeane regarded this position as a shocking failure "to respond to the moral and political aspects of this Polish repression." There were abrasive discussions in Washington, with Cap Weinberger and Bill Casey backing her position and Haig fighting back. Jeane noticed that "when someone disagreed with him he would take out the black briefing book he carried with him and just read the talking points again—louder." The infighting between them on a variety of issues became so bad that one White House aide shrugged and said, "All we can do is stand on the sidelines and hold their jackets."

Because of her impassive façade, calm demeanor and single-minded sense of purpose, people assumed that Jeane enjoyed the combat—the infighting and backbiting and damaging leaks. But in 1981 she blurted out almost plaintively to a writer from a women's magazine: "I'm not someone who is personally tough. I'm just not." The president understood her predicament, and at the end of a particularly bruising meeting at which Haig attacked her, he ostentatiously walked over to put an arm on her shoulder and tell her she was doing a good job.

---

The final showdown came with the Falklands War. By the time it erupted, Jeane was recognized as a Latin American expert inside the administration. She had visited Argentina briefly in the summer of 1981 and met with General Leopoldo Galtieri, who had visited the United States a few months earlier and committed Argentina to support the Contras. After he took control of the country in a coup late in the year, his support for the Nicaraguan resistance deepened to include training their forces on Argentine soil. Early in 1982, Galtieri thought to take advantage of what he regarded as his close ties to Washington to plan an invasion of the Malvinas, as Argentine irredentists insisted the islands should be called.

In what some regarded as a monumental self-contradiction for someone who frequently alluded to Munich, Jeane wanted the United States to remain neutral as Argentine noises—which she thought were nothing more than that—about military action grew louder. She understood why, aside from the Special Relationship with the British, there would be prejudice against Argentina: deep-seated antipathy toward the country's "suspected sympathies with the Axis in World War II, the thousands of 'disappeared,' the fact of military dictatorship." But looking at the situation in terms of American interests, she worried that if the U.S. backed Britain, it would run afoul of *Latinidad* (even Nicaragua sympathized with the Argentine claims), set back the Contras' cause, and imperil the fragile hemispheric consensus on the importance of isolating Cuba.

Haig later charged that she had known in advance about the invasion and let the Argentine UN ambassador think that "if his country continued to support the U.S. on Nicaragua there would be no American criticism in the UN on the landing in the Falklands." She denied this, stating emphatically in her draft autobiography that she had actually been caught out on the whole affair, underestimating the will of Argentina and the resolve of Britain: "I thought it inconceivable that . . . a European power would send a ragtag armada 8,000 miles to fight for a place inhabited by 1,000 sheepherders." If Britain had not resisted decolonization in Rhodesia and Hong Kong, why would it draw a line in the sand in this godforsaken place?

But there was no doubt that she had been strongly courted by the Argentines, who were very much aware that she had written a well-regarded book on their country and read between the lines of "Dictatorships and Double Standards" to find an endorsement of their position. Well in advance, the Argentine ambassador scheduled a dinner in her honor for April 1, 1982. The next day, three hundred of his country's marines landed on the windswept islands, catching the British and Jeane herself off-guard. In her draft autobiography she wrote of speaking to the British foreign secretary, Lord Peter Carrington, a week or so later at a party at Henry Kissinger's, where she mentioned not having expected it: "Carrington expressed delight at my acknowledgement. He felt better, he said, to know that I too had been taken by surprise."

It was true that she continued to meet with the Argentines outside of official channels in the days ahead, as Haig later charged. But she did so with the knowledge and support of the national security advisor Bill Clark. It was also true, however, that in these discussions she always warned that in the event of a war, there was no doubt that the United States would choose the British rather than neutrality.

In the weeks ahead, as a British task force sailed toward South America, Jeane worked hard to save the situation. She met with the Argentine foreign minister Nicanor Costa Méndez and pushed him to accept the list of concessions that Margaret Thatcher had privately indicated she was willing to make—some of them so generous that Jeane actually believed Thatcher would be repudiated by her own Conservative backbenchers if and when they became known. But she got nowhere.

By the end of April there were continual air skirmishes. On May 2, the British sank the Argentine light cruiser *General Belgrano*, with 323 men lost. After a round of shuttle diplomacy, Haig made it clear that he supported the British, and that he was speaking for the president as well. Jeane continued to try to negotiate a cease-fire. But the Thatcher government refused to consider it unless Argentina withdrew its forces. Jeane was up until three in the morning just before the major British invasion on May 21, begging Costa Méndez to accept the offer. She came away feeling defeated and told aides that "the Argentines' lack of realism was shocking."

A few days later, she took key staff members to dinner at a Szechuan restaurant and told them that Haig had just telephoned and "yelled at her for twenty minutes about all this." When they expressed dismay, she shrugged, "My father used to yell at me and my brother. Now, one of my sons, my middle son, has taken to yelling at me. And so I've gotten used to it. I just let them press on and that's what I did to Haig."

But she was less sanguine about the invisible campaign of leaks that her opponents at State were waging against her. "I don't know how to handle it," she told an interviewer from *People*. "As a member of the National Security Council, I express my views and then a grossly distorted version is leaked to the press. I hate being the object of this kind of public attack. I feel that I'm being set up."

She was putting in sixteen-hour days, seven days a week, constantly commuting between New York and Washington to attend meetings of the NSC, the National Security Planning Group, and the administration's Crisis Management Team. According to her childhood friend Phyllis Smith, Jeane called her in Mount Vernon late at night several times during this period "desperate to talk about old times or anything else not connected to current events." On one of these calls Jeane said, "There are times when I am so tired when I get into bed that I think about getting into a nightgown and brushing my teeth and washing my face, but I just can't do it and so I kick off my shoes and just crawl beneath the covers." It was around this time that she was hospitalized at Georgetown overnight with heart symptoms. She worried that it was the disease of her youth returning, but exhaustive tests showed she was suffering from stress.

As British troops drove toward the Falklands capital of Port Stanley, the focus turned to the UN, where the Spanish and Panamanian delegations had introduced a resolution for an immediate ceasefire. In NSC meetings in Washington, Jeane argued that the United States should abstain. She noted that Britain had always pursued its own interests at the UN—especially on Middle East questions—and the U.S. owed it no debt; and that since the British would veto the resolution in any case, it would be superfluous and costly with Latin allies for America to join in.*

The president, with Haig as part of his entourage, was at Versailles for an economic summit when the matter came to a head on June 4. Haig cabled Jeane to vote with Britain in vetoing the ceasefire resolution. She urgently requested reconsideration, giving Haig her reasons once again. There was no response as the deadline approached, and she voted "no," as ordered. Two minutes later, a message arrived from Haig ordering her to abstain. She told an aide to reply that the vote had been taken. A new message came back: "They want you to announce that your instructions were to abstain." Jeane saw that she was being set up and said that she wouldn't do it. Haig repeated the order.

In a gesture filled with defiance and subtext, Jeane got up and read briefly from an antiwar poem by the great Argentine poet Jorge Luis Borges, which she claimed somewhat implausibly had been handed to her that morning by one of her sons: "I offer you my ancestors, my dead men, the ghosts / that living men have honored in bronze: / my father's father killed in the frontier of / Buenos Aires, two bullets through his lungs, / bearded and dead, wrapped by his soldiers in / the hide of a cow." Then she told the astonished delegates, "My government has been rent by a clash of values, loyalties and friends. That clash continued even to the registration of the vote in this issue. I am told it is impossible for a

---

* Still defending herself eight years later, Jeane wrote an article for the *National Interest* suggesting that what she regarded as the inequalities of the Special Relationship were part of the equation for her. "British support was needed and not forthcoming in Vietnam and Central America. These experiences—later repeated in the British response to the U.S. landing in Grenada—left me wondering why the U.S. should necessarily stand with the UK on matters outside of NATO." She saw the harsh British criticism of the U.S. invasion of Grenada in particular as an incommensurate payback for the Falklands: "My most extreme position [in the Falklands matter] was that we should remain publicly neutral, which was a very different, much warmer position than that which the British assumed toward us [in the Grenada matter]."

government to change a vote once cast, but I have been requested by my government to record the fact that were it possible to change our vote we should like to change it from a veto—a 'No,' that is—to an abstention."

She was criticized in high places in the aftermath of the drama. (She heard, for instance, that Vice President Bush, with whom she had never felt comfortable, had told Reagan that if he were president he would have asked for her resignation.) Yet the vote finally made by the United States—abstention—was the vote she had urged all along. And in discussions with the national security advisor, Bill Clark, who was with Reagan in Europe, she discovered that Haig had not briefed him or the president about the conflicting orders he had issued on the resolution. Angered that Reagan had been made to look like a bystander in his own foreign policy, Clark agreed to bring a full account of the matter to the president, including details beginning to emerge that Haig had been following the UN debate over an open line from France and had intentionally delayed answering Jeane's urgent request for reconsideration of the no vote in an effort to embarrass her.

Five days later, Jeane gave a speech at the Heritage Foundation in which she charged that America had "not been effective in defining or projecting in international arenas a conception of our national purpose," adding that U.S. diplomacy was perceived as "amateurish." Seeing this correctly as an act of war, Haig immediately mobilized all his assets in the press for a counterstrike. The following morning's *New York Times* contained an editorial denouncing Jeane, along with columns by James Reston and Russell Baker saying that she had supported the Argentines and was incompetent and should resign. The same message came from the *Washington Post*, and from Senator Charles Percy, the Republican chairman of the Senate Foreign Relations Committee.*

---

* How seriously Jeane took this latter charge is suggested by the draft of a "surprised and dismayed" letter to Percy in her archives, which she probably

The combat between Jeane and Haig was a unique bureaucratic slugging match in which neither of them made an effort to be discreet. At one point Haig tried to demean Jeane by telling the *New York Times* that she was merely "a company commander." Jeane snidely ridiculed him in return on *Meet the Press*, saying, "Such titles may be more meaningful to Secretary Haig, who is, after all, a general, than they are to me, a professor in my ordinary life."

On June 25, in one final act of clumsy Machiavellianism, Haig sent the president a letter of resignation, expecting it to be rejected, thus strengthening his hand against Jeane. But the White House had been increasingly suspicious of the secretary of state for more than a year, after his bizarre reaction when the president was hospitalized following an assassination attempt ("I am in control here!"). The resignation was immediately accepted.

Later on, Haig wrote in his memoir *Caveat* that the Falklands War was his "Waterloo." If so, Jeane had been his Wellington, winning out not merely by luck but as a result of a vigorous defense. It was a summary moment for her. Years later, when appearing at an event staged by the Independent Women's Forum, she was asked about the conflict that dominated the first two years of the Reagan administration, and responded: "I'm sure Alexander Haig thought he was going to wipe me out in the first nine months on the job.... It was important to me that he did not do it."

---

never sent. Hastily scrawled on yellow legal paper with cross-outs and angry elisions, it notes that she had been to Argentina "exactly twice in my life and met with the Argentine ambassador only four times, always for meals in the presence of others." She wrote that she supported a negotiated settlement because the U.S. was "caught between two friends" and because "arousing anti-Yanqui feelings would have profoundly negative effects in hemispheric politics." And she ended stonily: "Since my friendship with other countries has come into question, I should like you to know that I have profound identification only with the United States."

ABOVE: "I could say the alphabet backwards by the time I was three, thus establishing myself as undeniably promising."

RIGHT: She did plays, learned the Gettysburg Address and went to what was called the Schubert Music Class, where she learned to play "The Happy Farmer."

PHOTOGRAPHS COURTESY OF JERRY JORDAN
EXCEPT AS NOTED

ABOVE: Jeane's frontier grandmothers Victoria Kile and Ellen Jordan during the Depression. Despite hard times, there were always "crusty loaves of bread baked on a big wood stove in the kitchen, fried chicken that had been crowing and clucking in the yard a few hours earlier, and freshly churned butter."

ABOVE: Jeane with her father and brother. Fat always called her "Sister," even before Jerry came along.

RIGHT: Jeane with Leona and brother Jerry in uniform. "Even my mother agreed that my brother would have more opportunities than I and had more respect for male attributes."

LEFT: Jeane's high school graduation picture. One classmate thought her capable of "being recklessly in love."

RIGHT: Anne de Lattre, age 19, Jeane's first "serious intellectual friend" at Barnard, who helped her become a Francophile.

ABOVE: Evron Kirkpatrick, 40 years old when Jeane met him and "the most famous unfamous man of his day."

BELOW: Jeane and Kirk after their marriage. He was the Pygmalion who intellectually sculpted her in a way that brought her fully to life.

ABOVE: Jeane was pleased by her selection as UN ambassador on December 23, 1980. Alexander Haig was smiling too, but not for long. © TAYLOR/AP/AP/CORBIS

BELOW: The first Reagan cabinet. At one early meeting, Jeane saw a mouse scurry across the White House floor and thought to herself that "it was no more surprising that such a creature should be there than that I, a woman, should be."

ABOVE: Jeane with Israel's UN ambassador, Yehuda Blum. She saw the world body's "obsessive" vilification of Israel as based on "a systematic totalitarian assault on language and meaning."
© MARIO CABRERA/AP/AP/CORBIS

LEFT: Jeane speaking during a debate on Lebanon. For her, the UN was "that glass house where everyone throws stones."

ABOVE: Jeane examines a terrorist bombing in San Salvador in 1985, with U.S. Ambassador Thomas Pickering and an embassy guard. El Salvador was the place to start building a fire-wall against the forces she believed the Carter administration had allowed to become established in Nicaragua. © LUIS ROMERO/AP/AP/CORBIS

BELOW: Jeane with Henry Kissinger in Moscow on February 5, 1987, meeting Andrei Sakharov. "Kirkpatski, Kirkpatski, which of you is Kirkpatski?" Sakharov seized her hands emotionally and said, "Your name is known in every cell of the gulag."
© BORIS YURCHENKO/AP/AP/CORBIS

ABOVE: Jeane speaking to students at a Maryland high school *ca* 1991 with Margaret Lefever, her best and most loyal friend.

COURTESY OF MARGARET LEFEVER

LEFT: Attending the funeral of fellow Reaganaut Cap Weinberger on April 4, 2006. She was being slowly consumed not by any one disease, but by what doctors call "failure to thrive."

© PABLO MARTINEZ MONSIVAIS/AP/AP/ CORBIS

# Rich in Enemies

Jeane had not only kept her job, but also emerged as an improbable superstar for the administration. She had waged what amounted to a political campaign to define the UN in frequent appearances on Sunday morning television news shows and in dozens of speeches around the country in what was tantamount to a highbrow barnstorming tour. Her criticism of the cynical maneuvering of the organization's bureaucracies now began to strike a nerve with a public tired of the world body's anti-Americanism. People appreciated her blunt defense of national values and her willingness to take the fight to America's enemies, within the UN and without. Kirk liked to tell about walking down Fifth Avenue with her one afternoon when they had managed to shake her Secret Service detail. Just as the light changed and they were crossing the street, a truck driver pulled up to the intersection, rolled down his window and yelled, "Give 'em hell, Jeane!"

She now felt at home in the narrow Security Council meeting room filled with smoke from the Gitanes, Benson & Hedges and other international brands that littered the long rectangular conference table; when she spoke before the General Assembly, the gallery was filled with visitors hoping to see her slash away at her Communist opponents with erudition and heavy-lidded irony. This increased power was visible too inside the administration, where, as the new secretary of state George Shultz got acclimated, she acted in coalition with the CIA director Bill Casey and the national security advisor Bill Clark, and sometimes the defense secretary Cap Weinberger, to construct the hard line on the Soviets that, temporarily at least, defined Reagan's foreign policy.

She had also now "loosened up" personally, in the observation of her legal advisor and friend Allan Gerson. Her indifference to her personal appearance in her first days as permanent representative having landed her on *People*'s 10 Worst Dressed list for 1981, she allowed female aides and acquaintances to put her through a makeover that included more generous makeup and a tousled and shorter hairstyle with highlights. In grudging trips to the fashion ateliers of Seventh Avenue, she selected the designer Leamond Dean to outfit her in smart suits, frilly blouses, pashminas, and bangly costume jewelry that clanked like a tinker's cart as a result of her jerky body movements. She got oversized horn-rimmed glasses that she used as a prop, gnawing at the temples or resting her chin on them during moments of concentration.

But while she was better put together, she still traveled in a cloud of modified personal chaos. Her colleague Ken Adelman preserved a mental image of her arriving late for a meeting, packing a hodgepodge of State Department memos, copies of *Figaro*, political science papers and classified documents, which she dumped on a conference table and regarded with suspicion after seating herself.

Kirk was still a big influence. Her aide Jackie Tillman recalls that when some important issue came up, Jeane would often say, "I don't want to decide on this until I have a chance to talk to Kirk." He sometimes accompanied her on foreign trips, and to keep him from appearing to be a mere consort she would get the U.S. Information Agency to set up a speech for him. But when the plane landed he would be quickly shouldered aside by the foreign press and forced to stand on the periphery of the crowd, watching Jeane's impromptu news conference with a look of faint consternation on his face.

He and Jeane were guests of the king of Morocco on September 1, 1983, talking about North African issues, when an emergency call came from her aide Chuck Lichenstein saying that a Korean airliner had been downed by the Soviets after straying briefly into their airspace. It was already a bad day because of news that Scoop Jackson had died, and Jeane was in personal mourning as she hurried back to the United States. On the way, she learned that the Soviet government's assertions that the shoot-down had been accidental were belied by conversations between Soviet ground command and the fighter stalking the aircraft, recorded by a Japanese listening post and passed on to U.S. intelligence.

By the time her plane touched down, the U.S. Information Agency was putting together a video with an English translation of these communications, proving that the attack had in fact been hurried because the commercial jet was about to leave Soviet airspace. Jeane was working on her speech until the last minute when the video finally arrived. She rose to show it at the United Nations and in a moment of high drama said that the incident exposed the true face of the USSR and how "violence and lies are regular instruments of Soviet policy." The USSR's representative Troyanovsky gave a ritualized denial of the entire incident and then stood red-faced as Jeane handed him a copy of a TASS report, just published, acknowledging that an "unidentified" aircraft had indeed been shot down.

The response to KAL 007 may have been Jeane's Adlai Stevenson / Bay of Pigs moment, a dramatic high point in a four-year daily effort to delegitimate and embarrass the Soviet Union with harsh judgments that had largely disappeared from the American diplomatic vocabulary after détente; but the daily focus of this effort was the USSR's war in Afghanistan. She had made an early trip there in 1981, wearing her hat as a member of the National Security Council. She and her colleague Jose Sorzano flew into Islamabad, then got onto one of Pakistan's Soviet-built helicopters and headed to Afghanistan. The heat inside the helicopter was stifling and Sorzano asked for some air. The pilot said this was impossible because the Soviets had forgotten to include windows in designing the craft, a comment that brought a smile of confirmation to Jeane's face.

They landed in an arid and desolate area where tents had been set up with banners flowing from the openings and plush hand-crafted rugs on the bare ground within. Sorzano remembered Jeane standing in the blistering heat dressed in a skirt and high-necked blouse with a scarf on her head, while two hundred or so mujahedeen in robes and turbans with bandoliers over their shoulders milled around her. Speaking through an interpreter, she told them that a new president had been elected who was ready to support their efforts to reverse the Soviet occupation with real actions rather than just Olympic boycotts. Sorzano recalls her speech as eloquent but the response by a tribal leader, interrupted by shouts of *Allahu Akbar!*, as even more so. "Thank you for the food," Sorzano later paraphrased it. "We are hungry, but hunger is not our problem. Thank you for the medicine. We are sick, but sickness is not our problem. Our problem is that we've been invaded. But we are a people who believe in revenge. We will not stop fighting until we do to them what they have done to us. We will invade their country, rape their women, and kill their sons. We ask only that you continue to aid us with bullets and stand back and let us take our revenge."

She returned to the issue of Afghanistan over and over again in blistering speeches at the UN. "How far the Soviets are willing to go in their war," she told the General Assembly in 1981, "is indicated by the kind of weapons they have used there, including little booby trap mines ... frequently disguised as ordinary household items or toys. Children, naturally the least wary, are the ones most likely to pick them up. If they do, they risk being killed or having their limbs blown off." Two years later she charged that "the rising level of violence inflicted by Soviet occupation forces against Afghan civilians recalls images of Guernica and Lidice. The violence, which has included torture, mass executions, rape and civilian massacres has been painstakingly documented and strongly condemned by independent international humanitarian groups ...."

Sensing that the USSR was on the defensive for the first time since Vietnam, she also pressed the issue of "vicious attacks on Jews and Judaism that have polluted Soviet society" and made it "the world's largest center for the distribution of Jewish hate material." She argued the case of the dissidents and refuseniks with such vigor that years later, after she was long out of government, her name was still one to conjure with among members of this group. When she visited the Soviet Union during the height of *glasnost*, Andrei Sakharov came up to her delegation saying, "Kirkpatski, Kirkpatski, which of you is Kirkpatski?" When Jeane was pointed out to him, he seized her hands emotionally and said, "Your name is known in every cell of the gulag."

The USSR recognized her effectiveness and tried to blunt it. Later on, she told a *New York Times* reporter that she had been the object of a campaign by Soviet disinformation specialists who planted a series of lies that gained some traction in the UN's meeting rooms and corridors: that she had accepted diamonds from influential white South Africans; that she had personally ordered the doctoring of the audiotapes proving that the Soviets shot down KAL 007; that she secretly advocated breaking up India into a federation of countries. In 1982, the KGB forged a letter from the intelligence head of apartheid South Africa wishing her "best regards and gratitude" and successfully fobbed it off on the *New Statesman*.

She was enough of a thorn in the side of her enemies that there were strong rumors that some outside force, most likely Muammar Kaddafi, sworn enemy of the Reagan administration, had sent a hit team to get her. She was given a special steel-plated limo and a beefed-up detachment of Secret Service guards carrying Uzis inside Samsonite attaché cases. A career foreign service officer named Harvey Feldman later recalled showing up for an appointment at Jeane's office one afternoon to find her talking with animation to two young men. "No, no, no," she said. "I absolutely refuse. I will not wear this thing. Take it away!" After they left and Feldman had sat down with her at her desk, she said, "You are probably wondering what this is all about. They have a bullet-proof raincoat that they want me to wear. It is very heavy and very uncomfortable." Then, after a pause she said, "I guess I was pretty rough on them, wasn't I?" When Feldman said yes, she stood up and went to the door and called out to the two Secret Service agents, "Come back and I'll try on your damn raincoat."

But she never really accommodated to being overseen and would sometimes find ways to evade her keepers. When her close friend Anne Crutcher was on her deathbed in 1983 and Jeane came for a last visit, two Secret Service men passed the time by talking with the husband of Anne's daughter Colette on the front lawn. They told him that she was the most "problematic" of all the people they had guarded and was utterly unwilling to discipline herself the way political people should. One of them shot a sour look at the house and said, "She's probably getting ready to sneak out the back door even as we speak."

---

With Jeane now established as the premier champion of the administration's Cold War causes, there was talk of a "Kirkpatrick Doctrine." The ideas in "Dictatorships and Double Standards" about friendly authoritarian and hostile totalitarian governments were too tenuous—and transitory—to qualify as a foundational blueprint for foreign policy; but they were still taken seriously, as evidenced in U.S. caution toward the first expressions of anti-Marcos "People Power" in the Philippines in 1983. Paul Wolfowitz, assistant secretary of state and one of those pushing most forcefully for liberalization, went out of his way to say that the administration's actions didn't contradict Jeane's "theory" because the pressure on Marcos had been applied slowly and behind the scenes, with an awareness that there were democratic institutions in the Philippines to build on—a prerequisite the Carterites had ignored when they cut the shah adrift in Iran.*

The only doctrine that Jeane represented at the UN was the Reagan Doctrine, beginning long before the essayist Charles Krauthammer coined the term in commenting on the president's 1985 State of the Union speech. Reagan had said that the United States must not "break faith with those who are risking their lives on every continent, from Afghanistan to Nicaragua . . . to defy Soviet aggression and secure rights which have been ours since birth" and insisted that "support for freedom fighters is self-defense." Jeane saw the Reagan Doctrine *avant la lettre* as a sort of delayed response to the Brezhnev Doctrine, as propounded by *Pravda* in 1968 after Soviet tanks rolled into Czechoslovakia to stop the Prague Spring. In effect, the Brezhnev Doctrine held that the USSR had the right to intervene in the affairs of any country threatening to secede from socialist conformity, in addition to the right to help "progressive" forces establish Marxist regimes in other countries. In the years since 1968, Jeane believed, the United States and the West in general, "lulled by their confidence in détente, weakened by unilateral disarmament, passively accepting Soviet expansion," had given the USSR reason to believe that "history was on its side."

---

* Jeane would become known as an opponent of People Power, but this was an oversimplification of her position. Harvey Feldman, who traveled with her to the Philippines in 1983, later told of the toast she gave at the state dinner that Marcos put on for her, right after a Marcos crony and cabinet member had lost his seat in a regional election. "Jeane began her toast by saying in essence that in democracy one did not always get to win; sometimes one loses. . . . Then she went on to say that she was reminded of a story about Benjamin Franklin and the ending of the drafting of the U.S. Constitution. Franklin was asked by a woman after the session ended what kind of a government the drafters had given the U.S. He said, 'a democracy, if you can keep it.' Jeane said that this was the essence of democracy; it was necessary for every generation to keep it." Franklin actually used the term "republic," but Feldman got the moral of the story right: "To announce these words in front of Marcos in that palace, I thought was one of the most remarkable occurrences I ever witnessed."

After leaving government, Jeane would give several speeches about why she saw the Reagan Doctrine as a "principled, pragmatic response" to the menace of a growing Soviet power (especially ominous in the Western Hemisphere) in its assertion of "the moral and legal rights of people to defend themselves against incorporation into an empire based on force ... [and] the legal and moral right of the U.S. to assist those people." Such a doctrine was necessary because in "Nicaragua, Angola, Benin, Ghana, Congo, Mozambique, Guinea-Bissau, Cuba, Yemen, Syria, Ethiopia and so forth ... one finds extraordinary international brigades accumulated from East Germany, from Czechoslovakia, from Bulgaria, from Cuba ... from Vietnam, from the PLO, from all parts of the Soviets' worldwide empire brought to bear on the weak institutions and the relatively helpless people who almost invariably desire, above all, to be left alone to solve their problems."

She also liked the nice symmetry of it. "If the Soviet Union has a 'right' to give aid to client states, the United States has a 'right' to give aid to freedom fighters." Of course, there was one basic distinction to be made: "Force that liberates is not 'morally equivalent' to force that subjugates."

---

While Caspar Weinberger, Richard Perle and others were masterminding the 3-D chess game with the Soviets over issues such as the deployment of intermediate-range nuclear force missiles in Europe and the upcoming summit meetings, Jeane was all over the map, quite literally, in supporting the principles of the Reagan Doctrine. She continued to lead the rhetorical charge on Afghanistan. Her involvement in backing counterrevolutionaries such as Jonas Savimbi in Angola prompted the liberal *New York Times* columnist Anthony Lewis to write rancorously that "what really attracts Mrs. Kirkpatrick to Mr. Savimbi, of course, is that the Angolan government he opposes is Marxist. Moreover it is supported by 30,000 Cuban troops." To which Jeane laconically replied, "For once, I think Lewis is right."

But from the time she arrived at the UN until she left, the central front in her cold war remained Latin America—and more particularly, what she saw as the Siamese twin causes of backing the Contras against the Sandinistas in Nicaragua and supporting the government of El Salvador against the Marxist FMLN guerrillas. She never wavered in her view that the 1979 Sandinista takeover of Nicaragua was a Communist invasion of the hemisphere. As thousands of Cuban *internationalistas* and Soviet advisors poured into Managua to consolidate the revolution and turn the country into a forward operating base for guerrillas in El Salvador and elsewhere, Jeane fought to organize a U.S. response. The USSR desperately tried to disarm her—through stepped-up military assistance to the Sandinistas, and also through fronts such as the World Peace Council and its U.S. affiliates, including the Committee in Solidarity with the People of El Salvador. This group managed to convince some Democrats in Congress that the Sandinistas were simply "idealistic nationalists" trying to reform the brutal Somoza regime and defend against U.S. imperialism. All this only raised the stakes in Jeane's eyes.

El Salvador was the immediate concern: the Communists had not yet gained control, and a weak central government was caught in the crossfire between FMLN guerrillas and right-wing militias. The Salvadoran government was trying to oppose both these groups while also accommodating U.S. demands that it create democratic institutions and implement a land reform program designed in part by AFL-CIO specialists. While the international left pushed a narrative of "right-wing death squads" opposing "agrarian reformers," the situation reminded Jeane of stories her old graduate school advisor Franz Neumann had told about the slow strangling of the Weimar Republic by competing extremisms. "Murderous traditionalists confront murderous guerrillas— with only the government working to end this mutual murder," she explained in speeches at the UN.* For her, El Salvador was the place to start building a firewall against the forces that the Carter administration had allowed to become established in Managua.

In Jeane's first year at the UN, the FMLN staged its bloody "final offensive." When it failed, it was followed by the guerrillas' promise to overwhelm the election of 1982 with terrorism. Jeane attempted to rally support for the Salvadoran government by telling the UN General Assembly what she saw as the problem: "The men of the FMLN have assassinated ordinary citizens, imposed bloody reprisals against villagers unwilling to assist them. . . . They have bombed restaurants, buses, theatres, factories, food storage facilities, marketplaces, public utilities, bridges, and public buildings. They have occupied eight foreign embassies, kidnapped and killed diplomats, executed hundreds of presumed 'informers.' . . . They have sought reaction from the extreme right in the hope that it will ultimately lead to the revolution from the extreme left . . . ."

When critics of the administration's policy in El Salvador brought up the portent of "another Vietnam," she reminded them, in politically incorrect terms, that the analogy was double-edged: "God knows there are parallels enough. . . . In El Salvador, as in Vietnam, Congress calls the U.S. involvement into doubt, undermining the confidence of vulnerable allies in our reliability and their viability. And as in Vietnam doubts are continually voiced about whether the government of El Salvador is morally worthy of American approval or even of survival. . . . The crucial difference between Vietnam and Central America is that the Congress that cut off aid to Vietnam could say that it didn't know what would follow. Today's Congress cannot."

Despite the guerillas' attempts to disrupt the elections in El

---

* Shortly before joining the Reagan administration, Jeane had written that the problem confronting El Salvador was "Thomas Hobbes's problem—how to establish order and authority in a society where there is none."

Salvador, there was a huge—and courageous, given the violence—turnout that impressed even the skeptical American media. In February 1983, the president sent Jeane on another fact-finding trip to Central America—Honduras, Panama, Costa Rica and, most importantly, El Salvador. Arriving there, she found State Department representatives weakly parroting FMLN propaganda that it was necessary to create a "power sharing" agreement between it and the government, a position calculated to inflame the right-wing militias and put the government even more on the defensive. She asked one high-level figure from State posted there about this. He dismissed her concern by saying flippantly that the spread of Marxism in the region "wouldn't be perceived as a defeat if the U.S. didn't try to prevent it." Jeane scornfully condemned this comment as "solipsistic."

Catching a whiff of Carterism in this willingness to undercut an ally fighting a Marxist guerrilla movement, she made known her feelings about State's defeatism in a meeting with the president upon returning from the trip. Afterwards, Reagan grumbled in his diary about how the "State Department bureaucrats who made Castro possible are screwing up the situation in El Salvador." Then he added, uncharacteristically, "I'm really mad."

Perhaps because she was now "the leading theoretician of Central American policy in the administration," as one historian would later put it, Jeane's opponents in government and Congress unleashed a war of leaks to blunt her influence. In June 1983, she finally responded with an op-ed in the *Washington Post* titled "Pardon Me, But Am I That Hard-Liner the Anonymous Sources Are Talking About?" In it, she wrote acerbically about the "political melodrama" created by these leaks, "in which some bad guys—the 'hard-liners' are pitted against some good guys—the 'moderates'—in a contest for control of U.S. policy toward El Salvador and the Central American region." She continued, "In the current scenario, hard-liners are frequently named Clark and Kirkpatrick, though sometimes they are called Casey, Weinberger,

Stone, or even Reagan. Their principal activity is giving bad advice to the president. Because my name is also Kirkpatrick and I hold almost none of the views attributed to that Kirkpatrick, I desire to clarify just what kind of evidence I have given in the weeks after the president asked me to visit Central America."

Then she rehearsed the fact that she was for regional diplomacy, and emphasized that the "very hard line" she had taken was primarily on "hunger, malnutrition, infant mortality, illiteracy, and economic underdevelopment." She had not advocated a U.S. military *presence* in El Salvador, as the leaks suggested, but rather "continued military assistance at all levels adequate to meet and match the guerrillas' arms." She ended with a palpable hit: "if journalists were as suspicious of their favorite anonymous sources as they are of, say, the president, we would be better informed."

If El Salvador was the line that Jeane believed had to be held, its importance was always connected to and given resonance by what was happening in Nicaragua. So, while supporting Salvadoran centrists, she also continued a drumbeat of revelation about the depredations of the Sandinista regime in speeches before the General Assembly: the FSLN's "preventive arrests" of dissidents; the closing of Radio Catolica and threats against the Catholic Church; the censorship of *La Prensa*, the country's leading newspaper; the confiscation of the passports of opposition political leaders. "Thus, the dialectic of revolution unfolds," she concluded. "Liberation has already produced its antithesis in Sandinista Nicaragua."

But however rancid its smell, it was not just the first manifestations of "socialism in one country" that raised concern. From the beginning, revolutionary Nicaragua had been envisioned by its architects as a base to spread the Marxist-Leninist gospel throughout the region: "Within weeks after the fall of Somoza in July 1979, the Sandinistas began to cooperate in support of the Salvadoran insurgents by establishing training camps and the beginning of arms supply networks. . . . In 1980, after meetings in

Havana had unified Salvadoran Marxists into a single military command structure, the Sandinista leadership agreed to serve as a conduit for an arms trafficking system of unprecedented proportions. . . . Arms and ammunition for the Salvadoran insurgents reach Nicaragua by ship and occasionally by direct flights from Havana. . . . When a clandestine shipment of arms is captured or a safe house is found containing arms and terrorist supplies, it is often impossible to know with certainty whether the ultimate recipients are Guatemalan, Honduran, Costa Rican or Salvadoran terrorists, since the arms supply networks established by Cuba and Nicaragua are funneling lethal military supplies to terrorists and guerrillas in all four countries."

Softheaded international support for the Sandinistas bewildered Jeane. In a speech in England, she said, "From our side of the Atlantic it sometimes seems that in Europe there is more sympathy for the Nicaraguans who threaten the peace, independence and freedom of their neighbors than for the neighbors themselves. Sometimes it seems there is more 'understanding' for the thousands of Cuban and Soviet-bloc military advisors in Nicaragua than for the 37 or so U.S. military advisors in El Salvador who help that country fend off its would-be conquerors." The UN had been infected by the same logic: "Because it lacks power and powerful connections in the UN and is the object of a 'national liberation movement,' El Salvador is the target of resolution after resolution condemning its human rights practice. And because it has powerful connections, Nicaragua is never mentioned in human rights proceedings."

Afloat in what she saw as a sea of intellectual falsification at the UN, Jeane continued to pound away at the history of the Sandinista revolution: how it had been helped to power on U.S. aid in the amount of $24.6 million for food and $118 million in direct financial assistance, along with another $262 million in international aid—double the amount obtained by the Somoza regime in the preceding twenty years. (In one memorable moment before the Security Council, when the Nicaraguan representative accused America of being antagonistic to the revolution from the beginning, Jeane said, "The U.S. government did not attempt to prevent the Sandinistas' accession to power; it *helped* them.")*

Getting rid of the "faint-hearted bourgeois democrats" who were their fig leaf right after the overthrow of Somoza, the Sandinistas consolidated their power in a "coup d'état by installments"—a phrase Jeane borrowed from a famous description of the Nazis' coming to power. Then they developed a "pattern of systematic repression . . . familiar to all students of total power." She noted that the first Cuban advisors arrived the week after the Sandinistas seized power, and that the first Nicaraguan delegation traveled to Moscow within a matter of months to conclude a party-to-party agreement that pledged Nicaraguan support for Soviet policies all over the world. With a population of only 2.7 million people, Nicaragua had an active-duty military of approximately 25,000 plus another 50,000 reservists and militia, proportionately the largest force that Central America had ever seen. Over two thousand Cubans were training them in the use of Soviet T55 tanks, attack helicopters, amphibious ferries and transport aircraft.

In her coruscating critique of the regime, she went so far as to contest the foundation myth of *Sandinismo*, asserting that the revolutionary junta in Managua, in addition to its other betrayals, had even broken faith with its own namesake: "Augusto César Sandino was not a Marxist. . . . He supported nationalism and not

---

* In a 1981 essay titled "U.S. Security and Latin America" published in *Commentary* shortly before she took up her duties at the UN, Jeane was even more explicit: "What did the Carter administration do in Nicaragua? It brought down the Somoza regime. The Carter administration did not 'lose' Nicaragua in the sense that it was once charged that Harry Truman 'lost' China and Eisenhower Cuba, by failing to prevent a given outcome. In the case of Nicaragua, the State Department acted repeatedly and at critical junctures to weaken the government of Anastasio Somoza and to strengthen his opponents."

the Soviet Empire. On that basis he would have criticized [Nicaragua's] submission to Moscow's so-called internationalism, for he desired sovereignty for his country and desired a free country. He was very harshly criticized by communists while he was still alive for 'bourgeois' and 'counter-revolutionary' behavior . . . [and] because he refused to adjust his fight for 'country and liberty' to the plans of the communists. . . . It is precisely 'country and liberty' that the so-called Sandinistas have betrayed in imposing a Marxist-Leninist dictatorship over the Nicaraguan people."

At the same time she was publicly blasting the Sandinistas at the UN, Jeane, in her other role as member of the National Security Council, had been urging full support for the Nicaraguan Democratic Force (FDN), or Contras, since 1981. She had played a crucial role that year in the meeting of the National Security Planning Group that put up $19 million to make the Contras a fighting force. Her backing was never conditional, trimmed by apology, or rationalized as a situational expediency, as was the case with others in the administration. She described Enrique Bermúdez, much-vilified leader of the Contras, as a "great man." (Bermúdez returned the admiration, forming a 400-man unit that became known as "the Jeane Kirkpatrick Brigade.")* While the left campaigned to stigmatize the Contras—eventually the largest peasant army in the hemisphere, she frequently noted—as brutal renegades, Jeane always saw them as the "democratic resistance" against the curtain that the Sandinistas and their Cuban and Soviet sponsors were trying to pull down over Central America.

Because she was perceived as the worst enemy of the Sandinistas and the Salvadoran guerrillas, both beloved by the leftover left

---

* Jeane attended a funeral mass for Bermúdez when he was assassinated after being lured to a meeting in Managua's InterContinental hotel following the Sandinista defeat in the 1990 elections. She kept a Contra battle standard on proud and provocative view in her office at AEI until the end of her life.

from the 1960s, which reasserted itself in the mid 1980s, Jeane became its hate fetish. She first got a sense of how stigmatized she had become when she was invited to speak at the University of California, Berkeley, on February 2, 1983, soon after returning from her Central American fact-finding trip, but was shouted down by hundreds of hecklers, some holding placards stating "No Free Speech for War Criminals." After allowing herself to be removed from the stage for a moment because of the intimidating chaos, she insisted on returning and read her speech to the last word while pandemonium drowned out everything she said.

Later that month, she had to cancel the commencement address she was supposed to deliver at Smith College when administrators there refused to guarantee an orderly environment. ("If it's not going to be pleasant for the parents, the students, and also the speaker," she shrugged, "one shouldn't go.") In early March, she fought her way through a speech at the University of Minnesota while being interrupted by shouts of "Murderer! Nazi! Fascist go home!" And finally, in April, she turned down the honorary degree that Barnard had offered her months earlier because the faculty at her alma mater had subsequently voted to condemn her connection with anticommunism in Central America.*

The animus increased when she became the primary defender of the U.S. invasion of Grenada in October 1983—the summary moment in the tough response to the Marxist intrusion into the hemisphere that she had been urging for almost three years. The action was triggered by a coup of hardliners against the revolutionary government of Maurice Bishop, whose Marxist New Jewel Movement had taken power four years earlier and made the island an integral part of the Soviet-Cuban military buildup in the Caribbean. After Bishop was murdered, the Organization of

---

* Ruminating on these experiences later on, she said to me, "This was the time when I learned to count myself rich in terms of the number and kind of enemies I had."

Eastern Caribbean States (OECS) asked the United States to intervene. The American invasion resulted in 25 killed and 59 wounded among the Cuban forces stationed there, in addition to a large number of casualties suffered by the Grenadian revolutionaries.

The United States was fiercely condemned, particularly at the UN. In the days after the invasion, Jeane directed the defense, pointing out that "Maurice Bishop freely offered his island as a base for protection of Soviet military power in this hemisphere. The familiar pattern of militarization and Cubanization was already far advanced in Grenada. More than three dozen Soviet officials have been detained in just the past three days. Truly enormous arsenals of Soviet weapons have been discovered. The total number of Cuban military personnel in Grenada is still unknown, but it is clear that there were more than 1,000—more than one Cuban for every 100 Grenadians."

She took specific aim at the argument that the U.S. action was morally indistinguishable from the USSR's invasion of Afghanistan—an argument which ironically was developed by the Soviets: "Were the U.S. and OECS in liberating Grenada 'as bad as' the Soviets in invading Afghanistan? Is the U.S., in aiding the Contras, being 'as bad as' the Nicaraguans or Cubans or Soviets in destabilizing El Salvador's government?" Her answer— "assuredly not"—was followed by the kind of astringent argument she had become noted for in the world body: "To suggest otherwise is to deny the relevance of context and consequence to moral and legal arguments; it is like asking us to look only at the knife that cuts into the abdomen without taking into account whether the man wielding it is a surgeon or Jack the Ripper or whether the patient is likely to be cured or destroyed."

As the murmuring among Western Europeans grew louder, Jeane embraced her role as Reagan's *Femme de Fer*, a term coined by the French as an analogy to Margaret Thatcher's "Iron Lady." She arranged to speak in 1984 at London's Royal Institute for International Affairs, where she enumerated some of the possible reasons for Europe's cold shoulder: reaction to the Grenada invasion, conflict in Central America, enhanced American missile defense. Then she challenged the settings on her listeners' moral compasses: "If it is no longer possible to distinguish between freedom and despotism—the U.S. is a free country; between consent and violence—we are a society based on consent; between open and closed societies—we are an open society—then the erosion of the foundation of a distinctively western and democratic civilization is already far advanced and the situation is serious indeed."

---

It was not just her pivotal role in Latin American policy that put Jeane alongside Reagan himself at the top of the left's enemies list; there was also her gusto in embracing the dual role of quarterback and cheerleader for what she believed was a morally rearmed America. In the long half-life of the dissention over the Vietnam War, she said, the U.S. had seemed to be engaged in "an effort to commit suicide." But that era was over now, and "the suicide attempt failed." Moreover, "first aid has been administered; efforts to restore our health and capacity to believe in ourselves have taken hold."

But she seemed so committed to fighting the Cold War that she sometimes missed some of the subtleties of the changing battlefield. Partly because of the double standards that had surrounded such efforts in the Carter years, but also because of a constitutional wariness of trying to manufacture positive political change, she had remained slightly agnostic about the democracy promotion pushed by Carl Gershman, Elliott Abrams, Joshua Muravchik and others close to her. While they acknowledged that it was sometimes necessary to make alliances with the right-wing authoritarians against the Soviet bloc, they also believed it was necessary at the same time to encourage the growth of democracy in these countries, publicly and resolutely, if only because failure to do so would make them fertile soil for the toxic growth of Marxism-Leninism. Jeane was not so sure. When the Chilean Human Rights Commission asked her to distance herself from Pinochet, for instance, the most she would do was affirm the importance of "quiet diplomacy."* These differences with younger neoconservatives were subsumed at the time by the shared élan of Reaganism, but they would grow larger in years to come.

Far more fatal for Jeane was her obliviousness to the forces inside the administration centered on George Shultz, the secretary of state, that were beginning to coalesce against her. One of her aides later said to the journalist Michael Kramer, "We told Jeane to cultivate him. She wouldn't do it. She saw Shultz as a rival and her attitude was that she wasn't going to waste her time with people who bored her."

More patient than Haig and less of a sole practitioner, Shultz had worked to counter the alliance Jeane had formed with CIA Director Casey, Bill Clark and usually Cap Weinberger, with one of his own anchored by James Baker, the chief of staff, and Michael Deaver. It was a powerful combination. Deaver, the president's longtime image maker and friend (he had saved Reagan's life with the Heimlich maneuver after a peanut became lodged in his throat during a 1976 campaign flight) was now anxious to expand his writ into policy. Baker, regarded by Al Haig as by far "the more puissant" of the two, was the crucial figure in the Shultz coalition, approaching power struggles with a street fighter's savagery. He was also to some degree George Bush's man and shared the vice president's suspicion of Jeane as an "ideologue."

While he might have been temperamentally opposed to Jeane's

---

* Bill King of the University of Calgary has explored Jeane's ambivalence about human rights policy (with a focus on Chile) in "Elliott Abrams contra Jeane Kirkpatrick: The Neoconservative Shift in democracy promotion during the Reagan years," a paper dated January 6, 2010. He graciously shared a copy of this work with me.

hard-line positions, Shultz was not anxious for a confrontation in his first months in office, while he was still getting his footing in the administration. Yet the coming conflict between them was clear when, shortly after Shultz's appointment, Lebanon's president, Bachir Gemayel, was killed by a terrorist bomb, and Israel's allies in the Lebanese Phalange militia attacked the Palestinians' Sabra and Shatilla refugee camps as revenge for the killing but also to flush out PLO fighters hiding there. As Jeane related in her draft autobiography, the usually stolid Shultz came up to her with an agonized look on his face. "I don't know how you feel," he said, thrusting his palms toward her, "but I feel as though my hands are covered with blood. American weapons for Israel made possible the murder of women and children in the refugee camp." Jeane's reply was as unflinching as it was unsympathetic: "Well, I don't feel as if I have blood on my hands. We didn't kill anyone. And, as I understand it, Israelis didn't kill anyone either. I doubt that American weapons were used by the Phalangists."

The episode reflected a fundamental difference in worldviews that would bedevil the relationship. As *Newsweek* wrote not long after, "Shultz sees Israel as hard, abrasive, difficult. . . . Kirkpatrick, on the other hand, has always been a staunch defender of Israel, believing that for both strategic and cultural reasons it must be central to U.S. Mideast policy." It didn't help that Shultz called Jimmy Carter, already embarked on his long anti-Israel crusade, for advice on the Middle East. (In time, Shultz would become friendlier to the Israelis.)

Because she felt secure in her relationship with the president, and because Shultz was not abusive or overtly sexist toward her, as Haig had been, Jeane was late in understanding the changes afoot in the administration, which Shultz himself was pushing. Chief among them was the pressure for a "pivot" from confrontation to negotiation with the Soviets in Reagan's likely second term.

The chief spokesman for this position was Deaver, who later said self-effacingly that his only real accomplishment was to "light Reagan well" for the cameras at big campaign events. In the early days of the administration, Jeane had found him pleasant enough, someone with obvious campaign talents but "no interest or views on policy." She had failed to see that Baker had "turned" Deaver, encouraging him to be a player in the international match with the Soviets. Deaver's friend and protector Nancy Reagan wanted a "peace legacy" for her husband, and Deaver himself wanted a "new narrative" to bolster his own standing and keep Reagan from becoming a lame duck after his re-election.

In the spring of 1983, when she attended the annual Gridiron Dinner, Jeane was seated at the head table, as she later recounted in her draft autobiography, near Deaver, with whom she had previously only exchanged vague pleasantries.

"Well, I may as well tell you this," he suddenly leaned toward her during a lull in the proceedings. "You have to find out sometime."

"What's that, Mike?" she asked.

"The president may have an opportunity to make peace in our time."

"That would be wonderful," Jeane replied, ignoring the echo of Chamberlain's infamous pronouncement.

"Well, everyone notices you have influence with the president," Deaver said.

When Jeane shrugged noncommittally, he continued: "No, no, everyone notices. He always listens when you speak. He looks at you and his eyes light up. Maybe it's because you're a woman."

Jeane deadpanned, "Maybe it's because he's interested in foreign policy."

"Anyhow," Deaver ignored the comment, "when the time comes that the president has an opportunity to make peace we can't have you and Bill Clark around raising questions."

Jeane thought Deaver, a well-known drinker, was in his cups and didn't pay as much attention to the conversation as she later realized she should have.

A decisive moment occurred on October 13, 1983, when grow-ing pressure from Baker, backed by Shultz and Deaver, led the somewhat phlegmatic Bill Clark to step down from the position of national security advisor—for which he had never been tempera-mentally or intellectually suited—and take a cushier job as secre-tary of the interior. *Time* marked the sea change by noting snottily that Clark would no longer be "lumbering into the Oval Office every day pushing Cap's [Weinberger] and Kirkpatrick's schemes."

In Shultz's version of what happened next, there were only two serious candidates for the national security advisor's job: Jim Baker and Bud McFarlane, an NSC insider being pushed by peo-ple in the organization. Only when a stalemate developed did Weinberger and Casey propose Jeane as a compromise candidate. While paying a ritualized homage to her "capacity for passionate advocacy," Shultz said he felt she was not temperamentally suited to the position because she was incapable of being a "dispassion-ate broker."

In the slightly different version put forth by Jeane and her allies, Shultz had wanted Baker for the job and was literally within min-utes of succeeding when Casey, Weinberger, Ed Meese and Clark himself—all of whom regarded Baker as lacking in firm princi-ples—staged an intervention with the president and tried to block Baker with Jeane. According to this version, Reagan was ready to name her to the post, but then both Baker and Shultz threatened to resign if she got the job. (As Jeane's aide Jackie Tillman said, Shultz feared that if Jeane were the national security advisor, he would never be able to walk Reagan back from the decisions the two of them reached.) The result was that McFarlane was chosen.*

Jeane would later downplay how desperately she had wanted the job of national security advisor. She was tired of the UN and

---

* Warren Clark, a career foreign service officer who served under Jeane at the UN and became a friend, was told that the final and deciding voice against her appointment was that of Nancy Reagan.

what she had come to regard as its banality, and she was anxious to be back home in Washington with Kirk and her worrisome sons. Deeply offended by Deaver and Baker, she was in a sour mood when Reagan summoned her for a meeting to pour emollients over her rejection. Afterwards, he wrote in his diary, "We talked for an hour. She has wanted to come back to Washington from the UN for some time and hoped that she could be given Bill's job. I offered her a position as Counselor to the President on International Policy. I couldn't convince her it was a job where she'd have a real voice in making policy. Finally left it with me not accepting her 'no' and her promising to think about it."

Jeane understood Shultz's motives: "He saw an opportunity to build strength with a president whose foreign policy he didn't necessarily share." But she remained bitter about Deaver and Baker, feeling that she had been victimized by, among other things, their sexism. ("And she *was*," her former aide Carl Gershman later said.)

The episode also caused her a moment of doubt about her hero. "One thing I didn't understand," she wrote in her unpublished autobiography, "was why Reagan didn't see how objectionable Baker and Deaver were. Like Iago. Why didn't Othello see who he really was?" But she stopped herself from going further: "I guess it's the heroic quality of a Reagan or Othello that made them vulnerable to the machinations of a Deaver or Iago."

Baker, whom Jeane regarded as uniquely devious and anti-Israel to boot, had been the more significant force against her. But she always blamed Deaver more for the outcome, perhaps because she regarded him as the less worthy opponent. Some twenty years later, she was accompanying her friend Margaret Lefever to church one Sunday morning when she saw him sitting alone on a stone bench—a broken man, ravaged by a long bout of alcoholism along with a federal conviction for having lied to a grand jury about lobbying while in the administration. According to Lefever, "Deaver stood up with an eager smile and started to come over, but she cut him dead, and he just stood there for a moment with a dejected look on his face, then sat back down."

Just before Christmas 1983, Jeane had another meeting with Reagan, who later wrote in his diary that she was "weary of the UN ... but she wants to do whatever will best help in my reelection." She agreed to stay at the UN, but leaked her feelings to the *Washington Post* for its postmortem on the struggle over who would be the national security advisor: "She feels like she was treated as a character in a novel or screenplay; first they wrote her into the plot as a prototypical right-winger and then, after she served her purpose as a device for furthering the plot, they tried to write her out ... by killing her off."*

---

For almost three years, Jeane had approached her job as if there were no tomorrow, but now she began to think about life after the UN. Others were thinking about it too. One of them was Faith Whittlesey, a strong conservative and a feminist who was serving as the president's assistant for public liaison. Whittlesey was upset over the way Jeane had been treated by her enemies in the administration, who now wanted to deny or at least diminish her role at the 1984 Republican convention in Dallas. Whittlesey

---

* I once noted to her in passing that not getting the job was possibly a blessing in disguise since she avoided all the obloquy that McFarlane suffered during Iran-Contra, including the humiliating role in congressional hearings, etc. "I very much supported that policy," she replied stiffly, implying that she would gladly have braved the ordeal. Indeed, at the June 1984 White House meeting when CIA Director Casey argued for such a work-around policy to compensate for Congress's defeat of funding for the Contras, she had agreed that "We should make a maximum effort." Shultz criticized her for backing what he believed was an "impeachable offense." Her commitment to finding the money was so strong that McFarlane later said in his own defense that if he had tried to stand against the Iran-Contra plan, Jeane, along with Casey and Weinberger, surely "would have said I was some kind of commie."

brought her to meet Mark Holtzman and David Carmen, two young activists working for Citizens for America, a lobbying group for the president's agenda, especially issues supporting what was about to become known as the Reagan Doctrine.

Discovering that the U.S. treasurer Kathleen Ortega (whose chief virtues were that she was Hispanic and not Jeane) had been chosen to deliver the keynote at the convention, Holtzman and Carmen, seeing an opportunity for guerrilla theater, set out to make the three minutes that Jeane had been grudgingly allotted into the high point of the event. They worked with her to craft a twenty-minute speech, ignoring the stipulated time limit. They smuggled signs with slogans such as "Run, Jeane, run" into the hands of a couple hundred key delegates on the convention floor. They built suspense by selectively releasing some of the key lines in her speech to the media. Jeane cooperated fully, giving Carmen the impression that she was contemplating her next public step.

After Ortega gave a lackluster address, which included an apology for not being as interesting as other speakers, anticipation built for Jeane's appearance. Wearing an iridescent blue-green suit that shimmered like peacock feathers on TV screens, she held the convention in the palm of her hand from the opening line: "This is the first Republican convention I've ever attended . . . ." She clinched the deal with her evocation of the Carter years: "Jimmy Carter looked for an explanation for all those problems and thought he found it in the malaise of the American people. But the people knew better. It wasn't malaise we suffered from. It was Jimmy Carter."

Underlining the difference between Ronald Reagan, who she said wanted to defeat communism everywhere, and his opponents, who wanted to accommodate it everywhere, she excoriated the "San Francisco Democrats" and the "blame America first crowd" in what became the speech of the political season. She had the delegates on their feet when she said, "When the Marines sent to keep peace in Lebanon were murdered in their sleep, the blame-America-first crowd did not blame the terrorists who murdered the Marines; they blamed the United States. But then they always blame America first …" The crowd picked up the refrain, "They always blame America first," as Jeane went through the litany of policies in which the left had undermined U.S. interests.

When she blithely exceeded her allotted time, the convention managers caucused frantically in the wings, trying at first to get her off by ordering the band to play, but giving up when she ignored the first few bars and the crowd continued to go wild. The appearance certified her as a superstar and jumpstarted discussion among the party faithful about a possible future in electoral politics.

She continued to ruffle feathers when she was asked to prep Reagan for his debates with Mondale. The foreign policy questions that had been provided by Baker's staff, especially those involving Central America, were inadequate in her view, so she wrote her own. She alluded to Baker's notoriously thin skin, as well as the recent flare-up over the national security advisor job, when she talked with the *New York Times* about the mock debate. "I corrected Baker," she said with faux tremulousness. "In public. I am pretty stoic but I feared for my life."

She had another private meeting with Reagan just before Christmas. He was still trying to find a job that would keep her in the administration. But, as *Newsweek* wrote, "many of the President's key aides resist a larger role for her in U.S. policy. Secretary of State George Shultz, National Security Advisor Robert McFarlane and outgoing Chief of Staff James Baker have fought off several proposals …."*

Just after the second inaugural, she was back in the Oval Office

---

* Chuck Lichenstein commented: "The President is fond of Jeane, but he wasn't willing to tear his Government apart to make a place for her. And he would have had to tear the Government apart, because wherever you set up Jeane—and I don't care what you call the job—you're setting up an anti-Secretary of State. Everyone who finds fault with Shultz would rally around Jeane and you'd have war."

again for what the president referred to as "D-Day" in his diary. "Sorry to see her go," he wrote, "and the conservatives who worry that I'll go soft will lose a lot of sleep." He tried to reassure them by arranging for Jeane to receive the Medal of Freedom shortly after her resignation.

Her last day at the UN was April 1, 1985. Her testimony before the House Foreign Operations Subcommittee a week earlier had been her valedictory. "During the last four years, the U.S. has grown stronger in the world and in the UN. As a consequence, the UN is stronger, we are safer and so are many nations dependent on us." She always defended U.S. membership in the UN, to the occasional consternation of conservative allies, but she was very much a realist about the institution where she had made an indelible mark. Asked by a reporter what she had learned during her tenure at the world body, she replied, "A great deal. I am in every way a sadder and wiser woman about the world."

It was a time of endings. She had clung to her identity as a Democrat all during the time she had served as a Reaganaut, as much because of its intrinsic importance to her as because of the tinge of bipartisanship it gave the administration. She finally changed her party registration to Republican in March and made the announcement on April 3, at a celebration party where Vice President Bush read a welcoming letter from the president in which Reagan recalled his own switch decades earlier. But while the decision brought a tepid closure ("No more hiding" was the best she could say of the event in the terse discussion devoted to it in her draft autobiography), it brought little pleasure.

Irving Kristol, Norman Podhoretz and other friends of hers had made this same crossing without remorse or a nagging vestigial nostalgia for the old days. But for Jeane, becoming a Republican would always evoke a touch of melancholy that she was never able to hide completely, even when making an aggressive case for its necessity. How ill at ease the subject made her was suggested by an aside in a speech given at about this time at the Heritage

Foundation: "It is true that I am a convert to what are known today as conservative associations. Like many converts, I do not find the experience easy. I would rather be a liberal." In the semi-coherent ramblings of her conversations with friends at the end of her life, she would suddenly raise the subject of leaving her ancestral Democratic and liberal home, and her terminal agitation would worsen.

———

A scholar, a woman, an expert on totalitarianism who refused to hide this light under a bushel and was always willing to draw her terrible swift sword to defend Israel and America: in these dimensions, at least, Jeane had not seemed cut out for the job of U.S. permanent representative to the UN. But she had held the job longer than anyone else except for Adlai Stevenson and Henry Cabot Lodge Jr., and had arguably exerted a greater influence on the world body than either of them. She had certainly achieved what she set out to do upon arriving there: take the "Kick Me" sign off the back of the United States.

Given that her steely defense of Reaganism had made her many enemies in the liberal establishment, there were plenty of negative reviews of her performance as she packed her bags. But the *New York Times*, which had always been chief among her critics, gave the devil her due when it acknowledged that she was "the first woman independently to achieve real power in the area of international affairs," an evaluation it would expand after her death when it said that "no woman had ever been so close to the center of presidential power without actually residing in the White House."

# THE END OF HISTORY

HER FORMER colleagues at Georgetown thought that they had perhaps seen the last of Jeane when she joined the Reagan administration, but one of her first acts upon leaving was to negotiate a return as Leavy Professor of Government. Teaching had always been a central part of her identity and she had always prided herself on being a good colleague who carried her full share of departmental duties. Immediately upon returning to Georgetown, she resumed these and plunged into undergraduate courses and graduate seminars with titles like "The Critics of Utopia" and "Culture, Democracy and Politics." She also returned to the American Enterprise Institute and became the superstar that the new president of the organization, Chris DeMuth, could use to raise money from big donors—thus helping AEI recover from near bankruptcy in 1986 and position itself as the premier conservative think tank in the years ahead.

While she was touching these home bases once again, something surprising happened: a bidding war broke out for the rights to Jeane as a public figure. It was the last thing she ever expected to happen, but suddenly she was a celebrity, deluged by lucrative offers from the media.

All the major newspaper syndicates invited her to write a column. Tom Johnson, publisher of the *Los Angeles Times*, stole a march on the others when he buttonholed Jeane at a party thrown in her honor by Henry Kissinger soon after she left the UN and convinced her to go with him for a guaranteed $100,000 a year. All the leading speakers' bureaus also stalked her, with Harry Walker, the most prestigious, winning out. "There hasn't been anyone hotter than Jeane, ever," the agency's Dan Walker said after she agreed to do fifty dates a year at $20,000 each; he then added that he had filled her schedule within a month of advertising her availability and indicated that he could easily have gotten a hundred engagements. Almost immediately she was appearing at conventions of corporations such as AT&T, General Foods, and the Illinois Bankers Association, in addition to doing a large number of pro bono speeches for local Republican groups.*

Her files contain copies of letters from Sterling Lord, Morton Janklow and all the other top New York literary agents who rushed her about doing a "big book." The legendary Irving "Swifty" Lazar, whose clients had ranged from Kissinger to Cary Grant, won out after an arduous courtship that at first seemed likely to fail. ("I respectfully urge you to have another meeting with me before making a final determination," he wrote on February 21, 1985. "It might be gainful for you and there is certainly nothing to lose.") Once chosen, Lazar fielded offers from Nelson Doubleday, Peter Osnos, Erwin Glikes of Free Press, and others. When he tried to get her to meet personally with publishers as part of a charm offensive, however, Jeane bridled, telling him that it was "too much like hawking one's own wares." Lazar finally accepted an offer from Michael Korda of Simon & Schuster for an advance of $900,000.

As the commitments piled up and Jeane found herself almost as heavily scheduled as she had been in government, she pleaded with a woman named Susan Marone to "help me run my life." She had tried to hire Marone years earlier to work for her at the UN, but Marone had declined because of a romantic involvement that took her away from New York. ("It will probably fail," Jeane had warned her dourly at the time, "and then you'll be stranded,"

---

* Colleges continued to be no-go zones. As late as 1994 she had to decline an honorary degree from Brandeis when several dozen faculty members opposed her for having backed the Contras during the Reagan years.

which, Marone later admitted, was more or less what happened.) This time she accepted the offer, learning to pack hairspray, candy bars, extra nylons and other gear as she accompanied Jeane on the speeches she gave all over the country during the next few years.

Worksheets in her files show that Jeane grossed $1.2 million in 1986, most of it from speaking. She ran into the journalist Sol Sanders, her old friend from Stephens College days, and told him with a kind of wonder, "Kirk and I have money now we never thought we'd have. It's amazing." They bought the stately Bethesda house. They also went shopping for a place of their own in Provence after so many years as summer renters, finally settling on a small house in the historic town of Les Baux. Over the next few years they would pour hundreds of thousands of dollars into the property, enlarging and transforming it into an *Architectural Digest* showpiece. Susan Marone recalls many hours spent on planes taking Jeane to speeches, looking with her through *House Beautiful* for ideas and poring over blueprints for additions to the French home: "She had a great eye for detail. She had stayed with Walter Annenberg at his Palm Springs estate and asked her architect to copy the way that huge walk-in closets connected to bathrooms there."

When Jeane turned sixty in November 1986, Happy Rockefeller threw a birthday party for her at the Sign of the Dove restaurant in Manhattan. That she had entered what one journalist called "The Prime of Jeane Kirkpatrick" was certified by the guest list: Barbara Walters, Walter Cronkite, Henry Kissinger and Kathleen Turner (but not Madonna, whose name Jeane ordered stricken). Richard Nixon played "Happy Birthday" on the piano. She became a cultural referent the following year when she was portrayed by Nora Dunn on a *Saturday Night Live* sketch—about a game show in which high school students were allowed to give flagrantly incorrect answers to difficult questions, over the furious objections of the experts posing them.

She still had a constituency in the administration. During the Iran-Contra affair, CIA chief Bill Casey grumbled about George Shultz's "weakness" and urged Reagan to replace him with Jeane, who would be "a leader rather than a bureaucrat." She herself took a hard line on the scandal, claiming that the real problem was the post-Watergate law requiring a Congress pathologically addicted to leaks to be informed of all CIA actions. But she hadn't forgotten that Shultz and Baker had blocked her for the NSC post with the hapless Bud McFarlane, now on the congressional hot seat. She twisted the knife, saying that the most serious aspect of the affair was "the disorderly, informal, and sometimes amateurish manner in which various policies were made and implemented."

Always trying to keep the president from being maneuvered toward the center by Deaver and others who were attempting to soften his image, she picked up what she regarded as the listing standard of the Reagan Doctrine. After a trip to Central America to visit Nicaraguan refugee camps and a much-publicized lunch with El Salvador's besieged president, José Napoleón Duarte, she made what she called her "Contra Tour" at home: flying to venues all over the country in a private plane, giving free speeches and raising money for the Nicaraguan resistance. It was an implicit rebuke to the White House for not making congressional funding into a public crusade. After meeting in Miami with members of Misura, a faction of Nicaragua's Miskito Indians that had joined the Contras, she wrote to Reagan: "They badly need additional help. I don't have to tell you they are also very important to us for strategic reasons. They prevent the consolidation of the Sandinista control over a large area of Nicaragua's Atlantic coast."

When Bill Casey died from cancer in 1987, his widow asked Jeane to give the eulogy at his funeral mass. Bishop John McGann, officiating at the service, shocked the mourners by starting the proceedings with criticism of Casey for his central role in the "violence wrought in Central America" by administration policies. When it came Jeane's turn to speak, she raked McGann over the coals with a spirited appreciation of Casey's life, especially his views of Central America. Ronald Reagan was watching from the front row. In his diary entry that evening he noted with awe that she "got a big hand," and he expressed admiration for her sharp reprimand of the bishop: "First time I've ever heard [that] at a funeral."

Given her visibility, it was inevitable that the question of running for office should come up. Jeane was for the Equal Rights Amendment and against a constitutional amendment prohibiting abortion, but nonetheless, as *Time* noted, she had "something like cult standing" with the Republican Party's "ruling right wing" and also with "moderates of both parties because of her habit of speaking her mind." George Will, always one of her boosters, wrote a column about the 1988 nomination titled "I Dream of Jeanie." Asked about seeking office, she usually gave politic "no intention" statements. But in an interview for the *Los Angeles Times* a month after she left the UN, she sounded more like a politician than an ingénue: "If I thought I could make a big difference to major problems, then I suppose I would have to try."

In fact, she had been making appearances in support of other candidates, drawing large crowds and raising considerable money and making herself known among the Republican Party faithful. Some political professionals gave her low grades for her inability to glad-hand and for her "gloom and doom" speeches about the Cold War. (One of them said, "You can't sound like Whittaker Chambers, which she does.") Yet this moral seriousness actually appealed to her audiences, as did the stump speech she crafted on themes that fit her political assets—realigning parties, the Democrats' appeasement of the Soviets, a concluding riff on why freedom "works." She even threw in some drum-roll laugh lines, such as this one about a discouraging moment during her time as UN ambassador: "I told someone things were so bad I had half a mind to get into politics, and he said, 'Don't worry, that's all you'll ever need if you do.'"

By the summer of 1987, a boiler-room operation led by Joshua Muravchik was looking into primary schedules, qualifications, etc. It soon became a larger group, including Lyn Myerhoff and her husband Harvey, an industrialist and philanthropist in Baltimore who would eventually become a leading financier of the Holocaust Museum. They had befriended Jeane in part because of her stand on Jewish issues and now strongly backed a presidential bid, throwing parties for her where she met wealthy conservatives such as Peter Coors and T. Boone Pickens. (Norman Podhoretz remembered one seasick venture with the Myerhoffs on their yacht, along with his wife Midge Decter and the Kirkpatricks, in which Lyn tried to convince Jeane to run by assuring her that money for a campaign would not be a problem.) The Myerhoffs took the lack of a no from Jeane as a yes, and they commissioned Herman Pirchner, president of the American Foreign Policy Council, to evaluate her prospects. He wrote a brief analysis advising her to put together position papers, especially on the social issues, to use in fundraising. Eventually, Arthur Finkelstein, a political consultant who had helped Jesse Helms and Alfonse D'Amato get elected to the Senate, was also brought into the picture.

Although Jeane herself insisted that these efforts were "exploratory" at best, she and Kirk met with the boys to discuss Doug's alcoholism and other family vulnerabilities that would bring media scrutiny if she announced. She got permission from all of them to go forward.

In early October she traveled to Nicaragua to underline her foreign policy strengths. The *New York Times* report of the visit admitted that admirers had greeted her upon her arrival at the Sandino Airport in Managua as if she were "a film idol," although Sandinista officials had warned that she was the "envoy of death." Over a thousand cheering Nicaraguans attended her speech— "unparalleled" because no other supporter of the Contras had ever made such a public appearance. Speaking in Spanish, Jeane reviled the government as a dictatorship and said that the Contras were "fighting for the right to live normal lives free of oppression and reprisals." The *Times* said that "she drove a wildly cheering crowd to the brink of delirium."

Back home, however, Jeane found such clarity hard to achieve. With time running out for a decision on the 1988 primary clock, she met with Meldrin Thompson, former governor of New Hampshire and its resident kingmaker, after a speaking engagement in Manchester. Thompson had been strongly courted by George Bush, Jack Kemp, Bob Dole, and all the other likely candidates, but he wanted Jeane and offered to back her if she entered the state's crucial early primary. As others would do in a variety of matters throughout her life, he discounted her inability to make up her mind, concentrating on her expressions of interest while ignoring the indications of ambivalence, and assumed she was in.

Mark Holtzman and David Carmen, the young Republican activists who had orchestrated her 1984 convention appearance, were also working with Jeane at this time. Carmen remembers what he regards as the turning point of her brief and indecisive career as a candidate. It came when the Republicans were preparing for the first debate between the candidates in the fall of 1987, to be hosted by William Buckley. Although not an announced candidate, Jeane called Buckley to ask if she could join, and he consented, intrigued by the theatrical value of having her walk unexpectedly onto the stage with the others. According to Carmen, Rupert Murdoch had agreed to serve as her campaign finance chairman if she became a candidate, and had a private plane ready to take her to the debate. But at the last minute she suddenly decided against the appearance and against the run itself.

Some thought that Kirk's declining health was the tipping point for her decision (although he had been very much in favor of her running). But there were other factors at work. As she told Carmen, "I've never seen a woman stand at a podium and do something like this. Running for the presidency? I don't have a role model."

When I once asked her about it, she gave another version of this failure of feminine will. She had been driving near her new Bethesda home one day when she pulled up at a stop sign next to a station wagon in which a housewife was struggling to control two small children in the back seat while still paying attention to traffic. "For some reason, this struck me as a sort of epiphany. I was more like that woman than I was like the men who'd already announced they were running. I thought to myself that you've got to have a certain competitiveness to do what they're doing and I didn't have it."

Those who wanted her to run "blitzed her with Golda Meir and Margaret Thatcher arguments," according to Jose Sorzano. "But they didn't budge her." In the end, her brand of feminism—that of an individual boldly pursuing her destiny while staying within the boundaries of tradition—was an insufficient foundation for an act of such audacity as seeking the presidency. And however flattering the attention had been, Jeane knew herself well enough to understand that the constant fundraising and campaigning and *managing* would involve the sacrifice of her private life far beyond anything she had experienced at the UN—and all at a time when Kirk was aging and Douglas was descending deeper into his troubles. In any case, she considered it probably beyond her abilities.

Jeane had never been close to Vice President George H. W. Bush. (Early in her UN days, colleagues remember her returning from a meeting in Washington with a concerned look on her face. When asked what the problem was, she replied, "I'm very worried about the vice president. He has influence and he's almost always wrong.") Once she decided that she wasn't running, she initially backed her close friend Jack Kemp, who apparently promised to make her secretary of state if elected. When Kemp's campaign failed to gain traction, she decided that Bob Dole would be better than Bush on Cold War issues and endorsed him. When Dole finally withdrew and Bush asked for her support, Jeane wrote that she would back him against the Democratic nominee, adding somewhat distantly, "And I am willing to say so in public places."

Some of the diehards backing her tried to initiate a draft for the vice-presidential nomination at the New Orleans convention. "Jeane Kirkpatrick for Vice President" caps, whistles and balloons were all manufactured; state delegations were bombarded with arguing points. Jeane didn't stop these activities, but when she arrived in Louisiana and saw that supporters had a large billboard reading "I Love Jeane" on the highway leading into the city, she quickly wrote Bush to say that whoever put it up was "acting without my consent or participation." She also put a stop to what would have been this group's cheekiest maneuver: flooding the convention hall during the vice-presidential nominations with beach balls emblazoned with the slogan: "Jeane Kirkpatrick, A Candidate With Balls."

---

The "big" book she was supposed to be writing was one area of clear failure amidst all this excitement. She had tried to craft an opening around a horrifying news event of June 15, 1987—the murder of Robert Stethem. He was a twenty-three-year-old Navy Seal who happened to be aboard TWA flight 847, bound from Greece to the U.S., when Hezbollah hijackers diverted it to Lebanon. There it sat on a runway for seventeen days while they negotiated to free Palestinian terrorists held by Israel. Midway through the ordeal, when the terrorists realized that Stethem was a military man, they brutally tortured and killed him in front of all the other passenger-hostages; then they dumped his body out of the rear of the plane onto the tarmac, in a scene captured by international camera crews.

This episode was indeed a key moment (perhaps more than Jeane realized) in the slow-motion transition from the threat posed by the Soviet Union to that posed by Islamist terror. Yet it was inert in her telling, an anecdote unconnected to either of these larger historical events and therefore unable to provide a framework that would shape her narrative.

The manuscript she painfully tried to assemble on her days at the UN was a collection of tenuously related chapters, started and abandoned and started again. A force field of formality and reticence surrounded the roughly one thousand draft pages she ultimately produced. Instead of presenting a lively account of her days in the cockpit of the UN, it was a dry sociology of the organization, unable to animate even those episodes such as the Falklands War in which she was deeply invested.

By the spring of 1987, with the deadline come and gone and nothing from the author, editor Michael Korda wrote a worried letter to Swifty Lazar, who relayed the editor's concerns to Jeane. Receiving no response from either of them, Korda became desperate: "If I do not receive a manuscript by August 15, complete and ready to go, we are almost certainly going to be obliged to terminate the contract for lateness." Again Lazar passed on the concerns to Jeane, who answered haughtily, "Korda wrote you, not me. I think it better that he be answered by you, not me. Frankly, I don't like the tone of the letter."

Apparently she never showed either her agent or her editor the hundreds of pages she had written. Lazar finally gave up, after writing a letter on September 23 complaining about her refusal to answer his phone calls. The closet drama ended on February 23, 1988, when Jeane's lawyer Ronald Rowland provided a copy of a release from the publisher terminating the contract, with full repayment of the portion of the advance she had received.*

Taking the loss was made easier by the money rolling in from

---

* Jeane was disingenuous in her discussions of this episode, implying that she had insisted on giving back the advance because she could not in conscience meet the publisher's vulgar demands for "kiss and tell." But in fact

her speeches. (This was a well that would never dry up; as late as 1999, Jeane lightly remarked to her friend Margaret Lefever, "Well, I'm up over a million again this year.") She also had her syndicated column to keep her in the political game. She wrote it into the mid 1990s, but it was most significant between 1985 and 1990, when it recorded her wary and zigzagging thoughts on the end game between the U.S. and the USSR and chronicled her worries that her successors in the administration were insufficiently committed to driving a stake through the heart of the Soviet monster.

Trying to grapple with events that moved with increasing velocity, she sometimes seemed hidebound in her own intellectual hide during these years. She was so worried that Reagan was being misled into the path of peacemaker by Deaver and others that she almost missed the significance of his strongest speech in 1987 at the Berlin Wall. (But she was not alone; George Shultz had objected to its strongest line, "Tear down this wall," as a potential "affront" to Gorbachev.) While still at the UN in 1984, she had traveled to the Philippines and, according to Ambassador Stephen Bosworth, "come away with a clear understanding of the complexity of what we were facing and [that] just to say that we supported Marcos was not sufficient." But now, replaying the tape loop of "Dictatorships and Double Standards," she fretted that a willingness to cut Ferdinand Marcos adrift might "pose strategic problems" for the U.S. When People Power reached South Korea and Chile, she would have similar initial reactions. (She once admitted to me that she should have been more perceptive about changes in the "objective conditions.")

Most of all, Jeane's syndicated columns reveal a deep unwillingness to trust the Soviets because she thought it impossible that

---

the correspondence with lawyers, agent and publisher shows that she dragged her feet on the repayment long after it was obvious that she could not complete the manuscript. She just hated giving the money back.

the Communist Party would ever give up absolute power. She kept a close eye on the Reagan administration's Cold War maneuvering, expecting the worst; and she circled suspiciously around the "new men" in the USSR, especially Alexander Yakovlev, former Soviet ambassador to Canada and architect of perestroika, whom she viewed as a sinister figure trying deviously to give communism a makeover for the modern age.

Gorbachev himself she regarded from the beginning as a "master chess player capable of pursuing a complicated global strategy," centered on a charm offensive directed at the gullible Europeans. It was hard for her to concede that the USSR—now falling behind in every way—couldn't afford a leader who was simply Brezhnev with a human face. It was also hard for her to see that Gorbachev was, in some sense, Ronald Reagan's creation: a desperate leadership gamble by the USSR to reform internally in a way that would allow it to compete with the U.S. as strengthened by the president.

She feared that summits between Reagan and Gorbachev would lead to Détente Part II. She warned that no such meeting with the Soviets had ever brought significant improvements, and that treaties resulting from all previous summits—ABM, SALT II, Helsinki Accords—"had been violated." As the Reykjavik summit unfolded, she worried as much about Reagan's offer for deep cuts in strategic and intermediate missiles as she did about Gorbachev's efforts to force the U.S. to give up the Strategic Defense Initiative. There was only one obscure pleasure for her in this event: the discomfort that the president's offer caused European allies who had poked a finger in the American eye in years of posturing about moral equivalence, but now panicked at the prospect that the American defensive shield that had financed their welfare states might be withdrawn.

In early 1987, she traveled to Moscow and had to rush out immediately to shop for long underwear because she had underestimated the severity of the Russian winter. She was slightly disturbed to find herself charmed by Gorbachev personally and struck by the qualified support being offered him by Andrei Sakharov and other dissidents, but she saw his changes as limited to building a "more efficient, creative, one-party Soviet state." Upon her return, she had lunch with the president to tell him about the trip, which he noncommittally called a "very useful and good session."

Others in her circle were beginning to see intimations of what would soon be called "the end of history." But despite what she had seen in the Soviet Union and what dissidents there were telling her, she let ideas trump experience—exactly the opposite of the reliance on the concrete and distrust of the abstract that had been the source of her intellectual power all her life. She couldn't get past her suspicion that perestroika was the most sophisticated of all the Soviet Cold War plots, and insisted that "the Soviet Union remains far more skillful than the United States and the West in political and psychological competition even while it is in economic crisis." In part, she was using doubt to inoculate herself against disappointment should the changes that seemed to be happening in the USSR turn out to be illusory. But she also genuinely feared that the U.S. was being outfoxed. At the end of the year, when Reagan himself had seen the handwriting on the Wall, Jeane was still nursing doubts because she had just finished reading Gorbachev's best-selling *Perestroika*, which she believed had revealed him as a classical Leninist: "flexible, adaptable, skillful in the pursuit and use of power, absolutely committed to 'the revolution,' to socialism, to a one-party state. . . . Again and again Gorbachev insists that his goal is the consolidation and perfection of socialism, not its modification."

Trying hard to see clearly through the dark glass of news from Moscow, she spied what she thought was a straw in the wind early in 1988 in the Politburo's rehabilitation of Bukharin, one of the original Bolsheviks who had been murdered by Stalin in 1938 during the show trials for his "right-wing deviationism." Since one of Bukharin's sins had been trying to extend Lenin's

New Economic Plan, with its very limited private enterprise, she speculated that Gorbachev had absolved him because he too was looking to Lenin for justification for the limited economic adjustments he was making.

Watching strikes being crushed in Poland midway through 1988, she again pointed out, Cassandra-like, that Gorbachev "has given no indication of any intention to forgo the monopoly of power established by Lenin." A few weeks later she warned that what appeared to be a Soviet retreat from Eastern Europe might be a ploy to "convince Western European nations to cut their ties to the U.S. and dismantle NATO." Yet she also had to admit that the world was "watching the Marxist governments of the Soviet Union and Eastern Europe relinquish control over some domains and begin to share power in others."

Only at the end of the year did she finally seem willing to accept the possibility that Gorbachev might actually "be ready to abandon efforts at total control, the distinguishing characteristic of the totalitarian state." This was a significant concession because it forced an interrogation of her own central premise in "Dictatorships and Double Standards." She was compelled to ask, with a measure of incredulity, "Is it possible that we are watching the early stages of an evolution of totalitarian states into authoritarian regimes?"

By early 1989, having dropped the idea that Gorbachev was Lenin in sheep's clothing, she briefly frightened herself with the possibility that Yegor Ligachev, the Politburo's chief ideologist, and his fellow hardliners might yet manage to stage a coup and reverse the changes in Eastern Europe. While willing to entertain the possibility that Hungary was putting the Brezhnev Doctrine into doubt by its unanswered economic and political reforms and gestures toward membership in the European Economic Community, she was still concerned that in the satellite states "Leninist 'socialism' [would] be supplanted by post-totalitarian regimes of which no example yet exists."

These fears stayed with her until September, when she realized that a watershed moment had occurred with the Soviet Union's admission that it had been responsible for the 1940 Katyn Forest massacre of Polish military officers and its renunciation of the Nazi-Soviet Pact, which had legitimated the USSR's occupation of the Baltic states. This was definitive evidence of something profound. Two months later, as the Wall was coming down, Jeane finally took yes for an answer, admitting that Gorbachev had decisively "abandoned the totalitarian project."

Jeane's real-time ruminations on the end of the Cold War show the truth of Hegel's observation that Minerva's owl spreads its wings only as night falls. Her reluctance to acknowledge the epic changes taking place was widely noted in the policy community, sometimes with a measure of ridicule. Yet it was also true that many of those who now criticized her had themselves been fearful of confronting the USSR forcefully enough to hasten its implosion; or worse, had believed that America was not morally better than the Soviets. And now they argued with deceitful flippancy that the USSR had been brought down by its own internal contradictions rather than by the Reagan administration's policies.

Jeane had studied totalitarianism all her life and was aware of its tensile strengths and subtle ruses for maintaining power. She had cut her intellectual eye teeth on documentary evidence revealing the psychological and political consequences of the gulag state. She had watched the USSR gather itself after the U.S. defeat in Vietnam and burst out of its traditional sphere of influence to pick up new clients around the world. Her pessimism about what was happening in the USSR differentiated her from Ronald Reagan, in that she believed the Soviet leaders' brutality gave them a huge advantage over the West. Like Jean-François Revel, whose book *Why Democracies Perish* she found "prophetic," she feared that the democracies might not have the will to persevere in the long twilight struggle. It is little wonder that when she saw the momentous changes leading to 1989, she often couldn't believe her eyes.

Yet as her skepticism subsided, she could take heart in the fact that there was an element of vindication in some of the things that were happening. This was most obvious in Central America, which had been the focus of her own efforts. El Salvador had not fallen. Nicaragua, no longer a threat because of the demise of the USSR, had reversed course in 1990 when the Sandinistas were forced to hold the election they had denied the people for the past decade. Jeane allowed herself to feel a moment of triumph when Violeta Chamorro ousted Daniel Ortega. One last time she celebrated the Contras, who had "risked their lives in a clear-cut freedom fight and, with the transition to democracy, will have attained their goals." She might also have been thinking of herself and other Reaganauts as well when she praised the fortitude of the Contra leaders, "who for a decade endured the frustrations of American politics to win support for their struggle."

Whether or not it signified "the end of history," the death of the Soviet Union put a period to the narrative that had defined Jeane's own intellectual life. She now had to become reacquainted with the self she had left behind when she first went to battle stations following the disaster of Vietnam and the triumph of McGovernism. As a friend later said, "She was like a rubber band which, after being stretched to its limit, snaps back to its original shape." She had been called (and called herself) a neoconservative, and would maintain the associations with others who had sheltered under this intellectual umbrella during the Reagan years. But she could not go the distance with the "second generation" of neocons who wanted the United States to aggressively capitalize on its victory over the Soviets to remake the world free for democracy. By her own choice, she stayed behind with a vigilant pragmatism resting on the bedrock belief, rooted in her Middle American upbringing, that we make things better in this world with great difficulty and make them worse very easily.

Looking at America's immediate future, Jeane saw—as she put it in an article that appeared in the *National Interest* in the summer of 1990—a "normal nation" able to return to "normal times" now that it had finally overcome the "messianic creeds" that had dominated the twentieth century. A half century of war and Cold War had given foreign affairs "an unnatural importance" in our national life. While it was important to "encourage democratic institutions whenever possible," she said, "it is not within the United States' power to democratize the world." Although she was out of sync with the triumphalist murmurings she heard among her former comrades-in-arms, she warned against an internationalism that "looks at the world and asks what needs to be done with little explicit concern for the national interest." Now that the USSR was dead, what she saw as America's goals were relatively simple: preserve our own freedom, independence and well-being; cautiously support the vitality of other democratic governments of the world; prevent violent expansionist leaders from gaining control of governments of major states.

The views she expressed in the *National Interest* reflected a concern that the country would be drawn into ever more "expansive, expensive" global projects, along with the fear, left over from the 1970s, that rushing to impose utopian values on the world usually wound up adversely affecting American interests. But if the piece was coherent with Jeane's thinking over time, it nonetheless struck some who had stood shoulder to shoulder with her in the Reagan years as the sudden declaration of a separate peace. A few months later, Charles Krauthammer explicitly contradicted Jeane in *Foreign Affairs*, writing about the opportunities of what he called "The Unipolar Moment"—the moment of unchallenged power that the United States had earned by defeating the Soviets. In fact, it was "an abnormal time," he said, insisting that "communism may be dead but the work of democracy is never done."

Krauthammer's words included a gracious homage to the achievements of intellectuals like Jeane ("many were heroic in the heroic struggles against fascism and communism"), but strongly criticized their current belief that "the time for heroism has passed." While Jeane saw a country returning in the post-Soviet world to the pursuits of culture, commerce and the social arts, and allowing foreign affairs to settle in alongside these priorities, Krauthammer believed that aggressively spreading democracy should "become the touchstone of a new, ideological American foreign policy." He chastised her with the reminder that "international stability is never a given" but rather the product of "self-conscious action by the great powers and most particularly by the greatest power." The hope for a stable future was not normalcy, however "compelling" that vision might be, but an America committed to "laying down the rules of world order and being able to enforce them."

Jeane did not rush to join the debate: she had been forced to leave one intellectual homeland already and was not anxious to repeat the experience. Over the next few years, she would join Jack Kemp and Bill Bennett in founding Empower America, widely viewed as a neoconservative social initiative, and would try repeatedly to re-knot the ties that bound her to the neoconservative worldview. But to some degree she was now merely a hesitant fellow traveler, who had to find her way through foreign policy issues without an intellectual roadmap filled with the bright lines that had previously shown her the way. In the future, the positions she took would feel ad hoc, and sometimes self-contradictory.

That she was increasingly a movement of one showed in her reaction to the first Gulf War. Her initial take on Saddam's invasion of Kuwait was that it did not require a strong American response. She wanted to let sanctions work and was not willing for the United States to step precipitously over the line that President George H. W. Bush proposed to draw in the sand. Her "grave reservations" prompted a lengthy phone call from Norman Podhoretz making the case for action. But even after she somewhat squeamishly allowed herself to be brought on board, she still hoped that airpower alone would be sufficient and opposed American boots on the ground until it was obvious that this action would be necessary to dislodge Saddam's forces, although after the war was won she said that the U.S. had erred in not taking the fight to Baghdad.*

She was critical of the willingness of her old foe James Baker, now secretary of state, to put Saddam's fate "not in the hands of the coalition that had defeated him, but in the hands of the UN Security Council." Her contempt for that body had only grown in the years since she was ambassador. She saw the UN chief Boutros Boutros-Ghali as a sinister manipulator trying to increase the organization's ability to control U.S. military action indirectly, and she was not surprised when the UN later failed "to support the use of force to enforce its own resolutions" against Saddam, thus demonstrating the "impotence" of its claim to be "the sheriff of the new world order."

When Bill Clinton ran for president in 1992, his campaign made overtures to Jeane in an effort to revive and remobilize the Coalition for a Democratic Majority. Max Kampelman, Samuel Huntington, Ben Wattenberg, Penn Kemble and Joshua Muravchik, among other alumni of the organization, supported his election. But although she was somewhat allergic to Bush, Jeane did not join them. ("I was not sufficiently nostalgic for the Democratic Party to believe what Clinton said," she later commented.)

From the outset she deeply opposed the new administration's conception of the United States "as potentially engaged everywhere in the world, as needed." Even worse was the fact that this engagement involved a loss of sovereignty because it was contingent on a philosophy of "assertive multilateralism." The only

---

* Her after-the-fact militancy would grow. A decade later, in a 1999 speech at Harvard's Kennedy School marking the establishment of a Jeane Kirkpatrick Professorship in International Affairs, she said that if the Gulf War had happened on Reagan's watch, he would have removed Saddam by force. Former Bush advisor Brent Scowcroft, also appearing at the event, immediately attempted to repudiate this position.

thing worse for the United States than acting as if it controlled a unipolar world, from her point of view, was pretending that it was just another nation in a multipolar one.

Somalia proved the case when the Clinton administration followed the UN into a venture that "blurred the lines between peacekeeping and nation building." Jeane believed the White House was suckered by Boutros-Ghali's twofold agenda of concentrating power in the UN through interventions around the world using American muscle, while also working to limit what the French would soon be calling America's *hyperpuissance*. She was aghast at the idea that U.S. troops should be put under UN command in Somalia and used for "a liberal agenda, namely, the rehabilitation of failed Third World states." She inveighed against the Clintonites' willingness to engage in "conflict resolution everywhere," and especially against their readiness "to risk American lives to achieve ambiguous goals in remote countries with which we have no significant ties."

The 1994 "humanitarian" invasion of Haiti seemed to her to be based on "some sort of Brezhnev Doctrine for democracy," with the Clinton administration acting as if it believed "the U.S. was responsible for protecting and restoring democracy around the world, regardless of the costs or whether American interests are at stake." In words recalling her pessimism in "Dictatorships and Double Standards," she criticized the idea that democracy was an "entitlement" in a column for the *Washington Post*, where she also attacked the notion that "international altruism" justified the invasion of "virtually any less developed country."

In Bosnia she did see a compelling interest for U.S. action, in part because the ethnic cleansing undertaken by the Serbs reminded her so much of events that occurred in the 1930s, back at the beginning of history. "We shouldn't forget that Benito Mussolini and his Black Shirts inspired Adolf Hitler . . . [by their] aggression against Ethiopia," she said in testimony before the House National Security Committee. She opposed the deployment of troops, but was for "lift and strike": lifting the arms embargo so the Bosnians could defend themselves, and using air strikes against the Bosnian Serbs to equalize the conflict. She again bitterly criticized Boutros-Ghali for calling this a "rich man's war" and ignoring it in favor of Somalia, and she criticized the Clinton administration's tendency to defer to the UN, joining Margaret Thatcher and others who also worried about the U.S. thinking it needed what Jeane called a "permission slip" from the international body before acting. (Her final judgment of Clinton was that he had allowed American forces to be "ambushed in Somalia, blown up in Saudi Arabia and shot down in Bosnia.")

In 1997, Jeane again found herself targeted by a theoretical ally when Robert Kagan published a piece called "Democracy and Double Standards" in *Commentary* (the title and the venue a deliberate taunt). Like Krauthammer, Kagan was a member of what would soon be called "neoconservatism 2.0" and a fellow partisan of the view that America had to use its "unipolarity" aggressively to spread democracy. He wrote stingingly of "a new pessimism, a new indifference, even a new distaste for democracy promotion" on the part of foreign policy "realists," Jeane chief among them. Kagan saw her as a metaphor for a failure of nerve about democracy and went back to her 1979 essay (which probably would not have been considered an appropriate target if not for her post-Reagan heterodoxy) to criticize her position there that Americans needed to be disabused of "the belief that it is possible to democratize governments, anytime, anywhere, under any circumstances." He saw a "return of the Kirkpatrick thesis" among people on the left whom she had skewered in 1979 and people on the right who were now withdrawing along with her, all of which showed that the policy winds were blowing toward "the resurgence of an older and more established tradition in foreign policy: namely realism." And this, Kagan said, was ironic because such realism represented a "strong repudiation of the policy followed by the Reagan administration, which made a very high priority out of promoting democracy in such places as El Salvador, Chile, the Philippines, and South Korea."*

While she was annoyed by Kagan's title and the place where the essay appeared ("A little too close for comfort, don't you think?"), Jeane seemed resigned to the fact that she had now become a primal mother who would be targeted by younger neocons in an Oedipal struggle over the future of American foreign policy. But she didn't give ground. In the "big policy book" she was still trying to complete, she would write incredulously about how America's attention on national security had been subsumed during the 1990s by its desire to promote democracy, "as if democracy could imbue chaotic societies and unstable governments with a respect for what we respected: the rule of law, basic human rights and a peaceful world order." But she chose to regard the attacks coming from the younger generation of neoconservatives as a family matter, linen not to be aired in public.

How consanguineous she continued to feel about this group was shown when she signed an open letter to President George W. Bush on September 20, 2001, circulated by the Project for the New American Century, preeminent foreign policy voice of neo-

---

* Kagan's piece was by no means the last time that "Dictatorships and Double Standards" would be exhumed as an arguing point. In 2006, the historian Niall Ferguson, examining its original and continuing relevance, gave it two cheers. He noted, among other things, that despite the view that its thesis was irreparably damaged by the fall of the USSR, it was in fact true that conservative authoritarian governments such as Chile, South Korea and Taiwan had democratized successfully, while the totalitarian former Soviet Union had backslid toward anti-democracy under Vladimir Putin. A few years later came the "Arab Spring" of early 2011 and the irresolute U.S. response, in particular, to the fate of Mubarak in Egypt and the subsequent rise of Salafism. Once again, Jeane's essay was frequently cited by contrarians in the policy establishment who wondered, as the Muslim Brotherhood maneuvered for control, if what came next in Cairo would necessarily be better than what had been overthrown—a regime that had at least been making slothful small steps toward an enlargement of civic space.

conservatism 2.0. Signed also by Charles Krauthammer and Robert Kagan, among others, the letter urged the president to prosecute the war on terror by all available means, including "a determined effort to remove Saddam Hussein from power" and engage in a "fight against Hizbollah."

---

Her publications throughout the 1980s and 90s were skimpy—mainly speeches and articles that formed the afterbirth of her years in the Reagan administration. She put a good deal of effort into publishing a two-volume collection of her speeches at the UN called *Legitimacy and Force* with the small publisher Transaction in 1988. A couple of years later came a collection of her syndicated columns titled *The Withering Away of the Totalitarian State . . . and Other Surprises.*

She remained heavily involved in public affairs throughout the 1990s—teaching, serving on boards, testifying before Congress, solicited for insights by the media—but seemingly without the urgent desire to put a fingerprint on events that she'd felt a quarter century earlier. For all her efforts to keep up with developing crises, she seemed to acknowledge that for the most part she had had her say. At the same time, she was being pulled down by the gravity of her family life, which embossed her last years with desolation and took her away from the public world that had once been her hiding place from such heartbreak.

Kirk had been the co-beneficiary of her celebrity following the Reagan years. He was an institution builder by nature, and after Jeane left the UN he had spent his time building a nonprofit called the Helen Dwight Reid Educational Foundation, which went by the unattractive acronym Heldref. It had been founded in the 1950s by his friend Helen Dwight Reid, a political scientist at Bryn Mawr, to support projects in education and international affairs. In the years since retiring from the American Political

Science Association in 1981, he had supervised the development of Heldref into a small publishing empire, consisting of a large number of scholarly magazines: *The Germanic Review*; *The Journal of Popular Film and Television*; *The Journal of Experimental Education*. Most were little-known and little-read: vehicles for junior professors at second-tier colleges who were trying to develop a publication record for tenure; acquired by university libraries to build their collections of periodical arcana.

Heldref was something for Kirk to do, but it was also something—academic work—that he and Jeane both believed in. They bought a stately Gilded Age mansion on 18th Street, a couple of blocks from the Mayflower Hotel, to house Heldref and a variety of other nonprofits in a warren of offices filling its four floors.* But beginning in the early 1990s, Kirk, still frail from the after-effects of Legionnaire's disease, suffered a series of strokes. At first he and Jeane were still able to travel every summer to the house they both loved in Les Baux-de-Provence. But by the mid 90s, that became difficult because of his diminishing strength. An acquaintance recalled visiting the Kirkpatricks in Les Baux in 1993, the last summer Kirk and Jeane were there together. The party dined at L'Oustau de Beaumanière, a Michelin two-star restaurant near their home. Everyone chatted energetically throughout dinner except Kirk, who was asleep much of the time with his chin on his chest.

All his life he had tried to make a religion out of political science. Now he became interested in Christianity and began wearing a large cross around his neck and attending Washington's Fourth Presbyterian Church. Jeane loyally accompanied him to the evangelical service many Sundays, although one close friend believed she was only "a pious agnostic."

---

* The building, another of the serendipitous financial moves that Jeane made late in her life, would be put on the market by her heirs for $16 million after her death.

Having brought Kirk back from the edge of death after his bout with Legionnaire's a few years earlier, she was now forced to watch helplessly as he died by degrees, at first relying on the elevator they'd earlier installed in the Bethesda home to get downstairs and then remaining in his bed. Knowing that Kirk didn't want to spend his last days in a nursing home, Jeane hired around-the-clock help.

Her three sons rallied around their dying father. But Jeane was still struggling with them, as well as with Kirk's mortality. In talks with friends, she sometimes dropped cryptic hints of the trouble all of them had had in orienting themselves and occasionally spoke enviously of the close three-generation family her brother Jerry now headed in Ohio.

Her middle son John, a large man like his grandfather Fat Jordan and now a successful lawyer, was the most dependable of the three, although Jeane often fumed about the way he "blundered" through life. In part this referred to broken marriages, but it also described what she regarded as a lack of responsibility in financial matters, which she and Kirk sometimes had to clean up for him.

With her youngest son Stuart, it was a different problem. According to a description of his life's journey that he later gave to an interviewer for the online magazine *Spiritual Traveler*, he had begun as a political science major at Georgetown, although his interests in this area were not those his parents would have considered legitimate: "Are you familiar with Herbert Marcuse's *One-Dimensional Man*? His analysis of technological society is that society shapes the apparent needs of people, and then people are bound by what they feel to be their needs. It's a very good description of our commercial society."

The celebration of someone like Marcuse, guru to the New Left, was bad enough; but when Stuart turned from there toward Eastern philosophy, Jeane regarded it is a betrayal of the Western tradition and a defection from the family's role and values. But as Stuart described it in *Spiritual Traveler*, this was part of a quest involving "quite a number of years in my late teens traveling from center to center, community to community, group to group—a Sufi group, a Gurdieff group, a Zen group, Dheravadfa and Mahayana groups. I have a complete love for the beauty of realization, and also the particular paths displayed throughout history, and throughout time, and throughout cultures."

That a child of hers would chose Eastern mysticism over Western rationalism was a blow to Jeane. Her friend Margaret Lefever learned how sensitive a subject it was when she innocently sent Jeane a couple of books on Buddhism she received as review copies in her job as librarian. In return she got a tongue-lashing over the phone: "Don't you ever send me another book on this subject! Do you understand? Never!"

Resembling Kirk (but with long blond hair, mustache and goatee, and ivory earrings), Stuart would become Traktung Rinpoche, leader of the Vajrayana Buddhist community in Ann Arbor, Michigan. Some of his followers believed him to be the reincarnation of Do Khyentse Yeshe Dorje, a Tibetan mystic who lived in the nineteenth century and was in turn an emanation of Dorje Trollo, who was pivotal in bringing Buddhism to Tibet. But the Dalai Lama refused to recognize his reincarnation. Asked about it in an interview, Stuart showed some of the Kirkpatrick combativeness: "What does the Dalai Lama have to do with it? Namkha Rinpoche, who is the holder of the family lineage of Do Khyentse Yeshe Dorje, recognized me." He added, "I however have nothing in particular for or against the Dalai Lama. He is not my Lama or my King, nor am I a rock star groupie."

When mentioning Stuart's spiritual calling, Jeane took a wan solace in the fact that when there was a schism inside his school of Buddhism, he was at least "the leader of the *conservative* faction."

John and Stuart may not have fulfilled Jeane's hopes for them, but Douglas was her tragedy. He was quiet like Kirk, but had, at least at the beginning of his life, a "winning personality," in the opinion of family friends. This made his fate all the more incomprehensible. By his early twenties, he had graduated from teenage binge drinking to full-fledged alcoholism. While still a student, he secretly married a beauty queen who was one of the runners-up to Miss America; everyone in the family hated her. When the marriage foundered and Douglas sank deeper into dysfunction, Jeane asked her brother Jerry to take him into his home in Ohio for a time during her UN years. After a few weeks, Jerry and his wife collected all the bottles of vodka that Douglas had hidden under his bed and elsewhere in the house when he was gone one afternoon and lined them up on the kitchen counter. When he returned, Jerry sternly lectured him, applying the term "drunk" to him for the first time in his life. (With Kirk and Jeane there had only been euphemistic talk about a "drinking problem.") The confrontation at least yielded an agreement from Douglas to seek professional help.

Jeane and Kirk traveled to Ohio during this time to see him. Kirk was philosophical: "Every family has problems like this." Jeane refused to adopt this fatalism. Instead, she joined her son in a cycle marked by her repeated interventions and his repeated professions of remorse and promises of change, which always ended with him sinking deeper into the hole he had been digging for most of his life.

He married a second time and again divorced. He managed to get a law degree but couldn't hold a job. He was in and out of detox and rehab centers over a twenty-year period, all of these treatments paid for by Jeane at an estimated cost, according to family and friends, of well over $1 million. Margaret Lefever remembers the ending of one of these rehabilitation stints, a five-month stay in a New Jersey facility. When he was about to be released, Jeane told Douglas over the telephone that she would drive up to get him. "You don't have to bother," he reassured her. "I'll be home in a couple of hours." Jeane said okay and began a long wait. She found Douglas dead drunk in a motel several days later.

The other boys resented the toll he took. Having isolated himself and his family in Michigan, Stuart commented bitterly to a family friend about Jeane, "She still changes Doug's diapers."

In a conversation about her son, Jeane said to her friend Jose Sorzano: "I know what I should do, but I can't bring myself to do it." When Sorzano asked what it was she should do, she answered, "Throw him out and not talk to him again. That would probably make him change. But I'm his mother and I can't do it."

Douglas couldn't stay away from her. Sometimes Jeane was afraid of him, and according to a family friend named Joyce Horne, she once locked herself in her bedroom and called the cops during one of his drunken bouts. But most of the time she couldn't stay away from him either. When her old friend Anne de Lattre came from France for a visit in the 1990s, Jeane took her on a macabre journey to see the apartment where Douglas's third wife Nora, whom he had met in a rehab center, committed suicide. A few days later, Douglas suddenly appeared at Jeane's house late one night, drunk, and passed out in the kitchen. The two women tried to move him, but he was too heavy, so they covered him with a bedspread, left him on the floor, and went to bed themselves.*

It was the tragedy that crossed party lines. In 1996, George McGovern published a harrowing account of his effort to deal with the alcoholism of his daughter Terry, who froze to death one night while drunk. Jeane called her old nemesis to offer condolences and wound up telling him about Douglas. They talked for

---

* Jeane foresaw a time when she would no longer be able to take care of Douglas, and she was now under no illusions that he could take care of himself. An amended copy of her will, updated a couple of years before her death, stipulated that while Stuart and John would get their share of the estate directly, Douglas would have a trustee "who shall from time to time pay for [his benefit] so much of the net income and principal as trustee in his sole discretion deems advisable. . . ."

a long time about missed opportunities and desperate gambits. The subject of "tough love" came up. McGovern told her he had tried to practice it with his daughter and failed. Jeane admitted that she hadn't even tried. It was a touching moment in which two bitter enemies on opposite sides of the American political divide found common ground at the end of their lives in shared grief over children they had been unable to save.

Jeane always believed that the leaves Douglas kept promising to turn over would be new. In 1995, when Kirk, now eighty-five years old, was entering his last days, Douglas lived at home for several weeks and became a dedicated caregiver. Jeane believed that his life might have been changed for the better by the profundity of the experience. Then Kirk died, and after the funeral Douglas suddenly disappeared again, "off on another drunken spree," as one friend said.

Kirk's death was the passing of her dragoman and lover and representative of a vanished world that Jeane had been allowed to share. She never felt that he had gotten his due as a public figure, and so she made sure that the funeral service highlighted his unique life and unique accomplishments. At the reception afterwards, a friend came up to offer condolences and said of Max Kampelman's eulogy, "Those were the perfect words." Jeane looked at him sharply and replied, "They were not *just* words."

Honoring her husband's memory—matter-of-factly and never allowing herself to sink into mawkishness—became a central part of Jeane's mundane life. She frequently cited Kirk in conversation. In the house at Les Baux where she was now a solitary presence in her summer trips, she always seemed to be looking around as if hoping to catch a glimpse of him. She would show visitors the elaborately tasteful collection of curios, artifacts and found objects the two of them had acquired in their years together, and would always conclude the tour in front of a woodcut on the wall of the master bedroom that she had been given during a state visit to Taiwan. It showed two surging horses leading a herd, independent from each other yet obviously profoundly in sync. "I've always loved this piece," she would say. "Somehow it reminds me of the relationship Kirk and I had. This was our life together."

# A TIME OF SUBTRACTION

JEANE TELEPHONED me shortly after midnight her time on New Year's Eve, Y2K. She was calling from our mutual friend Jim Denton's house and was jubilant that the dire predictions of collapse, which she took to be anti-Americanism in disguise, had been proven false. She concluded the brief conversation with an uncharacteristically ebullient, if still somewhat formal pronouncement: "I feel *very* optimistic about this new century!"

But in a brief chat a few months later, she sounded down and admitted that she was bothered by what she ruefully called her own "slow-motion collapse." It was not clear at the time what she was referring to, although medical records in the papers she left behind show that she was operated on for uterine precancer in the summer of 2000 and then suffered a broken pelvis a few months later in a fall she took while visiting her son John in Miami. In her annual visit to Les Baux-de-Provence in the summer of 2001, she began to suffer severe stomach pains. Anne de Lattre came down from Paris and tried to arrange treatment for her. But Jeane stubbornly insisted on returning to the United States. She became ill on the plane and was removed in a wheelchair at Dulles Airport, loaded into an ambulance and taken immediately to Sibley Hospital for treatment for a virulent amoebic dysentery, which left her in a weakened state for several weeks.

She had entered a time of subtraction. Partly because of this illness, but also because of what she bitterly described as the French "death tax" levied on her property after Kirk's passing, she decided that she could no longer keep the house in Provence. It brought something over $1 million when she sold it. But the transaction was a melancholy one, marking the end of the time of her life—the time saturated by things French—that had begun over fifty years earlier when she first traveled to Paris to escape herself and learn something of the art of living well.

In 2002, she finally retired from Georgetown. Having given up her syndicated column, she now devoted her attention to the book on foreign policy she had been struggling with for well over a decade.

Her hopes that the U.S. could be a "normal country" were dashed by 9/11. "It would be a very serious mistake for the United States not to respond with force . . . [to] protect our civilization," she said immediately after the attack. And, she added, "I don't just mean American civilization. I mean modern civilization." She strongly backed the operation against al-Qaeda and the Taliban in Afghanistan (and cooked an elaborate welcome-home dinner for her friend Anne Crutcher's grandson, a Navy pilot whose carrier was engaged there in the first days of the war).

But although she had impulsively joined other neocons right after 9/11 in calling for Saddam Hussein to be removed from power, she became deeply troubled by the prospect of a major land war in Iraq as it actually approached. Trying to remake that country, she feared, would not cure the deep disorder and chaos that infected it; and launching a full-scale invasion would be even more destructive of American national interest than the tepid, ill-conceived multilateral adventures she had criticized during the Clinton years for having bled U.S. sovereignty and sense of purpose drop by drop. The fact that she now shrank from an enterprise her neoconservative friends enthusiastically backed could only increase her sense of personal quarantine.

Despite her misgivings, which would grow dramatically as the war in Iraq unfolded in the years ahead, Jeane allowed herself to be persuaded to represent the United States at the UN Human Rights Conference scheduled for Geneva in March 2003, a few days before the invasion. She arrived to find the U.S. mission heavily guarded by military and police, as a massive demonstration took place in front of the old League of Nations building. Syria and Cuba were putting forward a resolution against any military action in Iraq. Jeane loyally worked to defeat it, although she refused to use the idea of preemptive self-defense in this effort as the administration had asked. (Her legal counsel from her days at the UN, Allan Gerson, who accompanied her to Geneva, later quoted her as saying, "It will never sell. No one will buy it.") Instead, she defended an invasion on the somewhat scholastic grounds that it would merely be a continuation of the first Gulf War because Saddam had violated the 1991 ceasefire that ended the conflict. She narrowly managed to defeat the Syrian and Cuban resolution. As a result, Arab hostility to the invasion was initially, in the words of the British paper *The Independent*, "comparatively muted."

She had done her duty. But when I had dinner with her in Washington a year and a half later, she didn't seem particularly proud of her diplomatic mission. By then, she had told Norman Podhoretz and other friends about her growing opposition to the war and the Bush Doctrine, but didn't feel that she should go public—which meant that she was on the sidelines during the biggest foreign policy debate since the end of the Cold War. She mentioned having heard that some of the "second generation" of neoconservatives were now favorably embracing the term "hegemon" to describe the U.S. position in the world. "I don't like that word," she commented. "It is a Chinese concept, not in any way an American one." The furtiveness with which she said this— looking around the nearly empty restaurant and lowering her voice—suggested how painful it was to have broken ranks.

———————

Her anxiety about the direction in which the country was moving found an objective correlative in her own personal life. She had looked forward to having grandchildren, perhaps as a make-up game for parenthood. In her draft autobiography, she wrote with unusual emotion: "I have beautiful quilts done by my grand-mothers that I will give to my first granddaughter." But soon after John and his wife had a little girl named Laura, whom Jeane was prepared to dote on, there was a fracture in the marriage and a bitter breakup. Jeane was denied access to the girl, although she lived with her mother only a few miles away in Maryland. For a while there were unclaimed presents at birthdays and under the tree at Christmas, and then nothing. Margaret Lefever recalls a time later on when Laura appeared on a local television program showcasing Maryland students. Jeane sat there watching her in silence, with a look of ineffable sadness on her face.

She also felt that she saw Stuart's children in Michigan too sel-dom. (He told family members that he didn't want to expose them to his brother Doug.) Yet this longing for extended family had a certain literary quality to it—a desire to perpetuate the con-tinuity that had begun in Indian Territory in Oklahoma over a hundred and fifty years earlier, more than a desire to interact with grandchildren per se. When she was actually with them—in this case, those John had by a second marriage—she was, he thought, stiff and formal, unable to reach out all the way to them emotion-ally. There was something off-key in Jeane's dedication of her last, posthumous book to the six grandchildren along with an admo-nition to honor and protect freedom.

In any case, it was Douglas who remained her preoccupation. Not long after Kirk's death she had installed him as executive director of Heldref, as part of yet another new beginning. But over time he had become a spectacle there. Employees once dis-covered him standing up dead drunk in the building's small ele-vator; another time, he crashed through the building's front door, badly cutting himself; he drank at work, sometimes vomiting on the walls and the rug of his office. The business of Heldref, which Jeane had supported by refinancing the increasingly valuable building in which it was housed, was in shambles, with bills unpaid although checks worth tens of thousands of dollars languished for weeks, uncashed, in Douglas's desk drawer.

---

In late 2004, Kate Campaigne, her last assistant at AEI, noticed that while Jeane was usually as sharp as ever, she occasionally seemed to be fatigued or struggling through a funk of disconnection, and was often out of the office without giving a reason for several days at a time. In the spring of 2005, Jeane finally acknowledged that she had suffered a mild heart attack that she had tried at first to ignore, despite suffering such serious vertigo that pillows had to be piled up all around her bed to break her inevitable fall when she got up at night.

After a pacemaker was implanted, she was immediately better, showing up at the office every day with alacrity. But by the fall, she began to sink again. Alarmed by her decline, her brother Jerry, the one family member on whom she could always rely, came to Washington and set up an appointment for a complete workup at Johns Hopkins University Hospital. Jeane underwent extensive tests and then returned with Jerry for the results a week or so later. Because of a contretemps, the doctor who had conducted the psychological part of the exam met with her before the doctor who'd done the physical. When he began to talk of "memory loss and possible dementia," Jeane immediately stood up and stalked out, not bothering to get the results from the other tests. She was furious at her brother for setting up the appointment, although he had done so with the assumption that there was merely some glitch in the pacemaker that could easily be fixed. "'Dementia' is not a compliment," Jeane told him icily on the drive home. (The diagnosis turned out to be false.)

On top of everything else, her status at AEI, the last position validating her continued relevance, was crumbling. The old sense of opulence that had characterized the organization in its earlier days had gradually been replaced with a more bureaucratic structure. A woman named Danielle Pletka, formerly an aide to Senator Jesse Helms, had been brought in to head the foreign policy department without Jeane's involvement, although this was theoretically her bailiwick. Jeane tried to ignore the fact that she was being supplanted. She knew that the years when she had been the star of the institution—the one who deserved the corner office with the private washroom and three assistants—were over. But she still felt she was a significant ornament to the organizational letterhead and hoped that the "big book" she was working on— some of the sections now over twenty years old—would rehabilitate her reputation.

Jeane finally submitted the book to the AEI Press in mid 2005. Months later, Kate Campaigne attended the weekly meeting of the scholars' assistants chaired by Danielle Pletka. When it was her turn to speak, she asked what was happening with the book. Pletka told her that AEI Press was passing on it. To justify the decision, Jeane was given a report written by an outside reviewer hired by AEI that disparaged the manuscript.

It was a blow, especially because AEI Press was not known as a first-tier publisher and had, in fact, functioned to some degree as a sort of vanity press for the organization's scholars over the years. Jeane's friends saw the rejection of the manuscript as part of a strategy to isolate her. According to another AEI employee, "There was a total lack of respect, which Jeane couldn't understand. Her name would come up in hallway conversations and Pletka would roll her eyes sarcastically. She thought Jeane didn't see this, but of course she did. Worst of all, she believed that this disrespectful behavior was sanctioned by those at the top of the organization."*

Kate Campaigne left AEI in March 2006 for another job. When she returned a few weeks later for a visit, Jeane's office had

---

* Pletka did not respond to several requests to be interviewed for this book.

been cleaned out. No one in the organization seemed to know what had happened. Jeane's longtime friend Joshua Muravchik, a productive foreign policy analyst at AEI who himself would be let go as part of what appeared to be a mini purge, later observed, "When anyone leaves AEI—secretaries, researchers, anyone— there is always a farewell party with wine and toasts and parting gifts. But nothing for Jeane."

When Campaigne finally reached her, Jeane said, "I just felt unappreciated and unwanted, so I took my things and left."

She tried to continue as if nothing had changed. As late as May 2006, she gave an interview to the *Washington Times* in which she took not too subtle aim at George W. Bush's foreign policy: "I don't think we have an obligation to engage in a new imperialism." In a valedictory tone, she also talked in the same piece about what she thought was her legacy: helping bring about a realignment in American politics and radically changing the atmosphere at the United Nations.

She continued to attend events, insisting on driving herself into the city from Bethesda. But she was clearly a menace to herself and others on the road. Meeting her at a Washington party and seeing how frail and uncertain she seemed, Ed Meese became so concerned that at the end of the evening he insisted on having his wife drive her home while he himself ferried Jeane's car back to Maryland.

The book was now her raison d'être. Annoyed at the treatment Jeane had received from AEI, Kate Campaigne had contacted a local agent named Teresa Hartnett, who read the manuscript and felt that the outside reviewer obtained by AEI had been wrong in denigrating it. Hartnett showed it to Sentinel, Times Books, HarperCollins and other large New York houses. The response was strong. Sentinel offered $300,000 on the condition that Jeane make her relatively mild criticism of the war in Iraq more explicit. Jeane refused, instead taking HarperCollins' $100,000 offer. She was delighted when Hartnett told her about the deal, saying with bruised surprise, "Maybe people actually still want to hear what I have to say."

In the late spring of 2006, Claudia Anderson, who had known Jeane all her life, arranged to take a home-cooked meal to her house. But when she and her husband Bill arrived with the food, they found Jeane and Douglas standing together on the driveway with their coats on. Jeane said, "We're going out, right?" Claudia reminded her that this had not been the plan and that she'd spent the day cooking. Jeane reluctantly invited them in for what became at times a surreal evening.

Douglas, normally even more silent and laconic than Kirk had been, was unusually talkative and even witty, attentive and indulgent toward his mother. Jeane made a strong effort to appear on point, but sometimes seemed to be caught in an intellectual undertow. When Claudia mentioned a dress that Saddam Hussein had given her during a state visit, Jeane, in an obvious effort to show that her memory was still sharp, insisted punctiliously that it had actually come from Tariq Aziz, Saddam's right-hand man. Anderson's feeling at the end of the evening was that there was something gallant about Jeane and Douglas propping each other up at what seemed the end of their trail.

A few weeks later, on July 14, 2006, Douglas was found dead from a heart attack in the hallway outside his condo. He was just fifty years old. His passing took the fight out of Jeane in a way that Kaddafi, Castro and the Soviet Union had not been able to. After his funeral, she met with John and Stuart and told them that she now wanted only three things: to celebrate her eightieth birthday on November 19; to die before the end of the year; and to see her book published. "She was very emphatic," John recalled. "She was very much her old self, setting the terms of her end."

Only the last of her three wishes was denied her. Despite

efforts to speed its production, *Making War to Keep Peace* did not appear until a few weeks after her death. But it put her back in the limelight briefly, although for reasons that she might not have wished. She intended the book as an inquiry into the use of the American military when vital national interests were not at stake, and more particularly as a critique of the misuse of the American military in misbegotten multilateralist adventures, of internationalist power grabs by the UN, and of futile efforts to plant democracy in barren soil.

Most critics ignored all this and focused on her chapter condemning the war in Iraq, which she said had been undertaken for "no compelling reason" and which she frankly admitted "troubled me deeply." She believed the Bush administration had failed "to do due diligence required for reasoned policy making because it failed to address the aftermath of the invasion" before it took place. But the real reason for her dismay went back to "Dictatorships and Double Standards." Iraq lacked "the requirements for a democratic government: rule of law, an elite with a shared commitment to democratic procedures, a sense of citizenship and habits of trust and cooperation." Going to war to build a democracy there simply violated what Jeane regarded as reality.

Reviewers seized on the woman-bites-dog aspect of *Making War to Keep Peace*: queen of the neocons criticizing a neocon war. From the left there was joyous schadenfreude because the book offered a perfectly fashioned stick with which to beat the Bush administration and neoconservatism itself. For some of her former allies, there was puzzlement about what happened to Jeane Kirkpatrick. It was a question they wouldn't have asked if they'd known her better.

---

Like others, Jeane's agent Teresa Hartnett called her frequently in the Indian summer of 2006 as her health continued to decline.

They would talk about the manuscript, which was then going through a final and substantial editing. It was a subject that always gave her pleasure. But during these conversations with Hartnett, Jeane sometimes slipped away from the subject at hand into streams of consciousness mingling sharp observations, stoical reports on the clinical effects of shortness of breath, disorganized obiter dicta, and sad wool-gathering reminiscences about a miscellany of subjects from her past, one of which was all the friends she had lost when she became a Republican.

Winter was settling in early when Jeane celebrated her eightieth birthday on November 19. She was being slowly consumed not by any one disease, but by what doctors call "failure to thrive." Too weak to get to the elevator near her bedroom, she was carried down the stairs by her son John to attend the party organized by the family. She beamed at the small gathering there—friends of a lifetime to her and Kirk who had also been comrades-in-arms in the battles that had defined her public career: among them, Max Kampelman; Allan Gerson and his wife Joan Nathan, a noted food critic with whom Jeane had been able to share her love of cooking; her former assistant Jackie Tillman; Margaret Lefever and her husband Ernie. As the meal began, Jeane smiled broadly at the guests to drive away the melancholy of what was obviously a last supper while picking desultorily at the food. (She had already made it clear, as Margaret Lefever noted, that she "had decided to stop eating to hasten death.") After a couple of hours, the guests, mindful of Jeane's fragility, began to leave. She herself seemed shrunken, almost doll-like when John carried her back up to her bedroom.

In her last few days, she insisted that she was more than bone tired. She stared at the sere branches of the trees outside her windows while obsessively fiddling with her hair, snow white now, pushing it back from her forehead, finger-parting it roughly and trying to smooth it, demanding a barrette which she was unable to affix without help. Her long fingers, knobby at the joints with arthritis, moved over the bedclothes like spiders. She sometimes held the Medal of Freedom that Ronald Reagan had given her over twenty years earlier and seemed to want to put it around her neck. Having lost the ability to call up the names of people or objects as a result of a comprehensive anomia, she drifted in and out of sleep, almost purposefully drowsing off if visitors tried to talk her into alertness. Sometimes she would wake suddenly and speak sharply to the Buddhist nun named Tammy whom Stuart had hired to give round-the-clock care, but then quickly apologize. When Ricardo Barrantes—her "other son," she called him— brought his wife and daughter to say goodbye, Jeane smiled and tried to talk with her eyes, speech having at last failed her. As the end approached, Tammy, her last companion, put on a CD of Bach.

Jeane died on December 7, the date that had always lived in infamy for her generation and marked the beginning of the long war against two totalitarianisms that became their life's work.

———

The disappointments of her final years had been daunting, not only for Jeane herself but for those close to her who saw how near these sorrows had sometimes come to breaking her. Yet she never gave up, and her friends, for their part, never lost sight of the fact that these personal reversals were merely a footnote to a much larger story—of a woman who had so well prepared herself by a lifetime of exacting study, strenuous encounters in the public square and deep concern for the fate of her country that when she was unexpectedly invited onto the center stage of history she was able to play her part with brilliance and lasting effect.

The significance of this achievement was conspicuously present in the graceful memorial service staged by the American Enterprise Institute in February 2007, two months after Jeane was buried in a Maryland graveyard next to Kirk, with whom she always said she looked forward to spending eternity. Washington Cathedral was filled; the heavy security was justified when Vice President and Mrs. Cheney ducked into a reserved pew by a side door just as the ceremonies began.

Many of those present had their own private memories of Jeane's prickly eccentricities and impulsive generosity, her intense loyalty and fallible love. But they all agreed that George Will came closest to summarizing what her big little life would be remembered for in the future in his eulogy. Will recalled how Ronald Reagan had been presented with a draft of the speech that contained the first version of what would become one of his most memorable lines: "Now and forever the Soviet Union is an evil empire." The president, said Will, had immediately "deleted the first three words of that sentence—'now and forever'; then he and his sidekick Jeane Kirkpatrick set about deleting the Soviet Union from mankind's future."

THE CONVERSATIONS I had with Jeane Kirkpatrick stand in the background of this book, especially in the first few chapters. If I were to cite every sentence in the book that is grounded in these talks, the source notes would be boundless. I hope that the reader can infer from context and inflection where I relied on these interviews.

I profited from a day and a half's worth of conversations with Jeane's brother Jerry Jordan, who has a Velcro memory about events that occurred six or seven decades earlier and has taken upon himself the role of curator of things past with the Jordans. My friend Jim Denton led me to a heterogeneous and unorganized collection of materials—handwritten drafts of letters Jeane wrote that she may or may not have had typed and sent; a jumble of financial data; evidence of her brief flirtation with elective office; etc.—in the basement at Heldref, where she appears to have hurriedly transferred decades of accumulation from AEI. Perhaps too grandly, I have referred to this assemblage as the Heldref Files. Probably the most significant items in this little cache were tapes of the oral history Austin Ranney did with Kirk, in which this quintessentially taciturn man talked about his personal life more or less inadvertently as part of a discussion of his public life in political science.

Three people who knew Jeane well—Claudia Anderson, Margaret Lefever and Josh Muravchik—not only talked with me about her but also looked at the manuscript and tried to rectify some of its shortcomings. I am grateful to them and others who shared their experiences with Jeane. I am grateful also to the

Earhart and Randolph foundations, and to Roger Hertog, Paul Singer and Jim Piereson for supporting this project.

Finally, many thanks to Roger Kimball for wanting to publish this book and to Carol Staswick for making it more literate.

# SOURCE NOTES

## INTRODUCTION

*page*

xv "She is not someone I want" — *New York Times*, August 17, 1994.

## HEARTLAND

1f Duncan, Oklahoma — *The Encyclopedia of Oklahoma History and Culture*, published by the Oklahoma Historical Society, has an extensive section on the town and its origins.

3 "I'll make you cry" — Draft Autobiography, Part 2, p. 5.

4 Don Campbell remembered — Interview with Don Campbell, October 10, 2008.

7 "would have more opportunities" — Draft Autobiography, Part 2, p. 23.

9 Virginia Sharpe described — Interview with Virginia Sharpe Campbell, October 10, 2008.

11 "held herself well" — Interview with Phyllis Smith, October 29, 2008.

12 "read *The Federalist Papers*" — Interview with John Howard, October 20, 2008.

## BIG IDEAS

15f Youngdahl preserved a memory — Interview with Pat Youngdahl, December 10, 2010.

16 "gangly and quiet" — Interview with Sol Sanders, December 8, 2010.

17 "stunning good looks" — Interview with Margaret Lefever, August 22, 2007.

19 "I'm so *lonely*" — Interview with Anne de Lattre, April 3, 2009.

## KIRK

27 "the most famous unfamous man" — Jeane used this phrase to describe Kirk, although she didn't say who the original author was.

27ff Kirk's oral history — Taped by Austin Ranney on several occasions between September 21, 1979, and February 28, 1980. The details about Kirk's life in this chapter come from these interviews. Heldref Files.

31f  Willmoore Kendall — George H. Nash discusses Kendall's career in *The Conservative Intellectual Movement in America Since 1945*, 2nd ed. (Wilmington, Del.: ISI Books, 2006). See also *Willmoore Kendall: Maverick of American Conservatives*, ed. John A. Murley and John E. Alvis (Lanham, Md.: Lexington Books, 2002), especially the Introduction by William F. Buckley.

32  Howard Penniman — Interview with William Penniman (son of Howard), July 27, 2010.

35n  Bellow and Humphrey — Interview with Max Kampelman, October 17, 2008. See also Kampelman's *Entering New Worlds: The Memoirs of a Private Man in Public Life* (New York: HarperCollins, 1991), p. 60.

36n  "given funding for study" — Christopher Simpson, *Blowback: The First Full Account of America's Recruitment of Nazis, and Its Disastrous Effect on Our Domestic and Foreign Policy* (New York: Collier-Macmillan, 1988), p. 110.

38  "a lovely woman" — Interview with Max Kampelman.

39  "cast a shadow over Kirk" — Interview with Father Jim Evans, who also provided details about Kirk's first marriage, April 22, 2008.

## AMERICAN IN PARIS

42ff  Camus and Sartre — See especially Ronald Aronson, *Camus and Sartre: The Story of a Friendship and the Quarrel That Ended It* (Chicago: University of Chicago Press, 2005).

48  Sailed home as a couple — Interview with Jerry Jordan, April 5, 2008.

## "A LOUSY DECADE"

53ff  Kirkpatricks' social circle — Interview with Claudia Anderson, August 3, 2007. The daughter of Anne and Leon Crutcher, and a perceptive observer of the personalities of those involved in this social network, Anderson provided details about her parents as well as a copy of the eulogy Jeane delivered at her mother's funeral.

55n  Kendall and Strauss — The correspondence between them is reprinted in *Willmoore Kendall: Maverick of American Conservatives*, ed. John A. Murley and John E. Alvis (Lanham, Md.: Lexington Books, 2002), pp. 191–261.

57  "Fine, but Louie wants" — Interview with Joyce Horne, longtime assistant of Kirk's, June 20, 2008.

57  "a distant hugger" — Interview with John Kirkpatrick, November 18, 2009.

58  Jeane's orgone accumulator — Ibid.

59 "it ought to be read" — Harry Schwartz, "War Against the Mind," *New York Times Book Review*, October 17, 1956.

59 "special problems and special opportunities" — Evron M. Kirkpatrick, ed., *Year of Crisis: Communist Propaganda Activities in 1956* (New York: Macmillan, 1957), p. 2.

60f "It is now well known" — Jeane Kirkpatrick, ed., *The Strategy of Deception: A Study in World-Wide Communist Tactics* (New York: Farrar, Straus, 1963), p. xii.

63n "indescribable distress and anguish" — Allan Gerson, *The Kirkpatrick Mission: Diplomacy Without Apology: America at the United Nations, 1981–1985* (New York: Free Press, 1991), p. xiv.

64f The Winetasters — Interviews with Roy Godson and Karl Cerny, June 16, 2008.

65 "TV dodgeball" — Interview with Colette Crutcher.

65 "contemporary Caesarist movement" — Jeane Kirkpatrick, *Leader and Vanguard in Mass Society: A Study of Peronist Argentina* (Cambridge, Mass.: MIT Press, 1971), p. 3.

68 Kampelman on what Kirk did — Max Kampelman, *Entering New Worlds: The Memoirs of a Private Man in Public Life* (New York: HarperCollins, 1991), p. 161.

69n Lowi responded with a withering letter — Theodore Lowi to Victor Navasky, February 25, 1981, Heldref Files.

70 "Everything you say" — Interview with Father Jim Evans, April 22, 2008.

70 Cerny and dissertation — Interview with Karl Cerny.

71 Approaching Nelson Rockefeller for VP — Interview with Max Kampelman, October 17, 2008.

73 "But somehow the day" — Interview with Anna Kirkpatrick.

## Public Intellectual

75f "Kirk just closed the door" — Interview with Tom Mann, July 18, 2008.

77 "an intentionally generous" — Interview with Claudia Anderson, August 3, 2007.

78 "culture is ideology" — Jeane Kirkpatrick, *Political Woman* (New York: Basic Books, 1974), p. 20.

79 "the proportion of women" — Ibid., p. 4.

79 "fairly attractive, forty-eight-year-old" — Ibid., p. 29.

79 "Few of these legislators" — Ibid., p. 165.

80 "These women find much that is offensive" — Ibid.

80 "The authorities suspect arson" — Interview with Jose Sorzano, July 18, 2008.

81 Helped them too much at Sidwell — Interview with Tom Mann.

81f "God, I wish we had" — Interview with Jackie Tillman Harty, August 12, 2008.

83 42 percent of rank-and-file Democrats — Jeane Kirkpatrick, *The New Presidential Elite: Men and Women in National Politics* (New York: Russell Sage Foundation, 1976), p. 295.

84f Founding of CDM — Interview with Norman Podhoretz and Midge Decter, November 13, 2008; interview with Ben Wattenberg, November 19, 2011.

85 "the moral elevation of other countries" — *U.S. News and World Report*, March 21, 1981.

87 "rectitude specialists" — *The New Presidential Elite*, p. 102.

88 "issues of economic status" — Jeane Kirkpatrick, "The Revolt of the Masses," *Commentary*, February 1973.

90 "The U.S. has passed its historic" — Cited by Jay Winik, *On the Brink: The Dramatic, Behind-the-Scenes Saga of the Reagan Era and the Men and Women Who Won the Cold War* (New York: Simon & Schuster, 1996), p. 78.

91 More than fifty names — Interview with Joshua Muravchik, December 4, 2011.

93 "To oppose Soviet or Cuban involvement" — Cited by Peter Schweizer, *Reagan's War: The Epic Story of His Forty-Year Struggle and Final Triumph Over Communism* (New York: Anchor, 2003), p. 102.

94 "Weak is strong" — Draft Autobiography, Part 1, p. 5.

95 *Shabbos goys* — Interview with Ben Wattenberg.

96 "the Republican Party can only" — "Why the New Right Lost," Commentary, February 1977, reprinted in Jeane Kirkpatrick, *Dictatorships and Double Standards: Rationalism and Reason in Politics* (New York: Simon & Schuster, 1982), p. 181.

97 "The differences between neo-conservatism" — Jeane Kirkpatrick, "On the Celebration of Hubert Humphrey," The Wilson Center, 1980, p. 23.

97 Jeane at Social Democrats' conference — Interview with Carl Gershman, September 11, 2009.

REAGANAUT

99 "new Nicaragua through popular participation" — Cited by Peter Schweizer, *Reagan's War: The Epic Story of His Forty-Year Struggle and Final Triumph Over Communism* (New York: Anchor, 2003), p. 110.

100 "I've decided to work on" — Interview with Jackie Tillman Harty, August 12, 2008.

101 "The pattern is familiar enough" — "Dictatorships and Double Standards," *Commentary*, November 1979, reprinted in Jeane Kirkpatrick, *Dictatorships and Double Standards: Rationalism and Reason in Politics* (New York: Simon & Schuster, 1982), p. 26.

102*n* "the concern was limited to" — Jeane Kirkpatrick, "U.S. Security and Latin America," *Commentary*, January 1981.

102f Carter broached the topic of human rights — Gal Beckerman, *When They Come for Us, We'll Be Gone: The Epic Struggle to Save Soviet Jewry* (New York: Houghton Mifflin Harcourt, 2010), p. 365.

104*n* "theories ungrounded in experience" — "Dictatorships and Double Standards," p. 11.

104 "Well, it *was* heavily edited" — Interview with Sol Sanders, December 8, 2010.

105 "I found myself reexamining" — Ronald Reagan to Jeane Kirkpatrick, December 12, 1979, copy supplied by Jackie Tillman Harty.

107 "Your analysis is not true" — The participants in this meeting I spoke to—Jeane, Midge Decter and Norman Podhoretz, and Ben Wattenberg—all had slightly different versions of exactly what Carter said. The quotation here is from Jay Winik, *On the Brink: The Dramatic, Behind-the-Scenes Saga of the Reagan Era and the Men and Women Who Won the Cold War* (New York: Simon & Schuster, 1996), p. 100.

107 "I am not going to support" — Interview with Midge Decter, November 13, 2008.

107f "Governor Reagan is in town" — Interview with Richard Allen, August 30, 2008.

108 "The White House calling" — Draft Autobiography, Part 14, p. 6.

109 "He's not at all like" — Ibid., p. 12.

109 "Dick, I am ready" — Interview with Richard Allen.

110 "clearing the way for Democrats" — Richard Allen, quoted in *New York Times*, December 16, 2006.

110 Novak dinner — Draft Autobiography, Part 14, p. 14.

110 "He does not seek to dominate" — Ibid., Part 21, p. 1.

111 "Since we often find Republican policies" — Jeane Kirkpatrick, "Why We Don't Become Republicans," *Common Sense*, Fall 1979, p. 32.

111 "Yes, but you can't ignore" — Draft Autobiography, Part 14, p. 20.

112f "shared a view of the Soviet Union" — Ibid., p. 29.

113*n* "Apparently you have been warned" — Henry Kissinger to Jeane Kirkpatrick, undated and handwritten, Heldref Files.

113 Weinberger asks her to join him — Draft Autobiography, Part 14, p. 30.

114 Reagan call — Ibid., Part 9, p. 1.

114f Jeane and the Bilderberger Club — Ibid., Part 4, p. 3.

## Diplomacy without Apology

117  Backing the Contras — Jane Rosen, "The Kirkpatrick Factor," *New York Times Magazine*, April 28, 1985.

118  "why I gave up ping pong" — Draft Autobiography, Part 12, p. 9.

118  "an interesting if somewhat discursive" — Alexander M. Haig, Jr., *Caveat: Realism, Reagan, and Foreign Policy* (New York: Scribner, 1984), p. 76.

118  "work with that bitch" — Interview with Jeane Kirkpatrick, 1987, in *Frontline Diplomacy: The Foreign Affairs Oral History Collection of the Association for Diplomatic Studies and Training*. Also, Draft Autobiography, Part 12, p. 32.

118  "to agree to nothing" — Jeane Kirkpatrick, *Legitimacy and Force*, vol. 1, *Political and Moral Dimensions* (New Brunswick, N.J.: Transaction, 1988), p. 127.

120  "Temperamental once a month?" — "Women in Politics," a speech given to the Women's Forum, December 29, 1984, reprinted in *Legitimacy and Force*, vol. 1, p. 458.

121  "That my sentences are too short" — *Life*, April 1981.

121  "'Mr. President,' I said" — Draft Autobiography, Part 24, p. 102.

122  "Is you is or is you ain't" — Interview with Ken Adelman, October 20, 2008.

122f  Gershman speech — William King, "The Origins of Neo-Conservative Support for Democracy Promotion, 1960–1991," MA Thesis, University of Calgary, 2007, p. 113. See also Allan Gerson, *The Kirkpatrick Mission: Diplomacy Without Apology: America at the United Nations, 1981–1985* (New York: Free Press, 1991), p. 80.

123  "The secretary and I" — Interview with Jackie Tillman Harty, August 12, 2008.

123  "Why do you want to know?" — Ibid.

124  *Cet animal est très méchant* — Daniel Patrick Moynihan, *A Dangerous Place* (New York: Little, Brown, 1978), p. 101.

125  "a degree of falsification" — *Legitimacy and Force*, vol. 1, p. 216.

125  "unlarge, unpowerful" — Ibid., p. 217.

125  "The UN is their place" — Ibid., p. 196.

125  "have long since accepted" — Ibid., p. 200.

126  "political struggle is waged" — Ibid., p. xvii.

126  "a longstanding lack of skill" — Ibid., p. 218.

126  "good precinct work" — Draft Autobiography, Part 25, p. 7.

127  "We take the UN very seriously" — Ibid., Part 24, p. 10.

127  "I think you no more believe" — *New York Times*, October 13, 1983.

127  "It is not fair to judge" — *Legitimacy and Force*, vol. 1, p. 86.

127 "moral outrage has been distributed" — Ibid., p. 87.

128 "probably imperialist obfuscation" — "Israel as Scapegoat," reprinted in Jeane Kirkpatrick, *The Reagan Phenomenon, and Other Speeches on Foreign Policy* (Washington, D.C.: AEI Press, 1983), p. 115.

128 "At last a challenge" — Draft Autobiography, Part 25, p. 17.

128 "brass knuckles under the velvet gloves" — Ibid.

128 "A dog does not fight" — Ibid., p. 19.

128 "to lambaste American imperialism" — Jeane Kirkpatrick and Ken Adelman, "Stirring Up Trouble in Puerto Rico," *New York Times*, February 26, 2006. She tells the story of the 1981 battle in the UN in Part 30 of the Draft Autobiography.

129 "commented to me admiringly" — Interview with David Michael Adamson, 2002, in *Frontline Diplomacy: The Foreign Affairs Oral History Collection of the Association for Diplomatic Studies and Training*.

130 "I call for the expulsion of Israel" — Moynihan, *A Dangerous Place*, p. 154.

130 "the Holocaust is possible again" — Gerson, *The Kirkpatrick Mission*, p. 22.

130 Defending Yehuda Blum — Draft Autobiography Part 23, p. 24.

131 "A women's conference is suddenly" — *The Reagan Phenomenon*, p. 110.

132 "If it takes one nuclear missile" — Gerson, *The Kirkpatrick Mission*, p. 14.

133 "Back to office to meet" — *The Reagan Diaries*, ed. Douglas Brinkley (New York: HarperCollins, 2007), May 31, 1982, p. 87.

134 "I'm not someone who is personally tough" — *Glamour*, July 1981.

134 Reagan puts an arm around her — *New York Times Magazine*, April 28, 1985.

135 "suspected sympathies with the Axis" — Jeane Kirkpatrick, "My Falklands War and Theirs," *National Interest*, Winter 1989–90, p. 13.

135 "if his country continued to support" — Haig, *Caveat*, p. 269.

135 "I thought it inconceivable" — Draft Autobiography, Part 31, p. 5.

136 "the Argentines' lack of realism" — Ibid., Part 13, p. 22.

137 "My father used to yell" — Gerson, *The Kirkpatrick Mission*, p. 125.

137 "I don't know how to handle it" — *People*, June 26, 1982.

138n "British support was needed" — "My Falklands War and Theirs," p. 17.

138n "My most extreme position" — *Telegraph*, December 9, 2006.

138f "I offer you my ancestors" — Draft Autobiography, Part 31, p. 42.

139 Vice President Bush told Reagan — Ibid., p. 50.

139 Haig intentionally delayed answering — *New York Times*, June 8, 1982.

140 "Waterloo" — Haig, *Caveat*, p. 307.

140  "I'm sure Alexander Haig thought" — *New York Times*, December 20, 1984.

## RICH IN ENEMIES

142  Modified personal chaos — Interview with Ken Adelman, October 20, 2008.

143  "violence and lies" — Allan Gerson, *The Kirkpatrick Mission: Diplomacy Without Apology: America at the United Nations, 1981–1985* (New York: Free Press, 1991), p. 211.

143f  Jeane in Afghanistan — Interview with Jose Sorzano, July 18, 2008.

144  "How far the Soviets are willing" — Jeane Kirkpatrick, *Legitimacy and Force*, vol. 1, *Political and Moral Dimensions* (New Brunswick, N.J.: Transaction, 1988), p. 250.

144  "the rising level of violence" — Jeane Kirkpatrick, *Legitimacy and Force*, vol. 2, *National and International Dimensions*, p. 262.

145  Soviet disinformation — *New York Times*, August 17, 1994.

145f  "No, no, no" — Interview with Harvey Feldman, 1999, *Frontline Diplomacy: The Foreign Affairs Oral History Collection of the Association for Diplomatic Studies and Training.*

146  "She's probably getting ready" — Interview with Colette Crutcher.

147n  "Jeane began her toast" — Interview with Harvey Feldman, *Frontline Diplomacy.*

148  "principled, pragmatic response" — *Legitimacy and Force*, vol. 1, p. 422.

148  "Nicaragua, Angola, Benin" — *Legitimacy and Force*, vol. 2, p. 160.

148  "If the Soviet Union has a 'right'" — *Legitimacy and Force*, vol. 1, p. 445.

149  "For once, I think Lewis" — Ibid., p. 440.

149  "Murderous traditionalists confront" — Ibid., p. 118.

150n  "Thomas Hobbes's problem" — "The Hobbes Problem," reprinted in Jeane Kirkpatrick, *Dictatorships and Double Standards: Rationalism and Reason in Politics* (New York: Simon & Schuster, 1982), p. 85.

150  "The men of the FMLN" — *Legitimacy and Force*, vol. 1, p. 119.

150  "God knows there are parallels" — Jeane Kirkpatrick, "Central America: This Time We Know What's Happening," *Washington Post*, April 17, 1983.

151  "State Department bureaucrats" — *The Reagan Diaries*, ed. Douglas Brinkley (New York: HarperCollins, 2007), February 17, 1983, p. 132.

151  "the leading theoretician" — Jay Winik, *On the Brink: The Dramatic, Behind-the-Scenes Saga of the Reagan Era and the Men and Women Who Won the Cold War* (New York: Simon & Schuster, 1996), p. 254.

151 "Pardon Me, But Am I" — *Washington Post*, June 20, 1983.

152 "Thus, the dialectic of revolution" — *Legitimacy and Force*, vol. 1, p. 184.

152f "Within weeks after the fall" — Ibid., p. 107.

153 "Because it lacks power" — Ibid., p. xix.

154 "The U.S. government did not attempt" — Jeane Kirkpatrick, *The Reagan Phenomenon, and Other Speeches on Foreign Policy* (Washington, D.C.: AEI Press, 1983), p. 198.

154f "Augusto César Sandino" — *Legitimacy and Force*, vol. 2, p. 158.

156 "If it's not going to be pleasant" — *Newsweek*, March 21, 1983.

157 "Maurice Bishop freely offered" — *Legitimacy and Force*, vol. 2, p. 229.

157 "Were the U.S. and OECS" — *Legitimacy and Force*, vol. 1, p. 436.

158 "If it is no longer possible" — Ibid., p. 72.

158 "the suicide attempt failed" — Ibid., p. 27.

159 "We told Jeane to cultivate him" — Michael Kramer, "The Prime of Jeane Kirkpatrick," *New York Magazine*, July 6, 1985.

160 "I don't know how you feel" — Draft Autobiography, Part 33, p. 7.

160 "Shultz sees Israel as hard" — *Newsweek*, January 3, 1983. In the Draft Autobiography (Part 33, p. 3), Jeane says that while Shultz's opinions of Israel, like those of Weinberger and Vice President Bush, were initially "negative," he later came to be regarded as "a good and reliable friend" of the Jewish state.

161 "Well, I may as well" — Draft Autobiography, Part 21, p. 5.

162 "lumbering into the Oval Office" — *Time*, October 31, 1983.

162 "capacity for passionate advocacy" — George P. Shultz, *Turmoil and Triumph: My Years as Secretary of State* (New York: Scribner, 1993), p. 320.

162n Nancy Reagan's deciding voice — Interview with Warren Clark, February 28, 2012.

163 "We talked for an hour" — *The Reagan Diaries*, October 17, 1983, p. 188.

163 "He saw an opportunity" — Draft Autobiography, Part 21, p. 14.

164 "weary of the UN" — *The Reagan Diaries*, December 22, 1983, p. 206.

164n "impeachable offense" — Shultz, *Turmoil and Triumph*, p. 414.

164f Whittlesey was upset — Interview with David Carmen.

166 "I corrected Baker" — *New York Times Magazine*, April 28, 1985.

166 "many of the President's key aides" — *Newsweek*, December 31, 1984.

166n "The President is fond" — *New York Times Magazine*, April 25, 1985.

167 "Sorry to see her go" — *The Reagan Diaries*, January 30, 1985, p. 298.

168 "no woman had ever been" — *New York Times*, December 9, 2006.

## THE END OF HISTORY

169f "There hasn't been anyone hotter" — Michael Kramer, "The Prime of Jeane Kirkpatrick," *New York Magazine*, July 6, 1985.

170 "I respectfully urge you" — Irving Lazar to Jeane Kirkpatrick, February 21, 1985, Heldref Files.

170 "It will probably fail" — Interview with Susan Marone, August 1, 2007.

171 "Kirk and I have money now" — Interview with Sol Sanders, December 8, 2010.

172 Casey grumbled about Shultz's "weakness" — George P. Shultz, *Turmoil and Triumph: My Years as Secretary of State* (New York: Scribner, 1993), p. 837.

172 "They badly need additional help" — Jeane Kirkpatrick to Ronald Reagan, June 17, 1985, copy in Heldref Files.

173 "First time I've ever heard" — *The Reagan Diaries*, ed. Douglas Brinkley (New York: HarperCollins, 2007), May 9, 1987, p. 475.

174 Boiler-room operation — Interview with Joshua Muravchik, December 4, 2011.

174 Aboard the Myerhoff yacht — Interview with Norman Podhoretz, November 13, 2008.

174 Pirchner's brief analysis — Copy dated September 7, 1987, in Heldref Files.

175 She met with Meldrin Thompson — Thompson discussed the frustrating political courtship of Jeane in *Conservative Digest*, December 1987.

177 "And I am willing to say so" — Jeane Kirkpatrick to George H. W. Bush, June 4, 1988, handwritten copy in Heldref Files.

177 Candidate with Balls — Interview with Joyce Horne, June 20, 2008.

178 "If I do not receive a manuscript" — Michael Korda to Irving Lazar, March 24, 1987, copy in Heldref Files.

178 "Korda wrote you" — Jeane Kirkpatrick to Irving Lazar, April 10, 1987, copy in Heldref Files.

179 "come away with a clear understanding" — Interview with Stephen Bosworth, 2003, in *Frontline Diplomacy: The Foreign Affairs Oral History Collection of the Association for Diplomatic Studies and Training*.

180 View of Yakovlev as sinister — "Moscow's Anti-American Reformer," October 17, 1988, reprinted in Jeane Kirkpatrick, *The Withering Away of the Totalitarian State . . . and Other Surprises* (Washington, D.C.: AEI Press, 1990), pp. 38–41.

181 "more efficient, creative" — "New Thinking in the Kremlin," February 16, 1987, reprinted in *The Withering Away*, p. 19.

181 "very useful and good session" — *The Reagan Diaries*, February 24, 1987, p. 477.

181 "flexible, adaptable, skillful" — "Is He a New Kind of Communist?" December 13, 1987, reprinted in *The Withering Away*, pp. 21–22.

181f Politburo's rehabilitation of Bukharin — "Rectifying History—The Uses of the Past," February 15, 1988, in *The Withering Away*, pp. 34–35.

182 Gorbachev "has given no indication" — "The Limits of Pluralism under Perestroika," May 66, 1988, in *The Withering Away*, p. 45.

182 "watching the Marxist governments" — "Relaxing the Totalitarian Grip," October 31, 1988, in *The Withering Away*, p. 47.

182 "be ready to abandon" — Ibid., p. 46.

182 "Is it possible that we are watching" — Ibid., p. 45.

182 Ligachev and fellow hardliners — "The Logic of Freedom," March 14, 1989, in *The Withering Away*, pp. 58–60.

182 "Leninist 'socialism' [would] be supplanted" — "Is the Brezhnev Doctrine Dead?" March 20, 1989, in *The Withering Away*, p. 58.

183 Katyn Forest massacre — "Message to China, from Hungary," June 26, 1989, in *The Withering Away*, p. 70.

183 "abandoned the totalitarian project" — "The End of Totalitarianism in Europe," November 20, 1989, in *The Withering Away*, p. 78.

184 "risked their lives" — "Election Surprise," March 5, 1990, in *The Withering Away*, p. 232.

185f Krauthammer contradicted Jeane — Charles Krauthammer, "The Unipolar Moment," *Foreign Affairs*, Winter 1990–91.

187 Phone call from Norman Podhoretz — Interview with Joshua Muravchik.

187 "not in the hands of the coalition" — Jeane Kirkpatrick, *Making War to Keep Peace* (New York: HarperCollins, 2007), p. 39.

188 "as potentially engaged everywhere" — Ibid., p. 57.

188 "to risk American lives" — Ibid., p. 87.

188f "some sort of Brezhnev Doctrine" — Ibid., p. 113.

189f "a new pessimism, a new indifference" — Robert Kagan, "Democracy and Double Standards," *Commentary*, August 1997.

190n Niall Ferguson gave it two cheers — See *Telegraph*, December 17, 2006.

190 "as if democracy could imbue" — *Making War to Keep Peace*, p. 273.

192 "a pious agnostic" — Interview with Joyce Horne.

194 Traktung Rinpoche — See http://arborwiki.org/index.php/Traktung_Rinpoche. Also http://www.spiritualtraveler.com/spiritual_traveler/interviews/lama_traktung_rimpoche.asp

196 "changes Doug's diapers" — Interview with Joyce Horne.

196n Jeane's amended will — Copy in Heldref Files.

197  Call to George McGovern — Interview with John Kirkpatrick, November 18, 2009.

197  "Those were the perfect words" — Interview with Mark Lagon, April 13, 2011.

## A TIME OF SUBTRACTION

200  "It would be a very serious mistake" — Jeane Kirkpatrick, "The Case for Force," *Chronicle of Higher Education*, September 28, 2001.

201  "It will never sell" — Allan Gerson, "Not All Conservatives Hate the United Nations," *Guardian*, October 23, 2007.

202f  Douglas at Heldref — Interview with Jim Denton, August 1, 2007.

203  "memory loss and possible dementia" — Interview with Jerry Jordan, April 5, 2008.

204  AEI passes on the book — Interview with Kate Campaigne, October 20, 2008.

204  "total lack of respect" — Interview with Joshua Muravchik, December 4, 2011. Also, interview with Michael Ledeen, November 19, 2011. Ledeen too worked at AEI during this time.

205  "I don't think we have an obligation" — *Washington Times*, May 15, 2000.

205  Ed Meese was concerned — Interview with Ed Meese, September 11, 2009.

206  "Maybe people actually" — Interview with Teresa Hartnett.

207  "to do due diligence" — Jeane Kirkpatrick, *Making War to Keep Peace* (New York: HarperCollins, 2007), p. 300.

DESIGN & COMPOSITION BY CARL W. SCARBROUGH